P9-ELO-329

Managing UUCP and Usenet

Managing UUCP and Usenet

Tim O'Reilly and Grace Todino

O'Reilly & Associates, Inc.
103 Morris Street, Suite A
Sebastopol, CA 95472

Managing UUCP and Usenet
by Tim O'Reilly and Grace Todino

Copyright © 1990 O'Reilly & Associates, Inc. All rights reserved.
Printed in the United States of America.

Editor: Tim O'Reilly

Printing History:

February 1986:	First edition; sections on UUCP written by Grace Todino, Usenet by Tim O'Reilly.
November 1986:	Second edition. Updated to Netnews 2.11 by Tim O'Reilly.
May 1987:	Third edition. Updated for HoneyDanBer UUCP by Grace Todino and Dale Dougherty. UUCP sections reorganized and expanded by Tim O'Reilly. Index added. Revised page design by Linda Lamb and Dale Dougherty.
July 1987:	Fourth edition. Additional review comments incorporated. Some additional reorganization.
March 1988:	Fifth edition. Additional review comments incorporated by Tim O'Reilly.
October 1988:	Sixth edition. Minor revisions, mostly on SunOS 4.0, suggested by Guy Harris.
February 1989:	Seventh edition. Additional review comments incorporated by Tim O'Reilly.
December 1989:	Eighth edition. Updated for C News and Telebit modems by Jean Marie Diaz.
July 1990:	Ninth edition. Minor corrections.
January 1992:	Tenth edition. Added chapter on NNTP, appendices on UUCP for DOS and Macintosh systems, Frequently Asked Questions, and the Protocol specification. Many minor additions.

Many of the designations used by manufacturers and sellers to distinguish their products are claimed as trademarks. Where those designations appear in this book, and O'Reilly and Associates, Inc. was aware of a trademark claim, the designations have been printed in caps or initial caps.

While every precaution has been taken in the preparation of this book, the publisher assumes no responsibility for errors or omissions, or for damages resulting from the use of the information contained herein.

This book is printed on acid-free paper with 50% recycled content, 10-15% post-consumer waste. O'Reilly & Associates is committed to using paper with the highest recycled content available consistent with high quality.

ISBN: 0-937175-93-5 [7/92]

Table of Contents

Figures

Tables

Preface

UUCP stands for *Unix-to-Unix CoPy*. It is a collection of programs designed so that UNIX systems can communicate with each other. UUCP includes programs to:

- Transfer files between UNIX systems (**uucp**).

- Execute commands on a remote system (**uux**).

- Send mail to users on a remote system (**mail**).

Unlike many networking technologies, which require an investment in specialized hardware and software, UUCP is designed to use standard serial cables, modems, and telephone service. It can also run on many local area networks but does not require one. UUCP is used to create a *dial-up network*. That is, communications are established between systems only when users make communications requests.

Each system on a UUCP network has files that describe the other systems directly linked to it and what types of link are available. Creating these files is the major task of the system administrator. Once the communication links to the network are established, UUCP requires minimal supervision and overall administration.

Each computer system also provides for its own security by restricting remote use of the local system.

UUCP can also be used to connect to a network of systems called Usenet. Usenet is a bulletin-board network that uses the public domain Netnews software to exchange "news" about a wide variety of topics. Usenet includes thousands of systems, many of them using UUCP as their basic network protocol. Usenet is also connected through gateway systems to many computer networks, including the Internet. (Usenet is sometimes referred to simply as "the net," though this name more properly belongs to the Internet.)

The public domain Netnews software includes programs that allow users to read and post news messages to the net. In addition to providing for the interchange of news, a link into Usenet allows users to communicate by mail with users at any other Usenet site, even sites that are not directly known to the local UUCP network.

Scope of This Handbook

Managing UUCP and Usenet is meant for system administrators who want to install and manage a UUCP network or to connect to Usenet.

This handbook follows the *Nutshell* philosophy of presenting the concepts in an easy-to-read and logical manner. It is divided into the following sections:

Chapter 1,   *How UUCP Works*, gives a conceptual overview of how UUCP file transfers work, with an emphasis on how the UUCP programs make use of various configuration files that you, as the administrator, need to set up.

Chapter 2,   *The Physical Connection*, describes RS-232 cabling, the theory of serial communications, and the UNIX system files that control serial communications parameters.

Chapter 3,   *Setting Up a UUCP Link*, describes the UUCP configuration files and the procedure for establishing communication with other systems. This chapter assumes that you have already set up a physical link, as described in Chapter 2.

Chapter 4,   *Making Sure the Link Works*, describes in more detail the part of setting up a UUCP link that is as much art as science: figuring out the "chat script" used to log in to another system.

Chapter 5,   *Access and Security Considerations*, describes the mechanisms that you can use to increase or decrease the level of security for your system.

Chapter 6,   *UUCP Administration*, describes the UUCP administrative shell scripts that perform routine maintenance. It also covers tasks that the system administrator must carry out periodically to keep the system running smoothly.

Chapter 7,   *Introduction to Usenet*, gives an introduction to Usenet and the Netnews software.

Chapter 8,   *Installing Netnews*, describes how to install the Netnews software and how to get set up as a Usenet site.

Chapter 9,   *Administering Netnews*, describes routine tasks you will need to perform as Netnews administrator for your site.

Chapter 10,   *NNTP: Transferring News over the Network*, describes how to obtain, configure, compile, and administer the UNIX implementation of the Network News Transfer Protocol (NNTP), which is used for transferring news over TCP/IP and other high-speed networks.

Appendix A,   *Working Files*, describes the files used by UUCP in the process of transferring files.

Appendix B,   *Talking to Modems*, describes how to write UUCP support for modems, particularly Hayes-compatible modems such as the Telebit Trailblazer.

Appendix C,   *More on RS-232*, gives additional detail on the RS-232 standard.

Appendix D,   *Useful Programs and Shell Scripts*, contains several useful scripts that are mentioned in the course of the book. It also gives pointers to the location of other UUCP-related programs available in public domain source archives on the net.

Appendix E,   *UUCP for MS-DOS and Macintosh Systems*, describes several public-domain or low-cost UUCP implementations for non-UNIX systems, and also describes how one of these systems has been successfully configured to turn a DOS-based laptop computer into a travelling UUCP node.

Appendix F,   *Frequently Asked Questions*, answers some frequently-asked questions about UUCP and related networking topics, including how domain addressing works, how to find e-mail addresses for individuals on the net, how to use anonymous ftp, and how to get access to the Internet.

Appendix G, *The UUCP G Protocol*, describes the inner workings of UUCP's native *g* protocol. This appendix will help you to understand better how UUCP works, and why it sometimes doesn't.

After reading this handbook, you should be able to:

*   Set up a link to the UUCP network using either direct RS-232 or phone connections.

*   Add links to an established UUCP network.

*   Vary the level of security for your UUCP system.

*   Perform routine maintenance to ensure that the UUCP system is working properly.

*   Install the Netnews software and set up a link to Usenet.

This handbook assumes that you are at least superficially familiar with UNIX system administration and that you have superuser (root) privileges.

Versions of UUCP

The first UUCP system was built in 1976 by Mike Lesk at AT&T Bell Laboratories as part of a research project. It became such a success that an improved version developed by Mike Lesk, David Nowitz, and Greg Chesson was distributed with UNIX Version 7 in 1977 and became known as Version 2 UUCP. An update was released in 1981. Additional updates were incorporated by AT&T in System V Release 1 (SVR1) and System V Release 2 (SVR2).

Meanwhile, an independent set of updates was made at Duke University. While the Duke UUCP is no longer used, it became the basis for the versions shipped with the Berkeley Software Distribution from the University of California at Berkeley (BSD 4*x*), as well as with DEC's Ultrix and Sun's SunOS. The version of UUCP that was shipped with BSD 4.2 is sometimes referred to as Truscott UUCP, since its development was coordinated by Tom Truscott at the Triangle Research Institute. Despite its pre-eminence as a BSD system vendor, Sun actually does not ship the BSD implementation of UUCP. Prior to SunOS 4.1, Sun shipped a special UUCP version of its own. To make things still more complicated, SunOS 4.0 has significant differences from earlier SunOS versions. As of SunOS 4.1, Sun ships the standard System V Release 4 UUCP (see below).

With System V Release 3, AT&T began distributing a new version of UUCP that had been developed (in 1983) by Peter **Honey**man, **D**avid **A.** Nowitz, and **Brian E.** Redman. They rewrote UUCP to iron out some deficiencies in Version 2, make UUCP administration easier, and provide support for more advanced communications devices and networks. This version became popularly known as **HoneyDanBer** UUCP (derived from the authors' names) although it is more prosaically referred to as "Basic Networking Utilities," or BNU, in AT&T's official release of the product. We will refer to it by the latter name throughout this book.

BSD 4.3's UUCP is yet another significant update, incorporating some BNU features but retaining more continuity with other Version 2 implementations. The development of this version was coordinated by Rick Adams, then at the Center for Seismic Studies.

There are also minor differences in particular manufacturers' implementations. For example, older Xenix systems use a version of the SVR2 UUCP but has added a menu-driven configuration utility and its own method of modem support. Current Xenix systems use BNU.

BNU is largely backward-compatible with Version 2, so a UUCP network can contain both Version 2 and BNU sites. However, the names of the various configuration and control files have been changed.

If you do not know which version of UUCP you have, list the *usr/lib/uucp* directory and see if you have a file called *L.sys*. If you do, you have the "old" Version 2 UUCP. If instead you see a file called *Systems*, then you have BNU. If you have a Sun running SunOS 4.0, you will not see either file. You will find your *L.sys* file (as well as some other files normally found in *usr/lib/uucp*) in */etc/uucp*.

We have tried to make this book as version-independent as possible. Throughout, we will try first to describe the general case—the task or problem to be accomplished—and then explain the differences between what you need to do in Version 2 versus BNU, or on a BSD or Xenix system versus System V. Diversions from the main topic are clearly marked, so feel free to assume that what you read applies to all cases unless it is marked otherwise.

Conventions Used in This Book

The following conventions are used in this book:

Bold   is used for program names and command names.

Italic   is used for file and directory names when they appear in the body of a paragraph and to emphasize new terms and concepts when they are introduced. Italic is also used, in parentheses, to highlight comments in an example.

`Constant Width` is used in examples to show the contents of files or the output from commands.

`Constant Bold` is used in examples to show commands or other text that should be typed literally by the user. For example, **rm foo** means to type "rm foo" exactly as it appears in the text or example.

`Constant Italic` is used in code fragments and examples to show variables for which a context-specific substitution should be made. The variable *`filename`*, for example, would be replaced by some actual filename.

function(*n*) refers to the section of the UNIX programmer's manual in which the program is described. For example, *crypt*(1) refers to a page called *crypt* in Section 1.

%, $, # When we are demonstrating commands that you would give interactively, we normally use the default C shell prompt (%). We use the default Bourne shell prompt ($) if the commands we are demonstrating must be executed from the Bourne shell. We use the default superuser prompt (#) if the commands must be executed as root. Note that the superuser prompt can easily be confused with the comment character for shell scripts.

. . . stands for text (usually computer output) that's been omitted for clarity or to save space.

CTRL The notation CTRL-X or ^X indicates use of *control* characters. It means hold down the CONTROL key while typing the character "x".

All command examples are followed by a RETURN unless otherwise indicated.

Examples

In order to make the examples more or less consistent, we have used a hypothetical network, with systems named on a city/state scheme, throughout this book.

The local system is called *newton*. It is connected directly to systems *waltham* and *natick* and by a telephone link to *boston, newyork, calif,* and *japan*.

Examples of configuration files and commands are set off from the main text in smaller type. If there are commands that you have to enter to follow the example, these will be shown in bold type. System responses and the contents of files are printed in normal type.

NOTE

In some cases, due to space restrictions, we have been forced to split long lines in the examples into two lines. Whenever we have done this, we have indicated that we have done so by printing a backslash at the end of the interrupted line. Do not confuse this convention with the fact that in many UNIX programs, you can escape a newline and have the program treat the input as a single long line. In Version 2 implementations prior to BSD 4.3, the UUCP configuration files do not support this feature. All data must be on a single physical line unless we explicitly note otherwise.

Please note that even though we have tried to cover the main versions of UUCP, there may be differences in syntax from system to system. Each manufacturer sometimes makes minor enhancements in implementing the software for a particular system. Please refer to the UNIX reference manuals at your site if the examples do not work as shown.

As this book has had a long life, with many revisions, its examples come from many sources. However, the bulk of the examples come from systems we were using at the time early versions of the book were prepared. So, for example, most of our examples of Version 2 UUCP are based on the implementation shipped with the Convergent Technologies Miniframe. Most of the BNU examples were initially based on an AT&T 3B2/310, with later modifications based on the SunOS 4.1 and Interactive 386/ix implementations.

In the examples, we use the system prompt "#" to indicate when commands can only be executed as *superuser*, either because of file permissions or because a command itself is restricted. Commands that are shown preceded by the system prompt "$" can be invoked using your normal login id or when logged in as "uucp."

Acknowledgements

The tenth edition of this handbook includes a chapter on NNTP; this chapter was begun by Jean Marie Diaz (Ambar) and completed by Tim O'Reilly, with a great deal of help from Stan Barber, who gave up time on his vacation to review the draft and answer many questions. The tenth edition also includes an appendix on UUCP implementations for DOS and the Macintosh, which was written by Peter Mui of O'Reilly and Associates, and one on the UUCP g protocol, which was written by Jamie Hanrahan of Kernel Mode Consulting. Miscellaneous material previously published by UUNET under the title *UUNET Answer Booklet* has also been incorporated in this edition, most of it in Appendix F. Appendix F also includes a section on finding individual people's e-mail addresses that was written by Jonathan Kamens of MIT. Many thanks for permission to include this material. Many small corrections were submitted by Akio Kido and by Jeremy Epstein, and their suggestions triggered a thorough review of other out-of-date aspects of the book. Other improvements were suggested by Vern Hoxie, Philip Meese, Thad Floryan, and Greg Woods. In addition, Mark Taub provided a copy of the latest SCO UNIX documentation for our reference. Everyone's help in keeping this book up to date is gratefully acknowledged. Jerry Peek and Mike Loukides also made useful suggestions. Thanks also to Rosanne Wagger and Ellie Cutler who produced the tenth edition.

The eighth edition, which included coverage of C News, was prepared by Jean Marie Diaz. She also made minor corrections for the ninth edition. Thanks also go to Geoff Collyer and Henry Spencer, both of the University of Toronto, for their work on C News and for their review of Chapters 7, 8, and 9 for the eighth edition.

Guy Harris of Auspex suggested the corrections and additions made in the seventh edition. For the sixth edition, Rick Adams (then at the Center for Seismic Studies) and Carl S. Gutekunst of Pyramid Technology Corporation provided a large number of small corrections. In addition, Carl provided additional details on UUCP history and largely rewrote the section on the *USERFILE*. Clem Cole (then at Stellar Computer), Andy Tannenbaum of Interactive System Corp., Lyndon Nierenberg of Nexus Computing Corporation, and John Gilmore of Nebula Consultants reviewed drafts of the fourth edition.

Not to be forgotten is Mark Horton, who reviewed the original edition, which provided the base for the current work. In addition, at the time the original edition was being prepared, Masscomp kindly provided us with copies of the UUCP manual that they were developing and again provided us with review copies of their manual as it was being revised for BNU by Steve Talbott. Their help and support was greatly appreciated.

Thanks for help with the first edition are also due to Greg Chesson of Silicon Graphics, Steve Howard of the College of Business Administration at the University of Cincinnati, Barry Shein of Boston University, and Ross Alexander of Athabasca University, each of whom answered questions or provided missing information. For help with Netnews, thanks were due to Mark Hilbush of Case Communications, Barry Burke of Adelie Corporation, and Rick Adams, then at the Center for Seismic Studies.

Of course, the standard disclaimer applies: any errors that remain are our own.

Note to Our Readers

We see each Nutshell Handbook as reflecting the experience of a group of users. They are not written by "experts" but by people who have gone through a learning process similar to your own. Our goal is to share what we have learned from experience, so that you can become more productive in less time.

As publishers, this goal is reflected in the way we maintain the series by updating each title periodically. This allows us to incorporate changes suggested to us by our readers. The revision history of this book is printed on the back of the title page.

If you have a suggestion or solve a significant problem that our handbook does not cover, please write to us and let us know about it. Include information about the UNIX environment in which you work and the particular machine you use. You can send e-mail to *uunet!ora!nuts* (*nuts@ora.com*).

If we are able to use your suggestion in the next edition of the book, we will send you a free copy of the new edition.

1

How UUCP Works

Behind the Scenes
A Word About Modems
Setting Up a Link
Files and Directories
UUCP Login IDs

As you know if you have looked at the companion handbook, *Using UUCP and Usenet*, UUCP consists of a number of related programs.

The user has three main programs to work with:

* **uucp**, which is used to request a file transfer to or from a remote machine. It works much like **cp**, with added syntax for addressing remote machines.

* **uux**, which is used to request execution of a command on a remote machine. The commands that can be executed are usually limited for security reasons, but might include, for instance, printing on a printer attached to a remote machine.

* **mail**, which is not usually thought of as a UUCP program, but nonetheless understands the UUCP syntax for addressing remote systems and is closely

integrated with UUCP on all systems.* A related program called **rmail** (which is actually sometimes linked to **mail**) is invoked on a remote system to decide whether mail is to be delivered locally on that system or forwarded on to yet another system.

Different implementations of UUCP may support additional user programs; however, all have at least these three programs in common.

There is quite a bit more going on behind the scenes. A background program, or *daemon*, called **uucico** actually does most of the work transferring files or remote execution requests back and forth between systems. Another daemon called **uuxqt** is invoked on the remote system to process remote execution requests. And in order for these daemons to do their job, there are quite a few data files that need to be in place, giving information on the systems to be called and the mechanisms to be used to place the call. It is the job of the administrator to set up these files.

There are also a number of administrative programs that are run automatically but which may need manual intervention on very busy networks or if problems occur.

All of the above notwithstanding, UUCP is not difficult to set up. However, the setup instructions will make a lot more sense if you first understand how the whole system works. When it comes time to administer a running network, this understanding will prove even more important. So let's take a moment to look behind the scenes.

Behind the Scenes

UUCP is a "store-and-forward" network. That is, requests for file transfers or remote execution of commands on another system are not executed immediately but are spooled for execution when communication is established between the two systems. Depending on how the configuration files are set up, communication may be established immediately or may wait till a later time. (For example, many systems wait for evening, when rates are lower, to establish a telephone connection with a distant system.)

---

*A possible point of confusion: On BSD systems, there are two programs called **mail**: */bin/mail* and */usr/ucb/mail*. */bin/mail* is the original mail program from AT&T, which is closely integrated with UUCP. */usr/ucb/mail* is a mail user interface, which can work with a number of underlying mail programs, of which */bin/mail* is only one. A version of */usr/ucb/mail* called **mailx** is available on System V.

The **uucp** program itself does not copy files from system to system, nor does **uux** actually execute commands on a remote system. When a user invokes **uucp** or **uux** or sends mail to a user on a remote system, two things happen:

1. A work file containing information such as the name of the source file and the destination file, **uucp** or **uux** options, and the type of request (send, receive, or execute) is created in the directory */usr/spool/uucp*. Depending on the version of UUCP you are using and the command line options the user specifies, a data file may also be created which contains an actual copy of the file to be transferred. Data files are also created whenever you send mail to someone on a remote system or make a request for remote command execution.

2. The **uucico** program is invoked to actually make the transfer.

When **uucico** is invoked, it scans the spool directory for work files and attempts to contact other systems and execute the instructions in the work files.*

However, the work files contain only a small part of the information **uucico** needs to know in order to make a transfer. They tell **uucico** what to do, but not when or how to do it. This information is contained in a set of configuration files in the directory */usr/lib/uucp*, which it is your job as the administrator to set up.

Configuration Files

The most important of the files (or at least the one you will need to work with most often) is called *L.sys* in Version 2 UUCP, and *Systems* in BNU. It contains the list of systems known to the local system, together with instructions on how to reach each of them.

A typical (somewhat simplified) line in *newton*'s copy of this file might look like this:

```
boston Any ACU 2400 9999999 ogin: Unewton ssword: itsme
```

This line says that system *boston*:

- Can be called at any time.

- Over a modem connected to a telephone line rather than over a direct serial line (ACU=Automatic Call Unit).

- At a speed of 2400 bps.

---

*In BNU, a program called **uusched** does the scan for work and calls **uucico** only when a call needs to be made to another system.

- Using the telephone number 9999999.

- And logging in with login name *Unewton*.

- And password *itsme*.

If there are multiple ways to reach another system (e.g., two telephone numbers), there will be multiple entries for that system in *L.sys*.

Another file called *L-devices* (*Devices* in BNU) contains a one-to-one mapping between the actual communications hardware on your system (such as a direct serial line, modem, or network connection) and what device name **uucico** should use to access each device. For example, this file might contain a line like this:

```
ACU tty008 - 2400 hayes
```

which states that **uucico** can use the name *hayes* to refer to a Hayes modem connected to serial line *tty008*. Again, it is possible that there can be multiple connections of the same type (e.g., more than one 2400 baud modem.)* When **uucico** is calling a system or using a device, it creates temporary *lock files* to make sure no other copy of **uucico** tries to call that system or use that device at the same time.

If the connection uses a modem, **uucico** must look up how to dial the modem. The actual dialing instructions for modems are either hardcoded into UUCP (in some implementations of Version 2) or contained in an accessory file. (Files called *acucap* and *modemcap* are available in some Version 2 systems. In BNU, modems are described in a file called *Dialers*.) You must either use one of the preconfigured modem types or add dialing instructions for your modem.

There are also files that control which parts of your file system are accessible to a remote system and which commands can be executed by a remote system. In Version 2, these files are called *USERFILE* and *L.cmds*. In BNU, there is a single file called *Permissions*.

We'll talk about all of these files in detail later. For the moment, all that is important to understand is that a fair amount of information needs to be put in place before a simple file transfer can occur. Figure 1-1 shows the sequence of events for a successful call to another system.

---

*There are substantial differences between UUCP versions in the format of the *L-devices* file. See Chapter 3, *Setting Up a UUCP Link*, for details.

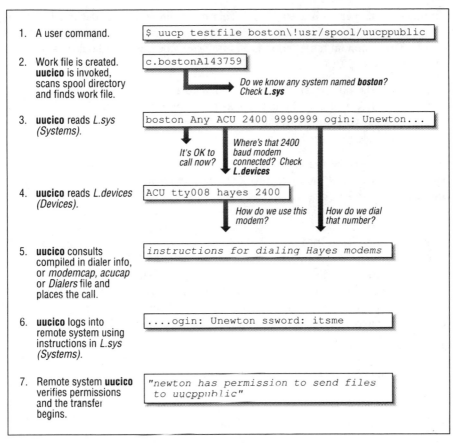

1. A user command.

   `$ uucp testfile boston\!usr/spool/uucppublic`

2. Work file is created. **uucico** is invoked, scans spool directory and finds work file.

   `c.bostonA143759`

   *Do we know any system named **boston**? Check **L.sys***

3. **uucico** reads *L.sys (Systems)*.

   `boston Any ACU 2400 9999999 ogin: Unewton...`

   It's OK to call now? *Where's that 2400 baud modem connected? Check **L.devices***

4. **uucico** reads *L.devices (Devices)*.

   `ACU tty008 hayes 2400`

   How do we use this modem? *How do we dial that number?*

5. **uucico** consults compiled in dialer info, or *modemcap*, *acucap* or *Dialers* file and places the call.

   `instructions for dialing Hayes modems`

6. **uucico** logs into remote system using instructions in *L.sys (Systems)*.

   `....ogin: Unewton ssword: itsme`

7. Remote system **uucico** verifies permissions and the transfer begins.

   `"newton has permission to send files to uucppublic"`

Figure 1-1. A successful file transfer

Possible Hitches

There are several reasons why the file transfer may not occur immediately. First of all, the *L.sys* (*Systems*) file may explicitly restrict outgoing calls to a particular time. Secondly, either the outgoing telephone line from system *newton* or the incoming telephone line on system *boston* may be busy.

If any of these things occur, **uucico** will not be able to make the connection. Instead, it will leave a status file in the spool directory (or in a hidden subdirectory in BNU) that contains the time last called and a message describing the status of the request. The next time **uucico** is invoked, it will try again, as long as a minimum retry period has elapsed.* This minimum period is designed to keep UUCP from tying up the telephone lines trying to call a remote system that is down. The minimum retry period is 55 minutes by default (one hour on some systems) in Version 2 UUCP.

BNU and BSD 4.3 use an "exponential backoff algorithm." That is, the retry period is shorter at first and lengthens as the number of failures increases. Both versions allow you to specify an alternate retry period on a system-by-system basis in the *L.sys* (*Systems*) file.

Note that the retry period is the minimum period within which **uucico** can try this system again, once it has been invoked. The retry period does not itself cause **uucico** to be invoked.

Connection: The Chat Script

When **uucico** is able to get through, it uses the last part of the line in the *L.sys* (*Systems*) file to log in to the remote system. This part of the line is often called the chat script, since it describes the conversation between the two systems. The chat script consists of alternating "expect" and "send" fields. For example:

- expect " ... ogin:"

- when "ogin:" is received, send "Unewton"

- expect " ... ssword:"

- when "ssword:" is received, send "itsme"

In this way, an automatic login can be performed. On the remote system, this presupposes that there is a login id in the */etc/passwd* file for a user named *Unewton*, with the password *itsme*. And the login shell for this user must be none other than **uucico**.

The two **uucico** programs, one on each system, work in tandem to make the transfer. First, they introduce themselves—in most implementations of UUCP, both systems must be known to each other. (That is, *newton* must have an *L.sys* entry for *boston*, and *boston* must have one for *newton*.)

---

*On most systems, **uucico** is invoked automatically for all systems (i.e., "uucico -r1") by **cron** at least once an hour. In addition, whenever someone makes a **uucp** or **uux** request to a particular system, **uucico** will be invoked for that system only (i.e., "uucico -r1 -s*system*"). If a status file exists and the retry period has not elapsed, **uucico** will quit without attempting the connection.

Next, the two systems must decide on which communications protocol to use. The choice of protocol usually depends on the type of physical communications link. For example, UUCP's default *g* protocol (named for its creator, Greg Chesson) does checksumming to produce a reliable transfer over an unreliable link, such as a telephone line, while other protocols do not need to do error checking, since they are designed to be used over reliable network links, such as TCP/IP.

Connection: The Transfer

After the preliminaries are out of the way, the actual transfer occurs. The **uucico** on the calling system is run in "master role"—it controls the link, specifying the request to be performed (send, receive, or execute). The receiving system's **uucico**, in "slave role," checks local permissions to see if the request can be performed, and if so, the transfer begins.

The sending system transmits packets of data; the receiving system sends back acknowledgements for each packet received. (Depending on the protocol in use, each packet may be checksummed; packets that did not come through correctly are resent.) While the file is being received, it is stored in a temporary file in the target system's spool directory. Once the transfer is complete, the target system's **uucico** copies it to the requested destination.

If any of the requests processed were for remote command execution (that is, **uux** requests), an execute file is created in the spool directory of the target system.

When the calling system's **uucico** is done with all of the requests it has queued for the remote system, it sends a hang-up request. If the remote **uucico** has any business of its own to transact (including requests for files needed for remote command execution), it refuses the hangup and the roles are reversed.

Hanging Up

When nothing is left to be transferred in either direction, the two **uucico**s agree to hang up. At this point, another daemon called **uuxqt** is fired up to scan the spool directory for any outstanding execution requests from remote systems. It reads the execute file(s) in its spool directory, checks that the remote system has permission to execute the requested command, and makes file transfer requests of its own if it needs additional files from the original system in order to carry out the command. If all went well, **uuxqt** forks a command to do what the user asked.

Throughout this entire process, the **uucico** programs on both systems write a variety of progress messages into a log file. Many errors are also written into a separate error logging file.

A Word About Modems

In the course of reading this book, you will come across the terms *ACU* (Automatic Call Unit) and *dialer*, as well as the more familiar *modem*.

To readers familiar only with modern so-called "smart modems" with built-in autodial capabilities using software commands and RJ-11 jacks for plugging directly into a telephone wall socket, these terms may be a little confusing.

A modem, strictly speaking, is simply a *modulator-demodulator*—a device for converting a string of bits on a serial line into audible tones for transmission across telephone lines.

Early modems were designed to be used in conjunction with an ordinary telephone. The call was dialed by hand, and then the telephone handset was placed into a device called an *acoustic coupler* so the modem could "talk" over the telephone.

Another device referred to as an automatic call unit, or programmable dialer, was used to place a call under computer control. The dialer was connected to the computer via a special interface defined by the RS-366 standard. A single dialer could service an entire bank of modems.

Keep in mind that UNIX was originally designed by the telephone company! According to our sources, in the early days of UNIX, direct serial connections were rarely used even for individual terminals. Everything was done by modem, even within the local office.

Banks of modems and separate dialers are still used with many large systems. Obscure though it may seem to many readers, there is a valid distinction between modem and dialer. It is not just a holdover from the early days of UUCP.

Another point to be aware of is that there are different protocols for modem communication and only modems that use the same modulation-demodulation standard can talk to each other. For many years, the Western Electric 103 (300 bps) and 212A (1200-bps) protocols were the prevailing standards. However, nowadays, few systems use modems slower than 2400 bps, and 9600 bps and higher speed modems are quite common. Many of these modems include automatic data compression and error correction. Some protocols to be aware of include V.32 (4800/9600 bps), V.32bis (V.32 with automatic compression), and V.22bis (2400 bps). Most of the newer modems are backwards-compatible, and support the older protocols.

Armed with a basic understanding of what goes on in a transfer, it is easy to understand what you must do to set up a link:

1. Establish a physical communications link between the two systems in question or, in the case of a dial-out link, between each system and a modem. (See Chapter 2, *The Physical Connection*.)

2. Give your system a name by which it will identify itself over the network. (See Chapter 3, *Setting Up a UUCP Link*.)

3. Create entries in the *L.sys* (*Systems*) file that describe when and how to reach the other systems with which you want to communicate. Each of the other systems must do the same for you. (See Chapter 3.)

4. Create entries in the *L-devices* (*Devices*) file to let UUCP know whether you are using a direct or modem link, which serial port is to be used, and, if you are using a modem, the type of modem (since different modems require different commands). (See Chapter 3.)

5. If you want to use a modem type that your system does not already know about, you must also write dialing instructions for that modem. (See Appendix B, *Talking to Modems*.)

6. Put in place security mechanisms, if required. You can control which files and directories on your system that remote systems have access to and which commands they can execute with **uux**. If you give each system a unique UUCP login instead of a single general-access login for all systems, you can control these permissions on a system-by-system basis. You (and the remote system administrator) must create the appropriate login ids in */etc/passwd*. (See Chapter 5, *Access and Security Considerations*.)

The exact procedures you will need to follow differ in places, depending on whether you are using Version 2 UUCP or BNU and on which implementation of Version 2 you are using. However, the basic thrust of what you need to do is the same on all systems. Keep your idea on the basic objectives, and the details will fall into place.

Files and Directories

UUCP has three primary directories:

- */usr/lib/uucp*, which contains the UUCP daemons, administrative shell scripts, and database files like *L.sys* and *L-devices*. In SVR4 and in SunOS at releases 4.0 and later, this directory contains only the UUCP daemons. The administrative scripts and database files have been moved to */etc/uucp*.

- */usr/spool/uucp*, which is used to store work files, data files, and execute files for spooled transfers. This directory is often referred to simply as *the spool directory*. In SunOS 4.0, the spool directory is */etc/spool/uucp*.

  Depending on the version of UUCP you are using, the spool directory may contain numerous subdirectories. See Chapter 6, *UUCP Administration*, for details.

- */usr/spool/uucppublic*, which is used to make sure that there is at least one place on every system to and from which UUCP can copy files. (For security reasons, it may be undesirable to give UUCP access to the entire filesystem.) This directory is often referred to as *the public directory.**

User programs like **uucp** and **uux** are kept in */usr/bin*.

UUCP Login IDs

As shipped, System III- or System V-derived UNIX systems include two login ids for UUCP in the */etc/passwd* file:

```
uucp::5:1:uucp:/usr/lib/uucp:
nuucp::6:1:uucp:/usr/spool/uucppublic:/usr/lib/uucp/uucico
```

The first is UUCP's administrative login. This is the user id that "owns" all UUCP files and directories and that receives mail about the progress of administrative programs. It is a normal login id, which has home directory */usr/lib/uucp* and

---

*AT&T documentation often refers to this directory by the name PUBDIR, without explanation. This is by transference from the UUCP source code which includes the line:

    #define PUBDIR */usr/spool/uucppublic*

just in case someone with source access wants to change the location of the public directory. In SunOS 4.0, this was linked to */var/spool/uucppublic*.

uses the Bourne shell by default. You should switch to this id to edit UUCP configuration files. It is used by the *cron* facility for running automatic UUCP maintenance procedures. On some systems, the administrative login is called **uucpadm**, and the working login is called **uucp**.

The second id in the password file is **uucico**'s working login. This is the login id that remote **uucico** programs will use to log in to your system. Notice that the home directory is */usr/spool/uucppublic* and that the login shell is */usr/lib/uucp/uucico*. This means that when a remote system logs in to your system, the program that is fired up is not the Bourne or C shell but, rather, another **uucico**, as we described above.

You can create additional working logins for **uucp** if you want. (This is often done for security reasons.) For example, you could have one login for all systems at your own site, and another for systems that dial in to you. You could then assign different levels of security to the two accounts. (We will give details in Chapter 5, *Access and Security Considerations*.) If appropriate, you can make all of these accounts members of the **uucp** group by listing them in the */etc/group* file.

BSD and older Xenix systems contain only a single login id—a working login with the name **uucp**. On these systems, you should edit the UUCP configuration files as *root* or create an administrative login as described in Chapter 5.

2

The Physical Connection

Building Serial Cables
Configuring Serial Ports
Communications Settings

The baseline of your UUCP network is the physical communication link. Until you have that link established, nothing else matters.

There are three types of communications links:

*   Direct (hardwired RS-232)

*   Modem (telephone)

*   Local area network (LAN)

For both direct and modem links, you will be using your system's serial (RS-232) lines as the communications medium. In the one case, you will be connecting a cable directly between two systems; in the other, you will be connecting a cable to your modem.

In this chapter, we will discuss RS-232 cabling, modems, and the UNIX system files that control the communication parameters for serial lines.

There are many different types of local area networks, each with their own setup requirements. We will not cover their physical setup here (although we will tell you in the next chapter how to set up UUCP to use a LAN that is already in place). See your documentation for details.

Building Serial Cables

The Electronic Industries Association (EIA) RS-232C standard (commonly referred to simply as RS-232) describes the serial cables used to connect computers or terminals to modems. By extension (really by bending, if not breaking, the standard), RS-232 cables have come to be used to connect computers to all kinds of serial devices—terminals, printers, ports on other computers, as well as just modems.

RS-232 cables consist of up to 25 wires, each with a specific function and each intended to carry a different signal. Only two of the wires are commonly used for data transmission; the rest are used for various kinds of control signals.

A piece of equipment (a computer or a modem) sends a signal across the cable by applying a small positive or negative voltage to a specific pin in the cable's end connector. The signal is carried across the wires in the cable to the corresponding pin at the other end, where it is detected by another piece of equipment. The voltage either may be held high (positive) as a go-ahead signal or may pulse quickly to convey data, with the sequence of negative and positive voltages being interpreted as binary codes.

Unfortunately, as it has now come to be applied, the RS-232 standard is rather broad and leaves a lot up to the equipment manufacturer. All that is "standard" is the function of each of the 25 pins found in the connectors on each end of a serial cable. All 25 pins are rarely used. Instead, different pieces of equipment require different signals to operate. To make things even more complicated, connectors with only 9 pins are becoming increasingly common.*

If you buy all of your equipment—computer, terminals, modems, printers, etc.—from a single manufacturer, you can probably also buy the exact cables needed to connect the various pieces. If, like most UNIX establishments, you mix and match hardware, you will probably end up building your own cables.

---

*In this chapter, we will assume you are using a standard 25-pin connector. Appendix C, *More on RS-232*, lists the pinouts for the 9-pin connector used on the IBM PC/AT.

We cannot describe here the mechanics of actually building a cable; what follows is a brief introduction to RS-232. You should be warned that RS-232 is a complex subject and seems to arouse near-religious opinions in some readers. We have tried to negotiate this subject with care. However, we are aware that some readers may find fault with our treatment, which reflects RS-232 as it is commonly practiced, rather than as it "should be" in an ideal world. Our objective is simply that, after reading this section, you should be able to figure out what kind of cable you need to connect either to a modem or directly to another system. You may then be able to buy the cable from an electronics supply store or, if you are handy with tools, build it yourself.

For more authoritative treatments of RS-232 and serial communications in general, we recommend *Technical Aspects of Data Communications* by John McNamara (Digital Press, 1982) and *C Programmer's Guide to Serial Communications* by Joe Campbell (Sams, 1987).

RS-232 Signals

Many of the signals defined by the RS-232 standard are rarely used. Table 2-1 lists the signals that are important for our present purposes.

Table 2-1. RS-232 Signals and Their Functions

Pin Number	Function	Direction DTE DCE
1	Frame Ground	↔
2	Transmit Data (TxD)	→
3	Receive Data (RxD)	←
4	Request to Send (RTS)	→
5	Clear to Send (CTS)	←
6	Data Set Ready (DSR)	←
7	Signal Ground (GND)	↔
8	Data Carrier Detect (DCD)	←
20	Data Terminal Ready (DTR)	→
22	Ring Indicator (RI)	←

Data Transmission

Only two of the 25 pins are used for data transmission:*

2   Transmit Data
3   Receive Data

These two lines are used differently by computers and modems. The RS-232 standard defines two types of equipment: Data Terminal Equipment (DTE) and Data Communications Equipment (DCE). Most (but not all) computers are DTE; modems are always DCE.

DTE uses pin 2 to transmit data and pin 3 to receive it, and DCE does the reverse.

To connect a terminal or computer to a modem or printer (DTE←→DCE), you want to make the connection *straight through*:

To make a connection between two computers (DTE←→DTE), you need a cables with lines 2 and 3 *crossed*:

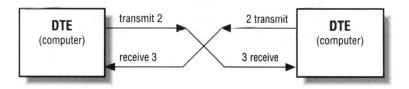

This is often called a *null-modem* or *modem-eliminator* cable.

Pin 1 is a safety ground and should be connected at one end (the host end of a computer-modem connection or either end of a direct link between two computers) and left unconnected at the opposite end of the cable. In a proper RS-232 implementation, pin 1 of the port is connected internally to the ground of the system. RS-232C actually says to connect at both ends, with the break done inside the modem. The proposed RS-232D standard says to connect only at the DTE

---

*The standard also calls for secondary transmit and receive lines, but they are rarely implemented.

end, as we have described here. But almost all manufacturers erroneously attach signal ground and frame ground inside the modem.*

Pin 7 is the signal ground. It provides the reference voltage against which other signals are measured. It should be connected straight through.

A pin is said to be "asserted" when a voltage greater than ± 3 volts (relative to signal ground) is present on the pin. On the data lines, a voltage more negative than -3 volts is considered a binary 1, and a voltage more positive than +3 volts is considered a binary 0. (Serial drivers usually assert voltages of ± 12 volts to allow a noise margin.)

On the control lines, a positive voltage is considered the "on" state and a negative voltage is considered "off." This is the direct opposite of the case for the data lines.

If you do not know whether a device is DTE or DCE, you can always tell by measuring the voltage on pins 2 and 3. The transmitter should always have a negative voltage, even when idle. If pin 2 is negative, the device is DTE. If pin 3 is negative, the device is DCE.

Hardware Handshaking

The remainder of the RS-232 lines shown in Table 2-1 are control lines. Some types of equipment (including modems) are not happy just to receive a stream of data. They need to feel more in control through a process called "handshaking." In handshaking, some preliminary communication between the two pieces of equipment must take place before data can be sent.

Let's consider what type of handshaking might be necessary between a computer and a modem in order to dial up another computer system.

First of all, on an outgoing call, the computer needs to know that the modem is available to make the call. Then the modem needs to tell the computer that it has made a connection.

---

*We have had a lot of controversy from our readers and reviewers over the proper use of pin 1. As noted in the latest BSD 4.3 UUCP documentation: "Proper earth grounding can make RS-23C connections virtually immune to electrical noise and lightning; improper grounding can make the system much more vulnerable. Whether or not pin 1 should be used is a tricky problem in electrical engineering, and sites that are very concerned about noise and lighting protection should have their entire communications network analyzed by a professional. At the very least, Frame Ground must not be confused with or connected to the Signal Ground, pin 7."

A computer (DTE) asserts pin 20 (Data Terminal Ready) to show that it is ready. A modem (DCE) asserts pin 6 (Data Set Ready). When the modem makes a connection with another modem on the other end, it asserts pin 8 (Data Carrier Detect) to let the computer know that a connection has actually been established. (Most UNIX systems ignore DSR and simply rely on DCD alone for this type of handshaking. In the case of UUCP, DTR is asserted when a program such as **getty** or **uucico** opens the device with an *open*(2) call. The *open* sleeps on the line until DCD is asserted by the modem or terminal on the other end of the line.) These voltages usually remain high during the entire transmission.

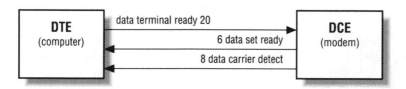

If the voltage on pin 20 drops, it tells the modem that the computer is unable to continue transmission, perhaps because it is down. The modem will hang up the phone if a call is in progress. If the voltage on pin 8 drops, it tells the computer that the modem no longer has a connection. In both cases, these pins give a simple "Yes/No" report on the state of the transmission.

This form of handshaking is sometimes referred to as *modem control*. As we will see later, on some systems, there is a UNIX system file that lets you choose whether or not to enable modem control on a serial line.

There is a further level of handshaking that is used to control the rate of data transmission. Particularly when transmitting large amounts of data at high speed, it is possible that one end of a link may try to send data faster than the other can receive it. To keep this from happening, there is a "flow-control handshake" that allows either end to prevent the other from sending any more data until it gets the go-ahead.

In the RS-232 standard, flow control is defined only for half-duplex connections—that is, for connections in which data can be transmitted only in one direction at a time. However, the standard has been adapted, *de facto*, for full-duplex communications as well.

In the half-duplex standard, the DTE asserts RTS when it wants to send data. The DCE replies with CTS when it is ready, and the DTE begins sending data. Unless RTS and CTS are both asserted, only the DCE can send data.

However, in the full-duplex variations, RTS/CTS is used as a kind of "throttle." The signals have the opposite meaning than they do for half-duplex communications.

Whenever a DTE device is able to *accept* data, it asserts pin 4, Request to Send. If the DCE is ready to *accept* data, it asserts pin 5, Clear to Send. If the voltage on RTS or CTS drops at any time, this tells the sending system that the receiver is not ready for more data: "Whoa! Hold on till I get my buffers cleared." Since this flow control handshake is implemented in the serial port hardware, it is considerably more efficient and reliable than the CTRL-S/CTRL-Q (XON/XOFF) handshake that can be performed in software.

If both types of handshaking are used, the entire conversation between computer and modem might look like this (where a plus sign signifies raising the voltage on the line and a minus sign signifies dropping the voltage):

Device	Signal	Meaning
Computer	DTR +	*I want to call another system. Are you ready?*
Modem	DSR +	*I'm turned on. Go ahead and dial.*
Modem	DCD +	*I've got your party, sir.*
Computer	RTS +	*Can I send data now?*
Modem	CTS +	*Sure. Go ahead.*
Computer	TxD ...	*Data sent out.*
Modem	... RxD	*Data received.*
Modem	CTS -	*Hold on for a moment!*
Modem	CTS +	*I'm ok again. Shoot!*
	...	*Previous four steps may be repeated, with either device in the sending role, and either device using flow control.*
Computer	DTR -	*I'm done. Please hang up.*
Modem	DCD -	*Whatever you say.*

Pulling the Wool Over Their Eyes

All of the above sounds good in theory, but in practice, it will not always work. Connecting a computer to a modem is generally easy, since a DTE to DCE connection is what RS-232 was made for. A straight-through cable connecting pins 1 through 8 and 20 (or all 25 pins) will usually do the trick. You should be able to get suitable cables at most computer or electronics stores.

Things can get quite a bit more complicated for a direct connection between two computers.

Just as the function of pins 2 and 3 is asymmetrical between DTE and DCE devices, so too is the function of pins 6, 8, and 20. A DTE device (a computer or terminal) asserts DTR (pin 20) and expects to receive DSR (pin 6) and DCD (Data Carrier Detect). A DCE device (a modem) asserts DSR and DCD and expects to receive DTR. If you connect two DTE devices with a straight-through cable, no handshaking can occur.

(On many UNIX systems, there is a clear symptom of this problem. The system asserts pin 20 when it wants to open a serial port. The success of the **open** call is dependent on getting back a response on DCD (or possibly DSR). The remote computer, not being designed as DCE, will never respond, and whatever process tried to read or write from the port will hang.)

To get around the handshaking problem, a null modem cable can cross some of the control lines as well as the data lines:

This allows DTR (pin 20) on each DTE interface to drive both DSR (pin 6) and pin 8 (DCD) on the other. That is, whenever either side asserts DTR, the other side thinks it is getting DSR and DCD.

Some publications suggest that you can fake out pins 4 and 5 by tying them together at each end of the cable. As a result, whenever the computer looks for a go-ahead signal, it gets it—from itself. This is really a poor practice. It will generally work if you are simply connecting terminals, since people cannot type fast enough to ever require the computer to cry uncle. (Even with terminals, there can be problems. For instance, a function key programmed to send a long string of characters—or a PC trying to upload a file—can send too fast for a loaded system to capture them all. Dropped characters can result, unless the system can rely on the flow-control handshake.)

For direct connections with UUCP, you should always connect pins 4 and 5, crossed so that the two DTE interfaces will converse correctly (unless, of course, one of the two computers has a DCE interface, in which case the cable should be straight through).

Here is the pinning for a full null-modem cable:

(You should only do this for a null-modem cable, since a modem really does require the DTR/DCD handshaking signals. If you use a cable like this with a modem, it will not know to hang up when the computer closes the port and drops (deasserts) DTR. This can result in very large telephone bills!)

A tip: if you are stringing cables through walls or ceilings, you should use straight-through cables with all necessary lines, then use secondary cables to do any null modem tricks. This will give you more flexibility in the long run.

Note also that though the official distance limit for RS-232 cables is 50 feet, in practice, they can be used over much larger distances. See Appendix C, *More on RS-232*, for details.

Like all generalities, the advice given above may be insufficient. Finding the right cable can be simple and straightforward. Or it can be a seemingly hopeless task for which no one has the right advice. You should be sure to read the documentation for the devices you are trying to connect. It may be difficult to translate the raw description given for each device into the information necessary to connect them to one another, but you will succeed if you persevere.

The use of a device called a breakout box can be invaluable if you are trying to build your own cable. (You can usually pick one up at any electronics supply store. A good breakout box is expensive but worth the investment if you plan to build cables.) The breakout box allows you to easily rearrange the wires in a cable for testing purposes and may include LEDs that display which signals are actually active at any point.

A final word of caution: many devices (such as terminals or modems) allow you to configure the serial connection by setting internal DIP switches. For instance, on a Hayes modem, if switch 1 is down, the modem will force its own DTR high, so that it can answer the telephone even if the computer itself is not asking for a connection. Don't do this! Check your modem to make sure someone else has not done it either, since it can complicate the search for the correct cable. Be sure to read the manufacturer's documentation for details like this that may affect the operation of the RS-232 link.

Once you have the cable, you have to connect it to a serial port. Your system has a number of serial ports, typically assigned to user terminals or printers. You need to find an available port or make one available, perhaps by removing a terminal.

You then need to configure the port, specifying whether or not it is used for dialing out, dialing in, or both (the difference being whether your system should put up a login prompt or not) and setting various communication parameters. Note that you will normally need superuser privileges to edit the files that control serial port configuration.

Naming Ports

Serial ports, like all devices on UNIX systems, correspond to special files in the directory */dev*. Serial lines usually have names beginning with the letters *tty*. For example, the special file for the eighth serial port might be called */dev/tty008*.

For convenience, you can also create a new special file for the device which has a name that you can identify more easily. The **mknod** command is used to create special files. It takes four arguments: the name to be given to the device, the type of device (in the case of a serial line, **c** for character device), and the major and minor device numbers of the device. These last two values differ from system to system. However, to create a new device with the same values as an existing device, you can simply use **ls -l** to find out the existing values:

```
# ls -l /dev/tty008
crw--w--w-  1 uucp  doc 0, 8 Jun 26 17:11 /dev/tty008
# mknod modem c 0 8
# ls -l /dev/modem
crw--w--w-  2 uucp  doc 0, 8 Jun 26 17:11 /dev/modem
```

See your documentation for details.* If you do this, it will be easy for you to remember which port you have the modem connected to. It will also be easier to change ports. You will not have to edit any UUCP configuration files—you can simply change the assignment. For example, to switch the modem to *tty009*, you might enter the commands:

```
# rm /dev/modem
# mknod modem c 0 9
```

Many systems still follow the convention of linking the serial lines attached to modems to names such as */dev/cul0*, */dev/cul1*, etc. (call unit line 0, call unit line 1, etc.). This is a holdover from the original design of UUCP, which calls for a separate dialer device, or ACU, (attached via an RS-366 connection). One dialer (usually connected to a line called *cua0*, *cua1*, and so on) might service a number of modems.

Throughout this book, we will refer to devices by standard port names (like *tty008*), but you should be aware that some systems may use other names.

Putting Up the Login Prompt

The **getty** program monitors serial ports on a UNIX system, starting a login process when activity is detected on the line (e.g., when a modem signals its presence by asserting DCD).† Just as there is a **getty** running for each terminal connected to the system, there needs to be a **getty** on the modem line when someone dials into your system. However, you do not want **getty** to monitor a dial-out line.

If **getty** is monitoring a dial-out line, it may respond to the login prompt put up by the remote system with a login prompt of its own, leaving the connection in a kind of "deadly embrace" as the two systems keep trying to log each other in. System performance degrades quickly as the two systems send repeated "login:" and "password:" messages at each other.

Up until System V Version 2.1, you could use a single port for either incoming or outgoing calls, but not for both. You had to set up two ports—one for outgoing calls and another for incoming calls. This is not too much of a problem for direct

---

*Note that some publications (including earlier editions of this handbook) suggest simply linking the special file to a new name with the **ln** command. While this will work on most systems, we have been told that this creates a security loophole and is not advised. It will not work at all on Version 7 or BSD 4.1 systems.

†A fine distinction: On BSD systems prior to BSD 4.3 and on Xenix systems, it is */etc/init*, not *getty*, that sleeps on the line. When DCD is asserted, *getty* is executed and prints the login prompt. In System V, *getty* sleeps directly on the line.

connections, although it takes up two ports, but for dial-out connections, it demands that you have two modems as well. The alternative is to disable the **getty** whenever you want to dial out and re-enable it when you are done, or to use **cron** to set a schedule for disabling/enabling the **getty** on one port at specific times during the day.

Starting with release 3, System V provides a version of **getty** called **uugetty** that allows the same port to be used both for receiving and for placing calls. The **uugetty** on the calling system will "step aside" so that no conflicts occur.

BSD 4.3 has a very different mechanism called **acucntrl** that has essentially the same effect. However, it only works on the Digital Equipment Corporation VAX. SunOS and Xenix have special workarounds of their own.

The configuration of the serial ports on UNIX systems is controlled by the following system files:

- */etc/inittab* (System III and System V)

- */etc/ttys* (BSD 4.*x* and Xenix Systems)

Once you have selected the serial port(s) that you are going to use for your dial-out line, you must modify the appropriate file on your system, as explained in the sections that follow.

/etc/inittab (System V)

The */etc/inittab* file has an entry for each serial port on your system. Entries look like this:

/etc/inittab

```
      id          type
      |           |
      001:23:respawn:/etc/getty tty001 9600
      002:off:respawn:/etc/getty tty002 9600
             |                    |
           level              process
```

Field	Function in */etc/inittab*
id	A one- to four-letter identifier which is used by *init* to label entries in its process table, generally (but not always) corresponding to the device name for the serial line. Port ids vary from system to system. Consult your documentation for details.
level	A string of characters consisting of [0-6,a-c], the *run level* of the process. The entry is considered *active* whenever the internal level of *init* matches *level*; otherwise, *init* terminates the process if it is running. When *level* is unspecified, it defaults to the string "0123456". A string such as "off" will cause no process to be associated with the line.
type	How *init* is to treat the process. *type* is one of the following strings: *off, once, wait, respawn, boot, bootwait, power, powerwait,* or *initdefault*. A detailed description of these options can be found in the *UNIX System Administrator's Guide* (or equivalent documentation for your system).
process	The program invoked when *init* activates an entry. For serial lines, the process is the **getty** (or **uugetty**) program that puts up the login prompt.

getty can take a number of options. One that you might find useful is **-t***n* for specifying a timeout value (in seconds). For example, with the option **-t60**, if a user attempts to log in but does not complete the login in 60 seconds, **getty** will automatically hang up the line. There are other options for **uugetty**.

getty takes as its first argument the device name of the serial port on which it is to run. (This is the name of the special file in the *dev* directory corresponding to this device.)

The second argument to **getty** is a label that is used to look up the appropriate entry in another file, */etc/gettydefs*, that contains serial communications parameters such as baud rate, parity, etc. The speed (baud rate) is conventionally used as the label, but other labels may be used as well or instead of the speed.

After editing */etc/inittab*, issue the command **init q** (**telinit q** on some systems) to force the system to re-read the file and make the changes.

Using a Bidirectional Port   *(BNU only)*

With BNU, a program called **uugetty** can be used in place of **getty** in the
/etc/inittab file. Even if you have only one dial-in/out port, you do not have to
manually disable and enable **getty**. The **uugetty** program is wise enough not to
put up a login prompt when the line is in use for outgoing calls.

The */etc/inittab* entry for a bidirectional port might look like this:

```
27:2:respawn:/usr/lib/uucp/uugetty —r tty12 2400
```

The **–r** option tells *uugetty* to wait to read for a character before putting up a
login prompt. If there is a **uugetty** on each end of the line, this prevents the kind
of "deadly embrace" that can result as two systems that are running **getty** try to
log each other in. The system that first does an explicit write to the line will be
the caller; the other system will respond with a login prompt. (We'll talk more
about this later when we discuss login chat scripts for **uucico**.)

You can edit the */etc/inittab* file manually using a standard text editor. SVR3 also
provides a menu-driven utility called *sysadm* that facilitates general system
administration. Use the *uucpmgmt* menu in *sysadm* and specify "bidirectional"
when you are prompted for the type of port.

Obviously, if you can set up a bidirectional port, you do not need to worry about
the monkey business in the next two sections that describe how to enable and disable ports. Go ahead to the discussion on communications parameters.

Using Two Ports   *(Version 2)*

To disable the **getty** for a dial-out port, you must edit the */etc/inittab* file. With
System V, you enable incoming calls by placing the word "respawn" in the third
field of the */etc/inittab* entry for your chosen dial-in port. The word "off" in the
third field disables **getty** for a port. For example, if you want to use port *tty007*
for dialing out and port *tty005* for incoming connections, you would modify the
inittab entries to read:

```
005:2:respawn:/etc/getty tty005 2400
007:2:off:/etc/getty tty007 2400
```

Using One Port   *(Version 2, System V only)*

In SVR2, if you are using only one port for both outgoing and incoming connections, you can temporarily disable **getty** when dialing out. Be aware that this is a
fairly awkward hack with a number of limitations.

The procedure involves specifying the run level (or *init* state) at which the port will be monitored by a **getty**. The *init* states are specified in the second field of the entries in the */etc/inittab* file. For example, an entry for port *tty007* might normally be configured as follows:

```
007:23:respawn:/etc/getty tty007 2400
```

The second field indicates that **getty** will be invoked if the run level is either 2 *or* 3. To prevent logins on *tty007* at run level 3, you would modify the entry to read:

```
007:2:respawn:/etc/getty tty007 2400
```

so that **getty** is enabled **only** at run level 2. Whenever you want the port to be used for dialing out instead of dialing in, enter:

```
# init 3
```

to disable **getty**. Now port *tty007* can only be used for dialing out. (The modem may still answer if someone dials in, but no login prompt will be displayed.)

To allow incoming calls again, type:

```
# init 2
```

Since only the superuser can switch run levels, this does not allow the average user to freely access the dial-out port.

It would probably be more convenient to establish a dial-out/dial-in schedule for a port and to disable/enable **getty** automatically. You can make an entry in the *crontab* file to automatically switch *init* states at specific times. For example, you might decide to spool all of your **uucp** requests until late at night and disable logins from 2 a.m. to 5 a.m. with the following lines in *crontab*:

```
0 2 * * *   /etc/init 3
0 5 * * *   /etc/init 2
```

(If you make a fixed schedule, remember to modify the *schedule* field in the *L.sys* (or *Systems*) file so that UUCP connections are made only during those periods when **getty** is disabled. See Chapter 3, *Setting Up a UUCP Link*, for details on the *schedule* field. See Chapter 6, *UUCP Administration*, for more information on *crontab*.)

A major drawback of using run levels to manage a single bidirectional port is that it will not work for more than one line (unless you use up a couple of run levels). Far and away the worst problem, though, is that there is no provision for checking whether or not some other process is already using the line. If a user is already logged in, he will not be amused when *cron* hangs him up to take the line away for UUCP's use.

/etc/ttys (Xenix and BSD 4.x Systems)

The */etc/ttys* file contains an entry for each terminal line on the system.

There are two versions in common use: the BSD 4.3 format and an older, more cryptic version still used by Xenix, SunOS, and other systems derived from earlier BSD versions.

Read the instructions below on the two *ttys* formats. Then when you have edited the file to your satisfaction, type:

```
# kill -1 1
```

to force *init* to reread */etc/ttys*.

---

ttys Format   *(BSD 4.3)*

BSD 4.3 */etc/ttys*

Field	Function in */etc/ttys*
devname	The name of the special file in the *dev* directory that corresponds to the device.
command	The command to be run by *init* when DCD is detected on the line. This is normally *getty* but could be another command, such as the command to start a window system. In BSD 4.3, *getty* is usually given with an argument that specifies the *gettytab* entry to be used for determining the speed and line characteristics. Since spaces and tabs are used to separate fields in */etc/ttys*, the command must be quoted if it includes an argument.
terminal type	The name of the terminal attached to the line. This should be the name as defined in the */etc/termcap* terminal database. The following additional keywords are provided to handle three cases in which a number of different terminals might end up logging in on the same line:

dialup   This line is connected to a modem.

plugboard   This line is connected to a board which allows different terminal cables to be swapped.

network   This line is a local area network connection.

Note that the presence of the terminal type field in the BSD 4.3 *ttys* replaces the */etc/ttytype* file that was used for this purpose in earlier BSD versions. Note that the terminal type specified here does not matter to UUCP and can be overridden by a user dialing in manually.

status   The word **on** if the *command* is to be executed or **off** if it is not. Additional flags may be specified after **on** or **off**. The word **secure** must be present to allow root to login on a particular terminal. The flag **window="command"** specifies a window system command to be executed by *init* before it starts *getty*.

comment   Comments can appear anywhere in the file. They are introduced by # and are terminated by a newline.

NOTE

SunOS 4.0 and later releases use a 4.3 BSD-style */etc/ttys* file, although for binary compatibility, it is called */etc/ttytab*. The *init* program generates a read-only */etc/ttys* file from it. You should be sure to edit *ttytab* rather than *ttys*. Older SunOS systems use the *ttys* format documented on the next page.

ttys Format

(Xenix, SunOS, etc.)
Older /etc/ttys

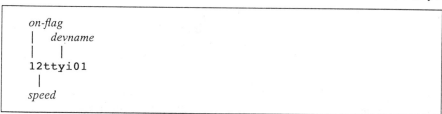

```
on-flag
 |    devname
 |     |
12ttyi01
 |
speed
```

Field	Function in */etc/ttys*

on-flag Either 0 (indicating that no *getty* should be forked by **init**) or 1 (indicating that a *getty* should be forked).

speed A code referring to a type of **getty** to fork. Version 7, Xenix, and BSD 4.1 have this information hardcoded in the **getty** program. BSD 4.2 and later systems use a definition in the file */etc/gettytab* for more flexibility. The *gettytab* entry describes the serial communications parameters for this port. Codes may vary from system to system; some commonly used codes are shown in the table below.

devname The name of the special file in the *dev* directory corresponding to this device. In SunOS, the device name indicates whether or not modem control is enabled on the line. See below for details.

Note that spaces should not separate the fields.

Table 2-2. Sample Speed Labels in /etc/ttys

Label	Description
0	Automatic baud rate selection
f	1200-baud
6	2400-baud
2	9600-baud
5	Dial-in 1200

The first character of each entry specifies whether a **init/getty** will monitor that line. If the first character is a zero (0), the entry line is ignored, no **getty** is spawned for that line, and the port is disabled for user login. An entry of one (1) starts a **getty** process for the line.

For example, two entries are shown below:

```
12ttyi01
02ttyi08
```

/dev/ttyi01 will have a **getty** at 9600 baud. */dev/ttyi08* will not have a **getty**.

Bidirectional Lines

BSD 4.3 includes a mechanism called **acucntrl** that is invoked by **uucico** to allow a line with a sleeping *init* on it to be used for call out. It does this by opening */dev/kmem* and scribbling on the kernel *tty* data structures in such a way that the **init** never wakes up. It runs only on a VAX, and if the **uucico** aborts without running **acucntrl** again to restore the line, it remains in the dial-out state.

SunOS has a mechanism of its own that allows a port to be used in both directions. The serial driver supports two "entry points" for each port.

If you open the device with a minor device number from 0 through 127 (usually corresponding to names *tty000* to *tty127*), the driver will monitor the serial interface for carrier detect and will only put up a **getty** when DCD is detected.

Minor device numbers from 128 through 255, usually corresponding to names of the form *cua0* to *cua127*, refer to the same physical device but allow the device to be opened even when DCD is not present.

Henceforth, we'll refer to these lines as the *ttyd?* and *cua?* lines, where the question-mark represents any arbitrary minor device number.

Once a *cua?* line has been opened, the corresponding *tty?* line cannot be opened. The reverse is also true. The net effect is that a modem can be attached to a line such as *tty000* (by convention usually renamed to *ttyd0*) and used for dial in and also used for dial out by referring to it with the name *cua0*.

To enable this kind of bidirectional port, here's what to do:

1. Create the *ttyd?* line simply by renaming or linking the desired tty. For example:

    ```
    # ln /dev/ttya /dev/ttyd0
    ```

2. Create the *cua?* line with *mknod* (since the minor device number must be offset by 128):

    ```
    # mknod /dev/cua0 c 12 128
    ```
    (for /dev/cua1, the minor device would be 129 and so on)

3. Enable logins for the *ttyd?* line by putting a line like the following in */etc/ttytab*:

    ```
    ttyd0 "/usr/etc/getty d2400"    unknown    on
    ```

4. Disable what Sun calls "software carrier detect" for the dialout version of the port (*/dev/cua?*). You can do this with the **ttysoftcar** command. For example:

```
# ttysoftcar n /dev/cua0
```

5. Use the *cua?* name in the configurations files for dial-out processes (such as **tip** and **uucp**). See the discussion of *L-devices* in Chapter 3, *Setting Up a UUCP Link.*

Xenix Serial Device Names
(Xenix)

Xenix runs on personal computers, which usually have only one or two serial ports. In DOS (and likely in the PC hardware documentation as well), these ports are referred to as COM1: and COM2:. However, there are expansion boards that provide additional serial ports.

You can tell how many ports Xenix thinks your PC has by looking at the information it displays when it boots. One of the lines should say something like this:

```
Standard serial board COM1: has 1 port(s)
```

Like every other UNIX system, Xenix uses special files in */dev* to refer to each of these ports. However, the naming conventions are somewhat different. Among other things, there are separate device files associated with each port for dialing in (with modem control) and for dialing out (without modem control. These device names are listed in Table 2-3.

Table 2-3. Xenix Serial Device Names

Device	Description	Use When Dialing...
tty11 or *tty1a*	COM1:, no modem control	out
tty12 or *tty1A*	COM1:, modem control	in
tty13 or *tty2a*	COM2:, no modem control	out
tty14 or *tty2A*	COM2:, modem control	in

Note that the device names for ports with and without modem control do not represent physically different ports and you cannot use them at the same time.

The alphabetic designations are for use with serial expansion cards. For example, you could access up to eight serial ports through COM1: by using the names *tty1[aA]* through *tty1[hH]*.

If you are using a line only for dialing out, you can use a device (e.g., *tty11* or *tty1a*) without modem control; if you are using a line for dialing in, you should use a device with modem control (e.g., *tty12* or *tty1A*).* If you are using a line for both dialing in and dialing out, you should use a device with modem control and then disable or enable a **getty** on the line as described below.

Temporarily Disabling/Enabling getty
(Xenix)

On a Xenix system, you can temporarily disable a line by invoking the **disable** command as superuser. For example:

```
# disable /dev/tty1A
```

If the line is already disabled, you will get an error message that you can safely ignore.

To allow remote systems to call in, use the **enable** command:

```
# enable /dev/tty1A
```

Your system can now receive calls from remote systems and will prompt for a login on */dev/tty1A*. You should wait at least 60 seconds between successive **enable** and **disable** commands to allow time for the files to be updated.

Communications Settings

In order to communicate over either a direct serial connection or a modem, two machines must be set up to share the same communication parameters. In most cases, these parameters have defaults that can be used without modification.

What this means is that all you normally need to do is to specify the correct speed in either */etc/inittab* or */etc/ttys* as described above. Other communications parameters will automatically be associated with that speed.

The speed is specified in bits-per-second (bps). This is often (erroneously) also called the *baud rate*, a holdover from the Baudot code used in telegraphy. (Properly speaking, the baud rate is the frequency of the electrical impulses on the communications line. It is equivalent to bits-per-second only if one bit is encoded per electrical signal. This is not always true. For example, both

---

*This runs contrary to the expected operation of the modem control serial lines. Theoretically, if you use a device without modem control, the call-out **uucico** will not have any way to hang up the modem when it is done and will have to assert DCD so that it can open the modem for dial out. Nonetheless, what we have shown here is the serial port usage recommended by SCO for use with Xenix.

"1200-baud" and "2400-baud" modems actually operate at only 600 baud but encode (respectively) two or four bits per signal.)

You should remember that the *speed* field is really just a pointer to another file where the actual communications parameters are set. Some systems use other labels than just the speed to point to the correct entry.

For a direct connection, the speed should probably be 9600; for a modem connection, it depends on the speed or your modem and the speed of the modems used by the systems with which you are communicating. (You have to go with the lowest common denominator. 2400 bps is probably the most common, although 9600-bps and even higher-speed modems are readily available.)

Serial communication occurs as a series of clocked voltage pulses over lines 2 and 3 of a serial cable. If a modem is involved, these pulses are converted to audible tones (modulated) for transmission over the telephone line then converted back into serial pulses (demodulated) by the modem at the other end.

The basic data unit is a byte—eight bits (or, in this case, eight serial pulses).* A byte is accompanied by two or three additional bits: a start bit and either one or two stop bits.

When no data is being transmitted, the signal on pin 2 (or the carrier tone on a modem) is equivalent to a continuous stream of binary ones. In a holdover from the early days of telegraphy, this is referred to as the MARK state. (In those days of electromechanical relays, constant negative voltage was the preferred idle signal; it resulted in the stylus making a continuous mark on a roll of paper, hence its name.) The start bit is a voltage equivalent to binary 0. By contrast to MARK, this state is often referred to as SPACE. After the start bit is received, both devices count the desired number of data bits and look for the stop bit, which is always binary 1 (MARK). Two stop bits are usually used at lower speeds such as 110 baud.

In the U.S., it is also possible to use only seven data bits. This is most commonly done in communications links transmitting only text files, since U.S. ASCII only uses seven of the eight bits of a byte. In fact, since some older UNIX utilities used the most significant bit in a byte as a flag, the Simple Mail Transfer Protocol (SMTP) used by Usenet and UNIX mail cannot support eight-bit character codes, so only seven-bit data is guaranteed to be transferred network-wide. Eight-bit character sets such as ISO 8859-1 are vital for European computing, though, so using seven bits is a parochialism we will all soon have cause to regret.†

---

*In data communications, the term "octet" is now used to represent this basic data unit.
†A workaround has been provided by the ISO 2022 code extension, which provides for encoding eight-bit characters in seven bits.

Serial links also have the option of using a simple form of error checking known as *parity*. Parity uses the setting of an additional bit to verify that what was sent out is the same as what was received. There are five possible parity settings:

Odd   The value of the parity bit, plus the value of the data bits, must always add up to an odd number.

Even   The value of the parity bit, plus the value of the data bits, must always add up to an even number.

Mark   The parity bit is always one.

Space   The parity bit is always zero.

None   No parity bit is sent.

Even or odd parity are the only settings that provide any error protection. The sending computer sets the parity bit to 0 or 1 depending on the value of the data bits. The receiving computer checks to make sure that the parity came out as advertised—odd or even. If line noise (e.g., on a telephone line) causes one data bit to be changed (appear 0 or 1 when it was not sent out that way), the parity will not come out right.

However, an even number of simultaneous errors in the same byte will cancel each other out. Since line noise usually occurs in bursts, parity is relatively useless as an error checking mechanism and has been superseded by various types of more complex error checking implemented in software. Nonetheless, it is a feature of serial communications that cannot be overlooked, since both sides must agree to use the same parity settings or no communication will occur.

One more important concept is that of the BREAK, which is sometimes referred to as a character but is in fact an interruption in the normal framing of characters (start bit, data bits, stop bit). A BREAK is a SPACE state that extends past the length of time normally required to transmit a character. Some terminals have a BREAK key that generates this condition, and in System V, BSD 4.2 and BSD 4.3, UUCP can generate a true BREAK. Other UNIX systems simulate a BREAK by changing the speed to a very low rate, sending NULL characters (all zeros), and then restoring the old speed in order to "break the frame" (i.e., keep the stop bit from being detected).

Serial Port Configuration Files

Some UNIX systems use one start bit and one stop bit, eight data bits, and no parity. Others use seven bits, even parity. However, whenever **uucico** starts up, it automatically switches the line to eight bits, no parity. (The simple error checking provided by parity is far inferior to the more complex error checking algorithms implemented in software by communications protocols like UUCP.)

What this means is that all you normally need to do is to specify the correct speed in either */etc/inittab* or */etc/ttys*. The rest of the settings should be set correctly without any intervention on your part. If any system with which you are communicating uses nonstandard communications parameters, though, you may need to create new entries in the file */etc/gettydefs* (System V) or */etc/gettytab* (BSD 4.2 or 4.3).

A brief discussion of these two files is given below. See your UNIX documentation for additional details on how to set communications line parameters. Some good places to start are the reference manual pages *termio*(7) (*termio*(4) on some systems), *tty*(4) and *stty*(1).

/etc/gettydefs (System V)

In System V, the file */etc/gettydefs* contains the definition of the communications parameters for a serial line. Each entry in the file has five fields separated by hash marks (#) and looks something like this:

/etc/gettydefs

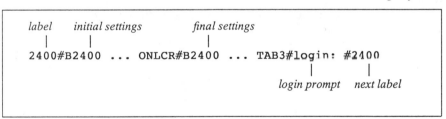

35

Field	Function in */etc/gettydefs*
label	The label that is used in */etc/inittab* to tell the **getty** process which *gettydefs* entry to read. This field is often, but not always, filled in with the baud rate of the entry. However, it can be any label that you find convenient, as long as there is a matching entry in both files.
initial settings	The *termio* I/O control codes that will be used by **getty** to initialize the line. These codes will be used until the *login* process takes over. Some of the codes you may need to change are listed below.
final settings	The *termio* I/O control codes that **getty** sets for the line before turning over control to the **login** program. These are the permanent settings that will be in effect when the user logs in. (The user can change settings with the **stty** command.)
login prompt	The prompt that **getty** will display on the screen. This prompt can include newlines by embedding the escape sequence \n. For example:

```
O'Reilly & Associates, Inc. CTIX 3.2\n\nlogin:
```

next label	The label to be used instead if the remote system (or user trying to log in) sends a BREAK or if there is an error reading the current entry. Many systems use this mechanism to create a linked list of entries at different speeds, so that a dialup line can be used by callers with modems at different baud rates. For example:

```
1200#B1200...IGNPAR#B1200...IGNPAR#login:#2400
2400#B2400...IGNPAR#B2400...IGNPAR#login:#9600
9600#B9600...IGNPAR#B9600...IGNPAR#login:#1200
```

The line will first be set to 1200 baud. If a user dialing in sends a BREAK, the speed will switch to 2400. If the user sends another BREAK, the speed will go to 9600 then back to 1200. Assuming the autoanswer modem has also been set up to cycle between baud rates, this line can service incoming calls at any of the three speeds.

You should not generally need to write a new *gettydefs* entry, and if you do, you may just want to copy one of the existing lines and modify a few parameters.

We do not have space here to discuss all of the possible I/O control codes that you can use in this file. However, Table 2-4 lists a few of the ones that might come up if you are trying to establish a telephone link with another system (especially a non-UNIX system that may not use the same default communications parameters.)

Table 2-4. I/O Control Codes in gettydefs

I/O Code	Meaning
B*nnnn*	Baud rate (e.g., B9600 for 9600 baud).
CLOCAL	No modem control on this line; it is a direct connection. Depending on the cabling you are using, this may be irrelevant. To be safe, use -CLOCAL when connecting to a modem.
CS*n*	Character size in bits. Usually CS7 or CS8.
CSTOPB	If set, use two stop bits. If not set, use only one stop bit.
HUPCL	Terminate program if device is closed. Be sure to use this on dialup lines.
IXANY	Allow any character to restart output stopped with CTRL-S (default is only CTRL-Q).
IXON	Enable XON/XOFF (CTRL-S/CTRL-Q) flow control. See **IXANY** above.
PARENB	Parity is enabled. If set, default is EVEN parity.
PARODD	If **PARENB** is enabled, use ODD parity.
SANE	Use default settings for a variety of options.

You should be extremely careful in modifying */etc/gettydefs*, since a corrupted file can make it impossible to log in to your system from any terminal. You should not modify the I/O control codes in any existing entry unless you are sure you know what you are doing.

Instead, you should copy the *gettydefs* file, then test that the entry you have created is legal by invoking **getty** manually with the **-c** (*check*) option:

```
# /etc/getty -c file
```

Even then, it may be a good idea to create a new entry and test it with a single serial line rather than replacing the entry used by all of your terminal lines.

/etc/gettytab (BSD 4.2 and 4.3)

BSD 4.2 and 4.3 systems use the file */etc/gettytab* to describe the characteristics that will be assigned to serial lines.

The *gettytab* file uses a format similar to the terminal database */etc/termcap*. That is, it defines a series of codes that describes the line characteristics. Some of the codes simply indicate the presence or absence of a characteristic. Others assign a string or numeric value.

Certain line characteristics are assumed by **getty**; others are set by an entry in /etc/gettytab labeled "default" that is read before any speed-selected entry.

The syntax of the *gettytab* file is far too complex to describe here. However, to give you a feeling for what the entries look like, a sample of several entries from a SunOS 4.1 system is shown below.

Each newline must be escaped, since each entry is actually a single line. Individual characteristics are separated with a colon. (Unlike many other examples shown in this book, the backslashes at the end of each line do actually appear in the file.)

```
default:\
        :ap:lm=\r\n%h login\72 :sp#9600:

2|std.9600|9600-baud:\
        :sp#9600:

D2400|Fast-Dial-2400:\
        :nx=D1200:tc=2400-baud:
```

The first line of each description contains the name(s) by which the description can be referenced. Multiple names can be separated by vertical bars (|).

For example, as shown in Table 2-2, an entry of *2* in an /etc/ttys entry points to the 9600-baud entry shown above.

In the default description, the capability **ap** says that it is ok to use any parity. The **fd** capability specifies the length of formfeed delay (necessary on old-style Teletype terminals). The **sp#** capability specifies the speed. The **im** (initial message) capability can be used to print a banner before the login prompt. (The login prompt itself can be customized with the **lm** capability, but since it is simply appended to **im**, setting either will do the trick. For example, the above **im** will be combined with the default **lm** built into **getty** ("login:") to produce the following prompt:

```
California Cool, Inc.

login:
```

The entries labeled *3* and *5* are linked entries for dial in. The **nx** capability specifies a linked entry to be tried if the first fails or the user enters a BREAK when trying to log in. The **to** capability specifies a timeout in seconds, after which the line will hang up if the user has not logged in. The **hc** capability causes a hangup on close, like HUPCL in /etc/gettydefs on System V.

You should not need to write *gettytab* entries. If you do, see *gettytab*(5) in your UNIX documentation for details.

3

Setting Up a UUCP Link

Summary of Procedure
Giving Your System a Name
Who You Gonna Call?
Multiple Systems Files
Dialing Prefixes
Aliases
Selecting the Device to Use
Modem Dialing Instructions

This chapter describes the various configuration files you need to edit in order to set up a UUCP network.

Summary of Procedure

Each system administrator should use the following procedure to set up a UUCP link between two systems:

1. Set up the physical connection, as described in Chapter 2, *The Physical Connection*. Be sure to edit */etc/inittab* or */etc/ttys* to enable or disable logins on the port and to set communications parameters.

2. Give each system a name that it will use to identify itself over the network. Use the **setuname** command (SVR2), **uname** command (SVR3), or **hostname** command (BSD 4.2 and 4.3) or edit the */etc/systemid* file (Xenix).

3. Edit *L.sys* (Version 2) or *Systems* (BNU) to supply data needed by **uucico** to call or be called by the other system(s). For each remote system, include the system's name, times when it is ok to call, device to be used for placing the call, telephone number if any, and the login sequence for **uucico** to use.

4. Edit *L-devices* (Version 2) or *Devices* (BNU) to supply additional information about the type and speed of the link.

5. Test the link to make sure it works.

With the exception of the first and last steps, this procedure is described in this chapter.

The procedure for setting up the physical link is described in Chapter 2. If you want to use a type of modem that is not known to your system, you will also have to write a modem description. The method for doing this depends on which version of UUCP you have. See Appendix B, *Talking to Modems*, for details.

The procedure for testing the link is described in Chapter 4, *Making Sure the Link Works*.

There are also a number of optional steps you probably need to perform to establish the file access and command execution permissions to be granted to the remote system. These steps are described in Chapter 5, *Access and Security Considerations*.

While this entire procedure may seem complex, it is only so for the first couple of links you set up. For example, once you have a modem connected to your system, all it takes to set up a link is for each system administrator to add one line to the *L.sys* or *Systems* file.

Conventions in Configuration Files

All of the UUCP configuration files adhere to the following conventions:

- A line beginning with a hash mark (#) is a comment (except in original Version 7 UUCP).

- The field separator is a space or tab. No spaces or tabs are allowed within fields.

- Unused fields should contain a dash.

- In BNU and 4.3 BSD, long lines can be continued with a backslash at the end of the line (followed immediately with a newline). *This does not work in most implementations of Version 2 UUCP.*

The Administrative Login

If your system has *uucp* as an administrative login, you should edit all UUCP files as the user *uucp*. This will preserve the original ownership and permissions of the files. To become *uucp*, type:

```
$ su uucp
Password:
$
```

NOTE

There may not be a password on the *uucp* account. If there isn't, you should create one. See Chapter 5 for details.

BSD and Xenix systems do not have an administrative login. You should edit the UUCP files when logged in as *root* or else create an administrative login, as described in Chapter 5. Even on other systems, it is wise to check the *passwd* file to make sure the *uucp* login does in fact have a normal shell instead of */usr/lib/uucp/uucico* before you attempt to switch to it.

Menu-driven Installation Utilities

Both Xenix and BNU (on the 3B2 at least) offer semi-automated methods of setting up the UUCP configuration files (steps 2 through 4 above).

On Xenix systems, you can use the menu-driven **uuinstall** utility to set up the files. If you just want to read the contents of the configuration files but not alter them, you can use the **-r** option of **uuinstall**.

On some systems, BNU comes with a set of menu-driven administration scripts called **uucpmgmt** that are used for basic editing of certain control files. The **uucpmgmt** menu is located under the **packagemgmt** menu of the simple administration (**sysadm** command) utilities.

On all systems with BNU, there is a shell program called **uucheck** that makes sure that the required files and directories are present. If the files exist, they normally contain sample entries that you can copy and modify when creating additional entries.

The installation procedures given in this chapter assume that you will be editing the UUCP control files manually. Neither of the menu driven systems does the complete job, and the manual procedure is quite simple in any case.

Giving Your System a Name

Each system in a UUCP network must have a name. As we have already mentioned several times, the names of other systems known to the local system must be listed in *L.sys* (*Systems*) for UUCP to be able to communicate with them. But what about a system's own name? Where does it come from?

As it turns out, each UNIX system may have several names. For example, in System V, there is the system name proper, which is often the manufacturer's name for the operating system (e.g., CTIX) and which will be displayed if you type **uname** with the -s option. There is the hardware name (**uname -m**). And there is the *node name*, which is the name by which the system is known to other systems in a communications network (**uname -n**). (In BSD 4.2 and 4.3 systems, the node name is referred to as the hostname and is displayed by the **hostname** command.)

Even the node name may not be the exact name used by UUCP. The node name is associated with the UNIX kernel and is not the property of UUCP. It may be used by other networks as well. Many implementations of UUCP limit the length of the system name to seven characters, in which case the node name will be truncated by UUCP. BNU and BSD 4.3 allow a name of up to 14 characters. BSD 4.3 actually allows a name of up to 64 characters, as per the DoD Internet spec. However, it truncates to 14 characters for UUCP. Some systems (including our own) truncate the name to six characters.

Also, the name you choose should be lowercase. While a mixed-case or uppercase name may work with UUCP, there are a lot of mail systems out there (including the ubiquitous **sendmail**) who believe that hostnames are case-insensitive. The dictum "Be conservative in what you generate; liberal in what you accept" applies here. The **uuname** command lists the names of all systems known to UUCP. With the -l option, it will list the node name of your own system. To check if there is a difference between the true node name and UUCP's name, use both the **uname** (or **hostname** on BSD 4.*x* systems) and the **uuname** commands. For example:

```
$ uname -n
sanfrancisco
$ uuname -l
sanfran
```

However, the full node name as shown by **uname** or **hostname** will still work in all UUCP commands and files. However, the truncated name will appear in messages and log files.

As shipped by the manufacturer, the system name and the node name are probably identical. You should create a unique node name for your system before linking it to other systems in a network.

If you are going to connect your system to Usenet, you should be careful to check that the name you want is not already in use. Ask your Usenet hookup (see Chapter 8, *Installing Netnews*) to check the **comp.mail.maps** newsgroup for names that might conflict. A quick and dirty way to do this (assuming news is spooled in the default directories) is:

```
$ cd /usr/spool/news/comp/mail/maps; grep name *
```

where *name* is the node name you propose to use. If a match turns up, you should probably adopt another name.

The exact method for defining the node name varies from version to version of UNIX. We will cover some of the most common cases here. If none of them seem to apply, consult your documentation for details.

---

setuname and uname -S
(System V)

In some implementations of System V, you can define your system name using the **setuname** command with the **-n** option. For example:

```
# setuname -n name
```

You must have root privileges to set the node name. The allowable length of the name varies from implementation to implementation. If you specify too long a name, it will be truncated.

setuname should be executed each time your system is rebooted. You can arrange for this to happen automatically by adding a **setuname** command to one of the system startup scripts such as */etc/rc*.

To define the name *newton* as the local system name, you would enter the following line in the */etc/rc* file:

```
setuname -n newton
```

In SVR3, you set the node name with the command:

```
# uname -Sname
```

Again, the best way to do this is to put the command into one of the system startup scripts (*/etc/rc2* in SVR3). On BSD 4.2 and 4.3 systems, the hostname (node name) is set with the **hostname** command. For example:

```
# hostname tiddlywinks
```

It is recommended that you put the command at the very top of the file */etc/rc*, so that the name is set before anything else is started. However, many sites set it in */etc/rc.local* instead. In SunOS, it is set in the file */etc/rc.boot*. Generally, a line to set the hostname already exists in one of these files. You simply need to edit it and reboot.

The **hostname** command with no arguments will display the current hostname.

/etc/systemid

(Xenix)

In Xenix, the */etc/systemid* file contains the node name of the local site and associates it with a micnet network site name, if any. (Micnet is a special type of network for linking Xenix systems.) You can use the **uuinstall** utility to define your system name or edit */etc/systemid* manually.

For example, if system *boston* was connected to a micnet network and known as *beantown* to micnet, the */etc/systemid* file would look like this:

```
boston
beantown
```

UUCP systems are usually created after a micnet network has been installed, so this file may already exist for a given site. In this case, you should add the node name to the beginning of the file on each system on the micnet network.

The micnet machine name is used only if your system is on a micnet network.

/usr/lib/uucp/SYSTEMNAME

On some earlier UNIX systems, the node name is defined in the file */usr/lib/uucp/SYSTEMNAME*. If this file is present, simply edit it to set the node name.

When None of These Work

On many systems, the node name is compiled right in to the kernel. Some systems (even those without source licenses) give you tools for modifying certain system configuration parameters and recompiling the kernel. If this is the case, the node name is probably defined in a file called */usr/include/sys/utsname.h*, */usr/include/whoami.h*, or */usr/sys/name.c*. Edit the appropriate file and recompile the kernel as described in your system's documentation.

If the name is compiled in and you do not have configuration support, don't despair. You do not need to patch the kernel with **adb**! Appendix D, *Useful Programs and Shell Scripts*, lists a C program written by Pat Wood of Pipeline Associates that works like **setuname** and allows you to patch the in-core image of the kernel when it is running.

Who You Gonna Call?

In setting up a UUCP link, you need to tell UUCP about the systems it will be talking to. You should determine what UNIX systems you want to use UUCP with, then talk to their system administrators and get the following information:

System node name   _____

OK times to call   _____

Phone number of modem _____

Login name for **uucico** _____

Login password   _____

You should provide the same information about your system. This information is placed in the file *L.sys* on Version 2 systems and *Systems* on systems that support BNU.

Note that it is also possible to set up one side of the link as a *passive* system—that is, one that can be called but will never originate calls of its own. If this is the case, the only information that needs to be added to the systems file of the passive system is the name of the system that will be calling. (In BNU and BSD 4.3; other implementations of Version 2 UUCP do not require that the name of the remote system polling you be known by your system. Each line in the system file represents one system that can be called by the local UUCP programs.

An entry for a modem connection to system *newyork* would look like the entry below. Note that in BSD 4.3 and BNU, a long line can be broken into two physical lines by escaping the newline at the end of the first line with a backslash (\ ).

This will not work in most implementations of Version 2 UUCP.

L.sys and *Systems*

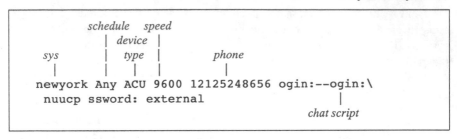

```
            schedule   speed
                | device |
     sys        |  type  |           phone
      |         |   |    |             |
   newyork Any ACU 9600 12125248656 ogin:--ogin:\
     nuucp ssword: external              |
                                     chat script
```

Field	Function in *L.sys* and *Systems*
sys	The node name of the remote system; must be unique (relative to other names in the same *L.sys* or *Systems* file) in the first seven characters.
schedule	When the local system can call the remote system. *Any* means any day of the week. See below for details.
device type	The type of device to be used for the call. See below for details.
speed	The speed in bits per second for the device. Some systems allow you to specify a range of speeds (e.g., 2400-9600) when conecting to a modem that adjusts its speed to match the modem that answers on the other end.
phone	The dialer sequence that will be used by the modem to call the remote system.
chat script	A string describing the initial conversation between two machines. It describes the login password and special character sequences needed to complete the login procedure.

When **uucico** is invoked, it first scans the system file for the name of the system to be called. It then checks if it is a valid time to call. If so, it checks the *device type* and *speed* fields and goes to the *L-devices* file for a device that matches.

uucico then checks to see if a lock file exists for that device in the spool directory (*/usr/spool/locks* in BNU), in which case the device is in use. If so, **uucico** checks to see if there is another device of the requested type and speed and uses it, if available.

If no device is available, **uucico** returns to the system file to see if there is another entry for the system in question. If so, the process is repeated. If not, the call is terminated.

Once an available device is located, **uucico** uses the telephone number (if appropriate) and chat script to actually make the connection.

The following sections give additional details on some of the fields.

schedule

The *schedule* field indicates when the local system can call the remote system. It consists of three subfields: the *day* of the week, an optional *time* of day when the system can call, and an optional minimum *retry* period for calling in when an attempt fails. BSD 4.3 and some later versions of BNU allow an additional *grade* subfield that allows you to control what type of transfers go out at a specific time.

The *day* and *time* subfields are written with no intervening spaces. The retry subfield is set off with a comma in Version 2 and a semicolon in BNU and BSD 4.3.

The *day* subfield is specified using the following keywords:

Any   means that the system can call on any day.

Never   means that the system should never call but should just wait to be called.

Wk   means any weekday. You can also specify individual days of the week using one or more of the keywords **Su**, **Mo**, **Tu**, **We**, **Th**, **Fr**, and **Sa**.

The *time* subfield is specified by two 24-hour clock times separated by a dash (–). For example, 1900-2300 means that a system can only be called from between 7 and 11 o'clock in the evening. The range can span 0000, so that a range of 0700-0500 means that the local system can call between 7 a.m. each day and 5 a.m. the next morning—that is, any time **except** from 5 to 7 a.m.*

If the time subfield is omitted, the local system can call any time of the day. However, the reverse case is not true. That is, you cannot leave off the day subfield and specify only the time. For example, if you want to call between 11 p.m.

---

*This is not exactly correct. **uucico** actually interprets this figure on a same day basis, so 0700-0500 actually means from 0000-0500 and from 0700-2359 on the same day. This is a fine distinction, which really has impact only when combined with a day specification. For example:

    Wk2310–0750

means 0000-0750 and 2310-2359 Monday through Friday—not 0000-0750 Saturday morning.

and 8 a.m. any day, you should be sure to enter Any2301-0759, not just 2301-0759.

A direct link would most likely be set up to run at **Any** time. However, for a dial-out line, you may want to restrict outgoing calls (particularly to systems outside your local area) to the evening in order to take advantage of lower telephone rates. (Be aware that your company clock may not match the telephone company's clock and give yourself a few minutes of grace on either end).

For example, to limit outgoing calls to system *calif* to 11:10 p.m. until 7:50 the following morning any weekday (when telephone rates are cheapest), you would write:

```
calif Wk2310-0750 ...
```

This does not mean that users can only invoke **uucp** or **uux** during those hours but, rather, that all requests will be spooled and not executed until that time.

In most implementations of Version 2, you cannot specify different times for individual days (e.g., weekday evenings, but all day Saturday and Sunday) except by creating multiple *L.sys* entries for a system, each with a different schedule field.*

```
calif Wk1800-2400...
calif SaSu...
```

In BNU and BSD 4.3, you can do this by separating day/time pairs with a comma. For example:

```
calif Wk1800-2400,SaSu ....
```

Some implementations of Version 2 UUCP do support a similar mechanism, using a vertical bar (|) as the delimiter instead of a comma.

In BSD 4.3, the keyword *Evening* is equivalent to *Wk1700-0800,Sa,Su*; *Night* is equivalent to *Any2300-0800,Sa,Su0800-1700*; and *NonPeak* is equivalent to *Any1800-0700,Sa,Su*. The NonPeak keyword was originally designed to match offpeak hours for X.25 public data networks. Unfortunately, though, both Tymnet and Telenet have changed their offpeak hours since this keyword was implemented, so it should no longer be used.

---

*Unfortunately, even this does not work in Xenix.

Grading. BSD 4.3 and some later versions of BNU also allow the day or time subfield to be followed by a maximum *grade* specification, set off by a slash. The grade is a single character in the range [0-9][A-Z][a-z]. That is, grade 0 (zero) has the highest priority, and grade z the lowest.

uucico normally processes work files (see Appendix A, *Working Files*) in grade order. The default grade for various types of requests varies from system to system, but is generally highest for uux requests, followed by mail, followed by news, with uucp requests last.*

Grading is used automatically to control the order in which UUCP requests, mail, and news, will be transferred. However, by setting a grade specification in the time subfield, you can actually keep certain classes of requests from being sent.

This feature allows you, for instance, to transfer mail messages even at peak times but Netnews only at night. For example, the schedule field:

```
bloom-beacon Any0900-1700/C ...
```

will allow only grade C or better to be sent during business hours.

Note, however, that setting the grade only controls what your site *sends*, not what it *receives*. For example, consider a UUCP connection between sites *ora* and *bloom-beacon*. Assume *ora* has some jobs queued for *bloom-beacon* at grade C (mail) and some at grade m (news). If *ora* calls *bloom-beacon* with the grade set to C, only the mail will be transferred from *ora* to *bloom-beacon*. However, any transfers waiting on *bloom-beacon* for *ora* will be sent, no matter what their grade.

In BSD 4.3, you can also invoke **uucico** with the *-ggrade* option, where *grade* specifies the lowest grade to be transferred. On SunOS 4.1 systems, the corresponding option is *-vgrade=grade*.

Note that if your uucp does not support grading, you may find the system dialing every time a user sends mail. In order to keep this from happening, set the time field to *Never* and use **cron** to periodically invoke **uucico** with the **-S** option (which overrides the time field). This should only be a problem on older UUCPs, since most newer ones are smart enough not to place a call for every mail message.

---

*The default grade for uux is generally A, for mail C, for news d, and for uucp n. If **rmail** is executed by **uux**, the grade for mail will be A. However, **sendmail** normally sets the grade to something lower, typically C. But this is highly site-dependent.

In UUCPs that support grading, you can change the grade of your transfer with the *-g* option to **uucp** and **uux**. Some versions of BNU support this feature; some do not. If you are unsure about your system, check the reference pages for **uucp** or **uux** to see if they support the *-g* option.

How often to retry?. The optional *retry* field indicates the minimum waiting period (in minutes) after an unsuccessful call to the remote system. The local system cannot try calling the remote system again unless the minimum waiting period has expired. By default, Version 2 will wait 55 minutes (one hour on some systems) before retries are allowed, while BNU and BSD 4.3 UUCP will use an exponential retry (starting with 5 minutes and growing larger as the number of unsuccessful attempts increases). Specify a retry period set off by a comma (or a semicolon in BNU and BSD 4.3) at the end of the *schedule* field if you want to override these defaults.*

For example:

```
japan SaSu,60 ...
```

limits overseas calls to system *japan* to weekends. If *newton* fails to login the first time, it must wait at least 60 minutes before it can try calling *japan* again.

You may want to have a shorter retry time for direct links than for dialup links. Be aware, though, that shortening the retry period may cause you to reach the maximum number of retries (default is 26) before a remote system comes back on line. Note also that changing the retry period will not cause **uucico** to be invoked any sooner. It just lets **uucico** know (once it has been invoked) when it can try the specified system.

device type

There are some differences between Version 2 UUCP and BNU in the way they use the *device type* field.

In Version 2, this field is used as follows:

- For modem links, this field contains the keyword ACU (Automatic Call Unit). When **uucico** goes to call another system, it checks the entry in this field, then goes to another file called *L-devices* for additional information about the device (such as the type of modem). If there is more than one ACU entry in *L-devices*, meaning that there is more than one modem attached to the system, **uucico** will use the first available modem.

- For direct links, this field contains the name of the special file in */dev* that should be used to call this system (e.g., *tty008* for */dev/tty008*). This is true of all Version 2 UUCPs except BSD 4.2 and 4.3, which use the keyword DIR.

  An entry must also appear in *L-devices* for this device, authorizing it as a legal port. See the discussion of *L-devices* later in this chapter.

---

*The retry subfield is not supported in the UUCP shipped with Version 7 UNIX systems.

- For TCP/IP (Ethernet) connections under BSD 4.3, the device is specified as TCP. The services name (or the port number) from */etc/services* (usually "uucp") goes into the speed field, and the remote system name is repeated in the phone number field. This is the name the machine uses on the network, which may be different from its uucp name. For example:

```
venture Any TCP uucp venture ogin:--ogin:  ...
```

Such TCP entries do not need any corresponding information in *L-devices*, since everything UUCP needs is in *L-sys*.

If there is no entry for UUCP in */etc/services*, you can add one. It should look like this:

```
uucp    540/tcp    uucpd   # UUCP TCP/IP
```

- BSD 4.3 also supports the following keywords:

Micom   A Micom terminal switch.

PAD   An X.25 PAD (Packet Assembler/Disassembler) connection.

PCP   GTE Telenet PC Pursuit. See discussion of *L-devices* for additional details.

Sytek   Sytek dedicated high-speed modem port.

In BNU, this field is used more consistently. It is always a pointer to an entry in the *Devices* file. Any keyword can be used, as long as there is a corresponding entry in *Devices*.

The advantage of looking up all devices in a device file is that it allows you to specify multiple paths for direct links as well as multiple modems. (In Version 2, you must create duplicate entries in *L.sys* with different device fields if you have multiple direct links to another system.) It also gives more flexibility in specifying additional information needed by the modem or other callout device (such as a local area network switch).

See the discussion of *L-devices* and *Devices* later in this chapter for details on how devices are selected.

Protocol selection. Early versions of UUCP, which were designed for use over noisy phone lines, used UUCP's native *g* protocol. The *g* protocol uses small, 64-byte packets that are checksummed and retransmitted immediately in case of error.

Because the *g* protocol imposes a great deal of unnecessary overhead on reliable links such as local area networks and X.25-based public data networks, several newer protocols have been added.

BSD 4.3 supports the *f* protocol, which uses 256-byte packets, and calculates a checksum for an entire file, rather than on a packet by packet basis. It is designed for "mostly error free" links like X.25 PAD-based networks. It can also be useful on the newer error-correcting modems.* For truly error-free networks, such as TCP/IP, BSD 4.3 provides the *t* protocol, which uses 1024-byte packets and a full eight-bit data path.

BNU has corresponding protocols for these two situations, called *x* (for X.25) and *e* (for "error-free"). They are not compatible with the BSD protocols, though some systems may support both.

In BNU, you can specify a list of protocols to be tried for a particular system as a subfield of the device field, separated from it by a comma. For example, you might have the following *Systems* file entry:

```
ruby Any TCP,eg ...
```

No, that ",eg" shown in the example just above isn't an ignorant technical writer's "slavish copying of an example" as one perplexed soul asked over the net after reading his company's manual. It means that for this connection, the local system supports the *e* and *g* protocols. They will be tried in the order in which they are listed. (Presumably, if you are specifying them on a system by system basis, you know that the corresponding system also offers these protocols, in which case the first will always be used. However, if you simply list all the protocols you support, in your preferred order, the remote system will be able to choose the one it in turn prefers. This process is described in further detail in Chapter 4, *Making Sure the Link Works*.) Protocols can also be specified in the *Devices* file, as described later in this chapter, and there, a protocol list does make more sense, because you may be connecting to many systems using the same device.

---

*One problem is that the *f* protocol uses only a seven-bit data path. Eight-bit characters are "quoted" to make them fit into seven bits. Bill Davidson of FPS Computing in San Diego pointed out on the net that this can cause quite a loss of efficiency when transmitting compressed files. On a test batch of compressed news, he showed a growth from 397803 to 655966 bytes as a result of the *f* protocol's eight-bit encoding algorithm. He also pointed out that when the data is again compressed by the compression algorithm in the modem, some, but not all, of the size is recovered. Because of the particular sequencing of the redundant characters, he found that Huffman encoding, as performed by MNP level 5 modems, was actually slightly more efficient than the LZW compression performed by V.42bis.

phone number

The fifth field contains the *phone number* of the remote system.

An equal sign (=) in the telephone number indicates a wait for a secondary dial tone (for example, 9 = would dial 9, then wait for the secondary dial tone on an outside line). In dialers that lack the logic to detect a secondary dial tone (such as the built-in dialer in a Hayes modem), the equal sign simply generates a pause. Note that this feature is not consistently implemented in all versions of UUCP. If it does not work, you may have to use whatever pause character is supported by the modem (e.g., "," or "w" for a Hayes or "K" for a Racal-Vadic).

A hyphen (-) usually generates a one-second pause, although it is a no-op in some implementations.

For a direct link in Version 2 UUCP, repeat the device name in this field. For a direct link in BNU, put a dash (–) in this field.

The telephone number may also contain an optional alphabetic abbreviation that is "expanded" in the *L-dialcodes* file (*Dialcodes* in BNU). The abbreviation typically specifies area codes and any digits needed to place an outside call. See the section "Dialing Prefixes" below for details.

If other devices besides modems or direct connections are supported, this field may contain whatever other information is necessary to complete the call over the device. For example, for a MICOM switch, the "phone number" might be the micom code for the site to be reached.

If your implementation of Version 2 UUCP supports other devices besides modems and direct connections, you should consult your documentation for details on how to "place calls" using that device.

chat script

The remainder of the line following the phone number contains a string of text called the *chat script*. The chat script defines the login "conversation" that will occur between the two systems. It consists of "expect-send" pairs, separated by spaces, with optional "subexpect-subsend" pairs separated by hyphens, as in the following example:

chat script

This line defines what the local system *expects* from the remote system and what it should *send* as a reply to the remote system, if the correct string is received.

The "expect" portion need contain only part of what is really expected. For example, if system *newyork* displays the following banner and login prompt:

```
newyork
Ghostbusters, Inc.
login:
```

the *expect* field may contain only the trailing portion of the login prompt, such as "ogin:" or even "in:". This is done to prevent failure if the remote system prompts "Login:" or "Password:" instead of the more common lowercase prompt. (Note that **uucico** actually will stop looking when it finds any part of the *expect* string. For example, "login" (without the colon) would also work. It is customary to use the last part of the string to make sure that the *send* string is not sent out too soon.)

A second or so after the expect string is received, the next send string is sent out. Each send field is followed by either a carriage return or a new line. (Which character is sent depends on the UUCP implementation. See Chapter 4, *Making Sure the Link Works*, for additional details.)

A very simple chat script might look like this:

```
ogin: nuucp ssword: help!
```

In other words, expect ... **ogin:**, send **nuucp**, expect ... **ssword**, send **help!**.

In Chapter 4, we will show you how to watch the progress of this conversation. It goes something like this:

```
wanted ogin:
got that
nuucp
wanted ssword:
got that
```

In actual practice, such a simple chat script is rare. At the very least, the chat script should use an optional "subexpect-subsend" sequence to give **uucico** more than one chance to log in. For example, assume that there was noise on the line, that was received by either system as real data before the login sequence was initiated. The simple chat would fail, where a script like the following might not:

```
ogin:--ogin: nuucp ssword: help!
```

This script says: expect "ogin:"; if you do not get it in a certain time, send nothing (-- here indicates a null subsend, though it does still cause a carriage return or linefeed to be sent), look again for "ogin:".

The difference between the normal expect-send sequence and the subexpect-subsend sequence is that a send occurs if the expect string *is* received, while a subsend occurs only if the preceding expect string *is not* received.

In order to define the chat script, you need at the very least to get the UUCP login name and password from the system administrator of the remote system and give him or her the same information for yours. If the other system will be a passive system—that is, one that never places calls to you but only receives them—the remote administrator needs only to put your system's name in its system file and to be sure permissions are set up correctly.

In addition, you may need to use one or more special character sequences if the remote system has any peculiarities in its login sequence. The escape sequences used in chat scripts are listed in Table 3-1. (In Version 7 UNIX, UUCP supports only "", EOT, and BREAK.)

Table 3-1. Chat Script Escape Sequences

Escape Sequence	Description
" "	Expect a null string.
EOT	Send an end-of-transmission character.
BREAK	Cause a BREAK. This is sometimes simulated using line speed changes and null characters. May not work on all systems.
\b	Send a backspace character. On BSD 4.2 systems, send a BREAK.
\c	Suppress newline at the end of the *send* string.
\d	Delay for 1 second.
\K	Insert a BREAK (BNU only).
\n	Send a newline or linefeed character.
\N	Send a null character (BNU only). Use \0 to send a null in other implementations.
\p	Pause for a fraction of a second (BNU only).
\r	Send a carriage return.
\s	Send a space character.
\t	Send a tab character (not implemented in BSD 4.3).
\\	Send a backslash (\) character.
ddd	Collapse the octal digits (*ddd*) into a single ASCII character and sends that character.

If a system requires a complicated chat script, the remote system administrator may well have already figured it out with another caller and may be able to give it to you exactly. If not, then you should use **cu** or **tip** to login to the remote system.

Watch closely what happens. For example, do you get a login prompt right away or do you have to press RETURN one or more times? Does the remote system always answer at the same speed? (As we saw in Chapter 2, it is possible to set up a line so that **getty** cycles through a number of possible baud rates until it finds one that matches. If this is the case, the user manually dialing in normally needs to press the BREAK key to switch speeds.)

For irregularities beyond the initial login, you may need to invoke **uucico** in a special debugging mode in order to see exactly what is going wrong.

Chapter 4, *Making Sure the Link Works*, includes a detailed discussion and examples of how to figure out the chat script for a neighboring system.

Multiple Systems Files

Newer versions of BNU support a configuration file called *Sysfiles*, which allows you to specify pointers to multiple sets of configuration files. While *Sysfiles* was designed to allow different dialing procedures for **uucico** and **cu**, it can also be used to split large *Systems* files into more manageable chunks.

The file includes two "service" definitions (one each for *uucico* and *cu*), as follows:

```
service=service name   systems=systems file list \
                       devices=devices file list \
                       dialers=dialers file list
```

where *service name* is either **uucico** or **cu**, and the various file lists are colon separated lists of filenames. Each service definition must be placed on a single line; however, escaped newlines are acceptable, as shown in the example.

Filenames are relative to */usr/lib/uucp* (or other UUCP home directory) unless you specify a full pathname. If no file list is specified for any of the three keywords (**systems**, **devices**, or **dialers**), the standard files are used by default. If multiple files are specified in a file list, they are searched in order.

For example:

```
service=uucico   systems=Systems.uucico:Systems \
                 dialers=Dialers.uucico:Dialers
service=cu       systems=Systems.cu:Systems \
                 dialers=Dialers.cu:Dialers
```

In this example, when *uucico* is invoked, it will first search the *Systems.uucico* file, then the standard *Systems* file; it will do the same for *Dialers.uucico* and

Dialers. By contrast, *cu* will start with *Systems.cu* and *Dialers.cu* before going on to the standard files.

To use *Sysfiles* merely to segment a large *Systems* file, specify the same file lists for both the *uucico* and *cu* services, and simply specify a search list of *Systems* files. For example, the following *Sysfiles* searches local, company-wide, and global *Systems* files, in that order:

```
service=uucico  systems=Systems.ma:Systems.ora:Systems
service=cu      systems=Systems.ma:Systems.ora:Systems
```

Chapter 4 contains an extended example that uses *Sysfiles* to define different *uucico* and *cu* configurations over a Starlan network.

Dialing Prefixes

L-dialcodes (Version 2) and *Dialcodes* (BNU) are used when you want to talk to a number of systems at one site that have a common dialing sequence. These files allow you to use a dialcode abbreviation in the *phone* field of the *L.sys* or *Systems* file.

A dialcode entry in this file contains a location prefix, the area code and any digits needed to get an outside line. For example, an entry in this file might contain:

```
paloalto 9=1-415-555
```

The corresponding system file entry might then contain the first five fields as follows:

```
calif Any ACU 9600 paloalto5555 . . .
```

When UUCP reads this entry, it refers to the dialcodes file and sends the dial sequence "9=1-415-5555555". As in the phone number field of the *L.sys* (*Systems*) file, the equal sign (=) after the "9" tells the dialer to wait for a secondary dial tone before dialing the rest of the number.

Note that the location is written in lowercase with no spaces between words (as in *paloalto* for Palo Alto).

According to David Nowitz's original paper on Version 2 UUCP, the purpose of the *L-dialcodes* file was not to save time in entering telephone numbers (for which it is not terribly useful) but to allow a common *L.sys* file to be used at a number of sites with different internal phone systems and area codes.

Another way to use *L-dialcodes* is to put *only* dial codes in *L.sys* and the actual telephone numbers here.

L.sys, which contains sensitive login and password information, can be readable only by *uucp*, while *L-dialcodes*, containing only the telephone numbers, can be readable by the world.

Aliases

In BSD 4.3 only, there is another configuration file called *L.aliases*, which allows you to define alternate names for sites in *L.sys*.

This is especially useful for trapping site names that have changed where new names have not become known to all remote users.

Entries have the form:

> *real_name   alias_name*

For example, if the system *risk* had changed its name to *venture*, you might include the line:

```
venture    risk
```

Then if a user types the command:

```
$ mail risk!adrian
```

uucico will actually queue the mail for the system *venture*.

Selecting the Device to Use

As mentioned above, the third field in each entry in the *L.sys* (*Systems*) file gives the name of a device to use when calling the system in question. (In BSD 4.2 and 4.3, it is not an actual device name but a pointer to *L-devices*.)

In Version 2 UUCP, for direct links, this "device" name is actually the device name of the serial port. But in BNU, and for a modem link in Version 2, it is a pointer to an entry in another file, called *L-devices* in Version 2 and *Devices* in BNU.

For a direct link, the *L-devices* (*Devices*) file must contain an entry specifying that the port is valid for UUCP to use. For a modem link, it must contain an entry that describes the port to which the modem is connected and the type of modem. If the link is direct, the buck stops there. However, if a modem is involved, yet another source must be consulted for instructions on how to dial the modem. We will look at modems later.

Creating L-devices Entries (Version 2)

Each port connected to a modem or direct cable to another system should be described in the */usr/lib/uucp/L-devices* file. An entry in this file contains four fields and has the following general format:

L-devices

```
   type        call unit
    |             |
   ACU tty008 - 9600
    |             |
   device      speed
```

Field	Function in *L-devices*
type	The type of link: usually *DIR* for a direct link and *ACU* for a modem connection, although additional types are sometimes supported. If there are multiple links of either type, additional lines with the same type label can be used. In BSD documentation, this field is referred to as the *caller*.
	The types of links supported vary from version to version. See your documentation for details. For example, in BSD 4.3, additional device types include DK for an AT&T Datakit network, MICOM for a MICOM terminal switch, PAD for an X.25 PAD connection, PCP for GTE-Telenet's PC Pursuit service, SYTEK for a SYTEK dedicated high-speed modem, and TCP for a TCP/IP (Ethernet) connection.
device	The name of the special file (such as *tty007*) in the */dev* directory that corresponds to the serial port used for the UUCP link.
	SunOS has separate device names for dial-in and dial-out serial ports. Usually, dial-out ports are given the name *cua?* while dial-in ports are given the name *ttyd?* (e.g., *ttyd0* and *cua0*). When a port is opened with the name *cua?*, the serial driver does not require carrier detect to be present on the line, and no **getty** is activated. (The **getty** is associated in */etc/ttys* with the corresponding *ttyd?* appellation for the same port. See Chapter 2, *The Physical Connection*, for details.)

call unit   If your system uses a true ACU, like a DN-11, UN56, Bell 801, or Racal-Vadic MACS, two separate devices are used to place the call: the dialer itself, referred to by a device name beginning with *cua*, and the data lines, referred to by device names beginning with *cul*.

If you are using such a dialer, you would place the device name of the dialer here and specify the data line in the *device* field.

If you are using a "smart modem" with a built-in dialer, fill in this field with a dummy value (such as - or 0).

Some implementations place a symbolic dialer name in this field instead of a call unit device. The dialer name points to the name of the *modemcap* or *acucap* entry that contains dialing instructions for a smart modem.

speed   The "baud rate" of the port for modems and direct links or the port number to use for local area network connections.

Let's look at an example. The local system *newton* is connected to system *newyork*, which has only a 2400-bps modem. The *newton* system has two modems, a Microcom MultiModem 224 (2400 bps) and a Telebit Trailblazer. A cable also connects port *tty005* on *newton* directly to port *tty001* on *waltham* at 9600 bps. Another cable connects port *tty006* on *boston* to port *tty008* on *newton*.

The *L.sys* file on *boston* would contain entries that read:

```
newyork Any ACU 2400 ...
waltham Any tty005 9600 ...
natick Any tty006 9600 ...
```

The *L-devices* file might read:

```
ACU tty008 2400 hayes
ACU tty009 9600 tb
DIR tty005  9600
DIR tty006  9600
```

This means that a 2400-baud Hayes-compatible modem (the Microcom) is connected to port 8 and a Telebit Trailblazer to port 9 and that direct serial lines are connected to ports 5 and 6. The direct lines will be used for calling specific systems as specified in *L.sys*. If an entry in *L.sys* calls for an ACU, **uucico** will use the first available modem listed in *L-devices*. (When a modem is in use, **uucico** (also **cu** or **tip**) create a lock file to keep other UUCP processes from using the modem.)

The corresponding file on system *waltham*, which is connected only to *newton* and has no modem links, might be:

```
DIR tty001 0 9600
```

This means that the cable from *newton*'s serial port 6 is connected to *waltham*'s serial port 1.

In BSD 4.2 and 4.3, there is a fifth field, which specifies the type of dialer. (There is a long list of supported dialers.) In BSD 4.3 only, additional fields can be used to construct a chat script similar to the one in *L.sys*. The difference is that the *L-devices* chat script is used for the conversation with the modem or other device, rather than with the remote system.

Older releases of SunOS use an entirely different convention for the dialer. They append the dialer to the type field. So you might say:

```
ACUHAYES  ttya  -  1200
ACUVENTEL ttyb  -  1200
```

and so on. In *L.sys* you can say:

```
waltham Any ACU 2400 9999999 ...
```

to get any ACU or:

```
waltham Any ACUHAYES 1200 9999999 ...
```

to get the Hayes dialer. (SunOS 4.1 has switched to BNU, so this information no longer applies to later releases.)

Creating Devices File Entries (BNU)

The *Devices* file contains information for direct links, automatic call units, and network connections.

Each entry must begin in column 1 of the *Devices* file. Otherwise, you will get an error message "NO DEVICES AVAILABLE" when you try to use that device. Each entry in the *Devices* file has the following general format:

```
type         device      speed
 |             |           |
waltham   tty006   -   9600   direct
ACU   tty23   -   2400   hayes \T
ACU   cul6   cual   1200   801 \T
            |        |            |
      dataport (dialer port)   dialer-token pairs
```

Field   Function in *Devices*

type   The *type* field describes the type of link and may contain one of the
             following keywords:

> **ACU**   For links made through a modem. The modem may be
>   directly connected to the computer or indirectly through
>   a local area network switch.
>
> **Direct**   For a line to a computer, modem, or LAN switch to be
>   used by **cu** only. Unlike Version 2, which allows **cu** to
>   call out over the same ACU as UUCP, BNU requires that a
>   separate entry be made for each dial-out line to be refer-
>   enced by the **cu -1** option. This does not mean that an
>   additional line is required but simply that there must be
>   an additional entry in *Devices*. See the example below.
>
> *network*   For links made through a LAN. On the 3B2, *network*
>   may be either *micom* or *develcon*, the only LAN switches
>   that contain default entries in the **Dialers** file. Other
>   switches may be used as long as they have correspond-
>   ing entries in the **Dialers** file.
>
> *sysname*   For direct links to a particular machine, where *sysname*
>   is by the remote machine name. This indicates that the
>   line associated with this *Devices* entry is for a particular
>   computer in the *Systems* file. The entry in the *type* field
>   must match the third field of the corresponding entry in
>   the *Systems* file.

As was the case with the *device* field in the *Systems* file, the *type* field can be followed by a comma and a list of protocols to be used for that device. Official BNU
protocols are *g*, *x*, and *e*, though many systems may also support the BSD 4.3 *f* and
t protocols.

dataport   The device name of the port to be used for making the connection. For direct serial links and modems, this field will contain the name of the special file in */dev* that corresponds to the serial port for the connection.

dialer-port An optional field that is used if the *type* field contains *ACU* and the ACU is an 801-type dialer (which, as we have pointed out, is a separate device from the modem itself). You then specify the device name of the 801 dialer in *dialer-port*. For non-801 dialers, this field is ignored, but use a dash (–) as a place holder.

speed   The *speed* field contains the speed of the device, if the keywords **ACU** or **Direct** are used. You can also use the keyword **Any** in this field, in which case the line will match any speed requested in the *Systems* file. The entry in this field must match the fourth field of the corresponding entry in the *Systems* file. If the device supports multiple speeds, you can specify a range (e.g., 1200-9600). If there are different types of devices, which may be used to place different types of calls at the same speed, you can precede the speed with a key letter (as long as it matches the *Systems* file entry). For example, C2400 and D2400 might be used to distinguish between calls placed over a Centrex or Dimension PBX.

dialer-token pairs
             The remainder of the line contains pairs of dialer names and "tokens." Each pair represents a dialer and an argument to pass to that dialer.

             If the computer is directly connected to the dialer or modem, there will be only one dialer-token pair. However, if the modem is accessed over a switch, there may be two or more pairs. The token given to the switch is whatever code is required to access the modem.

             Some dialer types (usually UUCP's original 801 dialer at the least) are already compiled into the software; others have entries in the **Dialers** file.

The dialers supported on the 3B2 are shown below:

direct   No dialer; the line is direct

801   Standard Bell 801 autodialer with Bell 212 or Bell 103 modem

penril   Penril modem

hayes   Hayes modem

ventel   Ventel 212+ modem

vadic   Vadic 3451 modem

network   One of the network switches described in the *type* field

TLI   Transport Level Interface Network (without STREAMS)

TLIS   Transport Level Interface Network (with STREAMS)

You can also use dialers that are not listed here as long as there are corresponding entries for them in the *Dialers* file.

SCO Xenix provides source for dialer programs, and instead of listing a built-in dialer, you can give the pathname of an executable dialer program. For example:

```
ACU ttynn - 300-2400 /usr/lib/uucp/dialTBIT
```

will use the dialTBIT program to dial a Telebit Trailblazer modem.

The token following the dialer name tells the dialer what to do. The token "\D" can be used to indicate that the telephone number given in the *Systems* file should be used. You can just leave the token field blank for the last dialer on the line. The token "\T" should be used if the telephone number undergoes "dialcodes" translation. There may be different tokens required for modems connected over a LAN switch. See your system documentation for details.

Here are some examples of valid entries in a *Devices* file:

```
ACU   tty23   -   1200   hayes
ACU   tty23   -   2400   hayes
ACU   cul5   cua0   300   801
ACU   cul6   cua1   1200   801
Direct   tty23   -   2400   hayes
waltham   tty006   -   9600   direct
ACU cui1i - 38400 MultitechMNP
TCP,te - - Any TCP -
```

A Hayes-compatible dialer on */dev/tty23* can be used at either 1200 or 2400 bps. */dev/cul5* and */dev/cul6* are Microcom modems with 801 dialers at */dev/cua0* and */dev/cua1* to be used at 300 or 1200 bps, respectively. There is also a Direct entry so that **cu** can use the Hayes modem on *tty23* at 2400 bps. There is also a direct connection to system *waltham* from */dev/tty006* at 9600 bps. The 9600 bps Multitech V32 Modem on */dev/cui1i* does automatic data compression, as well as speed matching with remote modems, so we send it data at the maximum speed of the port. The TCP device (on a Sun at least) supports both the BSD *t* protocol and the BNU *e* protocol, so we tell it to try *t* first, and if that is refused, to use *e*.

Modem Dialing Instructions

There are significant differences between Version 2 and BNU when it comes to the source of modem dialing instructions.

Keep in mind the distinction made earlier between modems and dialers. When UUCP was first developed, modems did not contain built-in autodialers. Modems had to be dialed either manually or with a special programmable dialer, such as a Bell 801 dialer, connected to the system via an RS-366 interface. The dialer placed the call and turned things over to the modem only when the connection had been made. Dialers such as this are sometimes still used, since a single dialer can service an entire bank of modems.

Once so-called "smart modems" containing their own programmable dialers were developed, things became more complicated, since each modem tended to have its own nonstandard dialing procedure. Individual UNIX system manufacturers modified the UUCP code to support the new types of dialers. However, users still had little choice but to use one of the supported modems.

At least two systems we know of, AIX and SCO Xenix, Versions 2.2.3 and up, took the step of separating out the dialer code and giving users instructions on how to write their own dialer programs. In many cases, though, adding a dialer is something you can do only if you have access to UUCP source code.

Other systems adopted a more general approach, taking the dialing instructions out of the UUCP code and putting them in an independent file called either *modemcap* or *acucap*. These files are modeled after the *termcap* facility for describing terminal types and, like *termcap*, are relatively difficult for novices to use.

BNU added a somewhat easier-to-use facility that describes modem dialing sequences in a file called *Dialers*.

As mentioned above, BSD 4.3 allows you to embed dialing instructions directly in the *L-devices* file.

If at all possible, you should use one of the modems that is supported by your system. Check the *acucap*, *modemcap*, or *Dialers* file, if present, for a list of supported modems. Look at your documentation if none of these files are present.

Modems Not Supported By Your System

If you want to use a modem that is not supported by your system, see Appendix B, *Talking to Modems*, for details on how to write dialing instructions for *modem-cap*, *acucap*, or *Dialers*.

If none of these files are available and you still want to use a different modem, don't despair. There is a trick for avoiding the built-in dialers by pretending to use a direct link, and embedding the dialing instructions in the *chat script* field of the *Systems* file.

For example, to dial a Hayes modem, your entry might look something like this:

```
newyork Any tty008 1200 tty008 "" ATZ OK ATDTphone CONNECT ...
```

That is, pretend that *newyork* is hooked up by a direct link on line *tty008* at 1200 bps. When it comes to the chat, expect nothing, send "ATZ," expect "OK," send "ATDT" followed by the telephone number, expect "CONNECT." From there, you would go on to the regular login chat.

This trick works quite well, and on a personal workstation equipped with a single modem, might well be the easiest way to set up UUCP.

4

Making Sure the Link Works

Testing with cu
Testing with tip
Testing with uucico -x
Checking the Log File
System Status Files
Testing with Uutry
Correcting the Chat
More Chat

The final step in installing a UUCP link to another system is to test the connection to make sure that you have indeed configured it correctly.

Before you try your first UUCP request, you may want to try dialing the remote system with **cu** or **tip** to make sure you can log in manually.

Once you have successfully logged in with **cu**, you are ready to test that **uucico** will be able to negotiate the chat script and successfully log in automatically.

If you are fairly confident that everything has been set up correctly, you can test the link simply by sending mail to yourself (*remote!yourhost!you*), or to the remote system administrator, or by trying to copy a file and checking to see if it came through.

If the mail or file does not get through or if you are interested in getting a better understanding of how UUCP works, you can run **uucico** manually, using the debugging option (**-x**) to display the progress of the transfer on your screen. The messages are fairly obscure, but with a little practice, they are easy enough to decipher. In addition, more understandable messages are written into the log file that **uucico** keeps for each transfer.

BNU provides a shell program called **Uutry** that invokes **uucico -x** for debugging. This program makes debugging somewhat easier.

In the discussion that follows, we have focused on Version 2. Though the messages are different in BNU (they are generally clearer), the process that **uucico** goes through is substantially similar. We have not explained the detail of every line of debugging output or log file message, in any case. Users of both versions should read the following sections. If you do have BNU, read the section "Testing with Uutry" below before you actually do any debugging.

After the discussion of the messages **uucico** gives and the process of debugging, we will spend some more time on the particular problem of writing complex chat scripts.

Testing with cu

Once you have the appropriate entries in *L.sys* and *L-devices* (or *Systems* and *Devices*), you should be able to call a system with **cu**. In SVR2 and later, you can simply type:

```
$ cu system
```

cu will look up the details on how to contact the system, just as UUCP does.[*] This will work even if there is no chat script for the system yet, so it is a good place to start if you need to figure out what chat script to use. (This will not work with **tip**, since **tip** uses files called */etc/remote* and */etc/phones* for associating system names and telephone numbers. Set up these files and then try the call. While *cu* may appear to be available on BSD systems, it is really just a link to *tip*. As a result, this will only work with System V implementations of *cu*.)

You can also use **cu** even without setting up *L.sys* or *Systems*, just so long as you have entries in *L-devices*. (If you are using BNU, there must be a **Direct** entry in *Devices* for the modem line as well as an **ACU** entry if you want to use **cu -l**.)

---

[*]See the companion handbook, *Using UUCP and Usenet*, for more complete instructions on using **cu** and **tip**.

Once you have the device file set up properly, you should be able to exercise a link by typing:

```
$ cu -l line
```

where *line* is the device name of the port to use. Again, this will work on all System V implementations of **cu** but will not work on Version 7 or BSD systems. On these systems, you can still use **cu** or **tip** to call a remote system; you will just not exercise the UUCP files in the process.

If you are connected directly to another system, you should be able to get the other system's login prompt. You may want to ask the remote system administrator for a valid login name that you can use, although this is not absolutely necessary, since getting as far as the other system's prompt and pressing RETURN a couple of times will tell you that you have the connection working.

If you get a message like "No device available" or "Requested device name unknown" then you do not have the *Devices* (*L-devices*) file set up correctly. Go back to Chapter 3, *Setting Up a UUCP Link.*

If, on the other hand, **cu** says "Connected," attempt to log in and out of the remote system. Depending on the system, you may have to press RETURN a couple of times before the prompt appears. (If no login prompt appears and everything seems right at your end, ask the remote system administrator to check that there is a **getty** on the line at his end and that the line is set up to use the same communications parameters at both ends.)

If you do get a login prompt, log in manually using the working **uucp** login and password you have been given for the remote system. You should get the message:

```
Shere=nodename
```

where *node* is the system's node name (hostname), as described in Chapter 3. (Some UUCPs will give variations of this message. For example, our Miniframes say "valid sys Shere.")

When you see this message, disconnect by entering a new line containing the tilde-period (˜.) sequence. (You must start on a new line, since a carriage return must precede any tilde escape in **cu**.) For example:

```
newton$ cu -l/dev/tty006
Connected
Waltham Electronics, Inc.   CTIX 3.2
login: nuucp
password:
```

```
Shere=waltham

-
.
Disconnected
newton$
```

To test a modem with **cu**, type:

```
$ cu -s1200 1-212-9999999
```

cu will use the first ACU defined in *L-devices* that runs at 1200 bps.

If you do not have *Dialers* (or *modemcap*, *acucap*, or one of the many other dialing schemes) set up yet, you may be able to connect directly to the modem and issue dialing commands.

For example, assuming that a 1200-bps Hayes-compatible modem is connected to */dev/tty008* (and that *L-devices* or *Devices* allows a direct connection to *tty008* as well as an ACU connection), you could use the following commands:

```
newton$ cu -s1200 -l/dev/tty008
Connected
ATZ
OK
AT DT 1-212-999-9999
New Yorker Graphics, Inc.  CTIX 3.2
login: nuucp
password:
Shere=newyork
-
.
Disconnected
newton$
```

If none of these things work, you may be able to use the **cu** command with the **-d** (debug) option to help track down the problem. In some versions of **cu**, the command:

```
$ cu -d -lline
```

allows you to call over a particular line and print diagnostic messages on the attempt.

Testing with tip

While *tip*, the BSD equivalent to *cu*, does not actually use the UUCP files for dialing information, you can use it to connect to another system and manually verify the login sequence. You can either add a system-specific entry to the *tip* configuration file */etc/remote*, or, if it exists, you can use the *hardwire* entry to connect directly to the modem. Here's an example of a hardwire entry:

```
hardwire:dv=/dev/cua0:br#9600
```

When you issue the command **tip hardwire**, you will be connected to the device on */dev/cua0*, at 9600 bps. You can then issue commands to the modem to dial another system.

Testing with uucico -x

You can invoke **uucico** manually, just like any other program. No work needs to be spooled by **mail**, **uucp**, or **uux** in order for a call to be made to another system. Of course, the schedule field in the *L.sys* (or *Systems*) file must allow calls at this time.

You can specify the name of the system to be called with the option **-s***name*. You must also use the option **-r1** to tell **uucico** to start up in Master role (that is, as the calling system). If you want to see what is going on, use the **-x***n* debugging option.

For example:

```
$ /usr/lib/uucp/uucico -r1 -x4 -swaltham
```

The debugging option **-x***n* provides different amounts of debugging information depending on the level number *n*.* The level number can be from one to nine. Level 1 gives the least amount of information, while level 9 gives the most. Level 4 usually provides enough information to locate the problem in the connection. Whatever level of debugging you specify, the output will always show the following phases of a file transfer:

• Connection setup and login

• Protocol negotiation

• Data transfer (if any)

• Shutdown

---

*In BSD 4.3 and BNU, you must have read access to *L.sys* (or *Systems*) to run **uucico** with debugging turned on. Other Version 2 UUCPs require your UID to be less than a magic value, which varies from version to version.

The debugging output normally goes to the terminal screen. However, since **uucico** ignores interrupts, it is a good idea to run it in the background and redirect its output to a file.* Then view the file with the command **tail -f**. (**tail** normally displays the last few lines of a file; the **-f** option tells it to ignore the end of file character, which lets it hang around and continue to display the end of the file as more data is added.) If you do this, you can interrupt **tail** and return to the shell if necessary. Otherwise, you will have to wait for **uucico** to finish.

If you are using the C shell, the output of the **uucico** program for our example above could be redirected to a file called *tmp.debug* in the current directory on the local system and viewed as follows:

```
% /usr/lib/uucp/uucico -r1 -x4 -swaltham >& tmp.debug &
% tail -f tmp.debug
```

and if you are using the Bourne shell:

```
$ /usr/lib/uucp/uucico -r1 -x4 -swaltham 2> tmp.debug &
$ tail -f tmp.debug
```

Note that if you use **tail -f**, **tail** will not quit even when the file has truly ended. You will need to interrupt **tail** (e.g., with CTRL-C) to get out.

In addition, if **uucico** has just failed to log in successfully, it will leave a status file called **STST**.*system* in the spool directory. (In BNU, status files are kept in a hidden subdirectory called *.Status* and simply have the name of the remote system.) This file will keep **uucico** from trying again for whatever retry interval is specified in *L.sys* (or the default value if no interval is specified). If you are making repeated attempts to get through, you will need to remove this file before you proceed. (The only exception is in BSD 4.3, which ignores the retry time when **uucico** is invoked with debugging in effect.)

You may want to construct your own version of the BNU **Uutry** shell script by saving the following commands in an executable file somewhere in your search path:

```
if [ $1 ]; then
    rm -f /usr/spool/uucp/STST.$1
    /usr/lib/uucp/uucico -r1 -x4 -s$1 2> tmp.debug &
    tail -f tmp.debug
else
    echo "Usage:  Uutry nodename"
    exit
fi
```

---

*This workaround is not necessary in BSD 4.*x* systems, since you can simply pause **uucico** with ^Z and kill or restart it as necessary.

Assuming that you give this script the name **Uutry**, all you will need to do then is to type:

```
$ Uutry system
```

The one thing to watch out for is that if your UUCP truncates node names, the name of the status file might not be quite what you think. That is, for a node name *waltham*, the name might actually be might be *STST.waltha*, in which case the **rm** command will not work unless you type:

```
$ Uutry waltha
```

A bad connection will produce system messages similar to the following:

```
finds called
getto called
call: no.i tty006 for sys waltham fixline - speed = 13
login called
wanted ogin: got ?
exit code 0
```

The attempt to contact *waltham* failed due to an incorrect chat script. It never got the login prompt it was expecting ("wanted ogin: got ?"). You should look into the *L.sys* file and correct the chat script. (See "Correcting the Chat," later in this chapter for details.)

The file */usr/spool/uucp/LOGFILE* will contain a message to the same effect:

```
walthamluucp (4/25-17:07:16) (C,14801,0) FAILED \
     (call to waltham )
```

A successful connection generates a large amount of output, as you will see in a moment. In order to make it easier to interpret, we have broken the output into sections, with each section followed by a brief discussion.

This output shows the conversation between two Convergent Technologies Miniframes running a SVR2 dialect of Version 2 UUCP. The exact messages you get from the **-x***n* option may vary depending on which type of device you are using to place the call, the chat script to log in to the remote system, and so on. However, the phases of transfer will always be the same.

Below we show a successful attempt to transfer a short test file to system *calif*. The file to be transferred is spooled using **uucp**'s **-r** option, which says to spool the file but not to start up **uucico**. This allows us to start up **uucico** manually.

```
$ uucp -r test calif\!/usr/spool/uucppublic
$ /usr/lib/uucp/uucico -r1 -x4 -scalif 2> debug &
$ tail -f debug
```

Connection Setup and Login

The first part of the debugging output shows the execution of the dialing procedure and chat script. The device is opened, then the dialing instructions and telephone number are sent to the modem. After the modem dials, the chat script is
executed.

The output from **uucico** is a little hard to read at first, since the reads and writes
are jumbled together and various nonprinting characters may show up as their
octal or hexadecimal equivalents (e.g., \015 or <0xd> for carriage return, \012 or
<0xa> for line feed, \0 or <0x0> for null). However, with a little practice, you
can pick out what is happening, especially if you know what you are looking for.

With that last comment in mind, let me prepare you by pointing out that the system file entry for *calif* looks like this:

```
calif Any ACU 1200 14157777777 ogin:--ogin: nuucp ssword: let_me_in
```

The device file entry (in our somewhat atypical CTIX implementation of UUCP)
looks like this:

```
ACU tty008 qubie 1200
```

qubie is a Hayes-compatible modem for which dialing instructions are kept in the
modemcap file. As described in Appendix B, *Talking to Modems*, the dialing procedure for a Hayes-compatible modem is to send the string "AT" (ATtention!),
wait for an "OK," then send "AT DT *phone number*" (ATtention! Dial Touchtone
phone number). For a pulse dialing phone line, the command would be AT DP.

It is a good practice to reset the modem (the Hayes **Z** command) before dialing,
so we actually start the dialing sequence with the command "ATZ".

Thus armed, let's look at the output from **uucico**.

```
finds called
getto called
call: no. 14157777777 for sys calif call fnc 14157777777
Dial 14157777777
mlock tty008
d_type tty008
open tty008
speed= 9
ioctl for /dev/tty008
dc - /dev/tty008, acu - /dev/qubie
sending <ATZ >
sending <AT >
writing phone <DT14157777777^M>
ACU write ok
dcdelay is 5
dcr returned as 6
```

```
login called
wanted ogin: ATZ<0xd><0xa>OK<0xd><0xa>AT DT14157777777\
    <0xd><0xd><0xa>CONNECT<0xd><0xa>got ?
wanted ogin: <0xd><0xa><0xd><0xa>California Cool, Inc.\
    <0xd><0xa><0xd><0xa>login:got that
wanted ssword: nuucp<0xd><0xa>Password:got that
valid sys Shere
msg-ROK
Rmtname calif, Role Master,  Ifn - 6, Loginuser - tim
```

The first ten lines or so are concerned with opening the device, setting the speed, and so on. We see reports on the various system calls made by **uucico**. If there were any errors at this point, we would instead see a message such as "NO DEVICE" (if the device file were set up incorrectly) or "OPEN FAILED" (if the port could not be opened for some reason such as no read permission for **uucp** on the special file in */dev*).

Then we see the messages:

```
sending <ATZ >
sending <AT >
writing phone <DT14157777777^M>
```

The modem echoes the commands that are sent and some status messages. However, **uucico** does not echo these messages immediately but first prints some messages of its own. As a result, the output looks rather scrambled.

The unscrambled sequence is as follows (with carriage return-line feed pairs shown on the page rather than as hex codes):

uucico	`wanted ogin:`
modem	`ATZ`
	`OK`
	`AT DT14157777777`
	`CONNECT`
uucico	`got ?`
	`wanted ogin:`
calif	`California Cool, Inc.`
	`Please login:`
uucico	`got that`
	`nuucp` (*This is actually echoed back by the remote system*)
	`wanted ssword:`
calif	`Password:`

```
uucico     got that
```
(password is not displayed)

Once **uucico** has logged in correctly, the two systems check to see if they know each other. The Slave prints the message:

```
Shere=nodename
```

where *nodename* is its node name (hostname), as described in Chapter 3, *Setting Up a UUCP Link*.

The Master replies:

```
Snodename - Qseq - xnum
```

where *nodename* is its node name (hostname), *seq* is the sequence number (see Chapter 5, *Access and Security*) or 0 if unused, and *num* is the level of debugging in effect.*

If the two systems agree to talk to each other, the Slave prints the message:

```
ROK
```

If the systems do not know each other or if any one of several security mechanisms (described in Chapter 5) is in effect, the call can be terminated instead. If callback is specified in *USERFILE* or *Permissions*, the Slave will refuse the connection, with the message:

```
RCB
```

meaning "I'll call back." If the Slave is Ultrix, SVR2, or BNU and the login name is missing from the *USERFILE* file or the *Permissions* file, the Slave sends the message:

```
RLOGIN
```

If the Slave is BSD 4.3 or BNU with NOSTRANGERS enabled and the Master hostname is not in the *L.sys* or *Systems* file, the Slave will send:

```
RYou are unknown to me
```

The "WRONG SYSTEM" (SVR2) or "WRONG MACHINE NAME" (BNU) message is produced by the Master when the hostname in the "Shere=*hostname*" message from the Slave is not the same as the Master thought it was calling. If this check fails, the Master does not even bother with its "Shostname" message; it just hangs up. This check only exists on SVR2 and BNU and does not work if the Slave

---

*Note that, as always, this conversation can vary depending on the systems involved. For example, in a conversation between our two Miniframes, the Slave says:

```
valid sys Shere
```

and the Master says nothing.

uucico is too old to put its hostname on the "Shere" message. Note that even on BNU, the name is checked only in the first six characters. Note also that each of these messages is preceded by a synchronization character (\020) which does not print on most terminals. Each is terminated by a null (\0) or a carriage return.

Protocol Negotiation

The two **uucico** programs now try to agree on a communications protocol:

```
rmesg - 'P' imsg > 20 Pgx  0 got Pgx
wmesg 'U'g
Proto started g
protocol g
```

The calling system first asks for a list of available protocols (low-level handshaking, error-checking, and data transfer methods). The list is communicated using a "P" message ("protocol list").

In this example, there are two protocols available, *g*, UUCP's own standard protocol, and *x*, a protocol which does no packetizing or error checking but simply sends a data stream. (This is for use on top of other data transmission protocols like X.25 or TCP/IP. Another protocol, the *f* protocol, which does a minimal amount of data checking (a single checksum on each file) is used for the same purpose.) The two systems agree to use the *g* protocol ("wmesg 'U'g").

The protocols that are supported are built into UUCP and may differ from implementation to implementation. In Version 2 UUCP, protocol selection is usually determined for supported device types when UUCP is compiled and is not something you as an administrator can modify. In BNU, a protocol list can be specified in either the *Systems* or *Devices* file.

Data Transfer

Next the actual data transfer (or other job processing) begins:

```
*** TOP *** - role=1, setline - X
cntrl 8
cntrl
cntrltim
setline - S
wrktype - S
 wmesg 'S' /work/nutshell/uucp_adm/test
rmesg - 'S' got SY
 PROCESS: msg - SY
SNDFILE:
-> 320 / 1 secs
```

```
rmesg - 'C' got CY
 PROCESS: msg - CY
RQSTCMPT:
notif 0
notif 0
```

During the work processing phase, four messages are used. These are specified by the first character of the message:

S   Send a file.

R   Receive a file.

C   Copy complete.

X   Execute a command.

In the example shown above, the Master asks to send the file (*wmesg 'S' /work/nutshell/uucp_adm/test*) and the Slave acknowledges ("SY"). If for any reason the file could not be transferred (e.g., wrong permissions), the Slave would reply "SN".*   While data is being transferred, it is stored in a temporary file in the spool directory, whose name begins with the letters TM. Once the transfer is complete, you should see a message like this:

-> 320 / 1 seconds

which shows the direction of the transfer, the number of bytes transferred, and the length of time it took.

The Master then awaits confirmation, in the form of a C message. The Slave sends CY, yes, the file made it across, once the data has been copied from the temporary file to its final destination.

---

*Any "No" message (SN, RN, CN, or XN) may optionally be followed by a number indicating the reason for the refusal. The most common values are:

2   Remote access to path/file denied.

4   Remote system cannot create the TM file. Usually means there is not enough space on the remote system.

5   Cannot copy the TM file to the requested destination. Depending on the system, the file may be put in the public directory, left in the spool directory, or deleted.

Role Reversal and Shutdown

When the Master finishes sending all queued files, it sends an **H** command, which asks the Slave to hang up the line.

```
*** TOP ***  -  role=1, setline - X
Finished Processing file: /usr/spool/uucp/C.califnA5148
wmesg 'H'
rmesg - 'H' got HY
 PROCESS: msg - HY
HUP:
wmesg 'H'Y
cntrl - 0
send OO 0,exit code 0
```

If there are jobs queued in the other direction, the Slave answers "HN" (for No), and the roles are reversed.

If the Slave does not have any files to send to the Master, it responds "HY" (for Yes). The connection ends with an "OO" message (over and out), as shown in the example above.

Checking the Log File

Throughout the entire transfer, **uucico** writes messages into a log file in the spool directory. (The exact name and location of this file may vary from version to version of UUCP. See Appendix A, *Working Files*, for details.) Normally, these messages are fairly brief, simply stating that a remote system was called and that a transfer was made. However, if debugging is turned on, the messages in the log file also get more extensive (at least on some systems).

For example, the logfile messages for the transfer shown above are as follows:

```
calif!tim  (4/26-11:16:05) (U,21653,0) QUE'D (C.califnA5148)
calif!uucp (4/26-11:16:14) (C,21655,0) C.calif (bldfl)
calif!uucp (4/26-11:16:18) (C,4413,0) OK (DIAL P14157777777< 6)
calif!uucp (4/26-11:16:26) (C,4413,0) TIMEOUT (LOGIN)
calif!uucp (4/26-11:16:32) (C,21655,0) SUCCEEDED (call to calif )
calif!uucp (4/26-11:16:34) (C,21655,0) Shere=calif (HERE)
calif!uucp (4/26-11:16:39) (C,21655,0) ora (send Myname)
calif!uucp (4/26-11:16:46) (C,21655,0) OK (startup)
calif!uucp (4/26-11:16:46) (C,21655,0) C.calif (bldfl)
calif!tim  (4/26-11:16:46) (C,21655,0) REQUEST \
    (S /work/nutshell/uucp_adm/test /usr/spool/uucppublic tim)
calif!tim  (4/26-11:16:46) (C,21655,0) REQUEST \
    (S /work/nutshell/uucp_adm/test /usr/spool/uucppublic \
    tim -dc D.0 664)
```

```
calif!tim (4/26-11:16:47) (C,21655,1) file removed in cntrl.c (D.0)
calif!tim (4/26-11:16:48) (C,21655,1) REQUESTED (CY)
calif!uucp (4/26-11:16:48) (C,21655,1) C.calif (bldfl)
calif!uucp (4/26-11:16:49) (C,21655,1) OK (conversation complete  tty008 23)
```

The first line is a record of the original **uucp** or **uux** job request. It shows the destination system and the login user who made the request, the date and time, the **uucp** job id, the action that occurred (QUE'D), and the name of the work file in the spool directory.

The remainder of the lines are all written by **uucico**. (Note that they all have the same job id.)

Take a moment to correlate the messages shown here with those in the debugging output for **uucico** shown above. Note that they show the same basic phases of transfer, though with less detail.

Another file to look at is the *SYSLOG* file in the spool directory, which shows the actual file transfers performed between systems. For example, for the above transfer, *SYSLOG* showed:

```
ventur!tim M (4/26-11:16:47) (C,21655,1) (0:0:42)  -> 320 / 1 secs
[23:1:6:14:1:0:1:0] [tty008,0,0,0,0]
```

(This file is most useful if you want to check up on what kind of transfers are being made to or from your system.)

System Status Files

While you are debugging, you will probably need to circumvent UUCP's normal retry mechanism.

Whenever a UUCP request is made, temporary system status files are created by **uucico** in the spool directory for each system. These files contain information about the status of conversation between two systems.

If two systems are conversing, the file entry for the remote system shows "TALKING" or "CONVERSATION".

Status filenames in Version 2 UUCP consist of the prefix *STST.* followed by the remote system name. For example, the status file for a remote system *waltham* would be *STST.waltham*. In BNU, they simply have the name of the system and are stored in the subdirectory *.Status*.

An entry in this file consists of six fields separated by blanks:

A System Status File

Field	Function in Status File
type	A code from zero to five indicating the status of the job. The code is also explained in the *status* field.
count	The number of call attempts made by the local system. It is incremented each time **uucico** tries to call the remote system.
UNIXtime	Time of the last connection attempt, expressed in *time*(2) format— that is, the number of seconds since January 1, 1970, GMT.
retry	The number of seconds that **uucico** must wait before another call attempt.
status	Status of the conversation.
system	The name of system being called.

Status files are deleted automatically in the course of normal operation, but when UUCP fails, they may remain and prohibit UUCP activity for a predefined period of time.

If a conversation ends abnormally, status files remain in the spool directory and *prevent further transfer attempts* for a period specified in the *retry* field of the *L.sys* file. You can modify this field to change the default time (55 minutes in Version 2; exponential in BNU and BSD 4.3). Status files allow 26 successive retries by *uucico*. After that, the files must be removed manually before **uucico** can try again.

While you are debugging a link, you will probably want to make a change to your chat script or other configuration information and retry immediately. The simplest way to do this is to manually remove the status file.

If you have problems debugging a link, do not forget to remove the status file before invoking **uucico** again.

Status files can also be read to find out the status of the transfer. See Chapter 6, *UUCP Administration*, for a listing of status messages.

Testing with Uutry

With BNU, you can use a shell program called **Uutry** to debug a new link. **Uutry** provides level 5 debugging. This can be reset using the **-x** *level* option. (Note that the name of this command begins with an uppercase letter.)

For example, to check that system *calif* can be called, the command is:

```
$ /usr/lib/uucp/Uutry calif
```

This starts **uucico** to call system *calif*. The debugging output is placed into a temporary file, and a **tail -f** command is executed. You can then press the INTERRUPT key (e.g., CTRL-C) to get back to the shell and return to the output later on. Or you can copy the output from */tmp/calif* if you want to save the output.

Uutry attempts to call a remote machine for five minutes before giving up. You also cannot invoke **Uutry** again until the retry period specified in the *Systems* file has expired. If you want to call the machine before the retry time, use the **–r** option. Alternatively, you can check the system status file for that machine (located in */usr/spool/uucp/.Status/machine*).

If you run into any problem, you can then attempt to transfer a file using the **-r** option of **uucp** (as shown in the previous section) and watch the debugging output.

It is not possible to show you all the problems you may run into while debugging a link, but the example of a transmission script shown in the previous section should help you. Just remember: wherever **uucico** stops, there lies your problem.

Correcting the Chat

In writing the chat script, you have to simulate the process of manual login. If the system administrator of the remote system cannot tell you from experience what the chat script ought to be, then you should use **cu** or **tip** to log into the remote system, as discussed in Chapter 3, *Setting Up a UUCP Link*. Pay attention to what keystrokes are required before a login prompt appears on your screen.

For example, to get a login prompt on one system, you might first need to press RETURN twice. Your chat script would begin:

```
""  \r\r ogin:
```

That is, expect nothing (""), send a pair of RETURNs (\r\r), and expect to get "ogin:". (\r\r will actually send either three carriage returns or two carriage returns followed by a linefeed. Depending on the system, **uucico** adds one or the other of these characters to every send string, unless you suppress it by ending the send string with \c.)

Another frequently encountered situation is that many systems support dialup lines at more than one speed. As we saw in Chapter 2, the **getty** process that controls the speed of the serial line can be set up to cycle through a series of different speeds each time it receives a break character.

So, for instance, the sequence:

```
ogin:-BREAK-ogin:
```

waits for "ogin:". If it gets it, **uucico** goes right on to the next send (e.g., "nuucp" in our first example). If it does not get it after a certain amount of time, it sends a BREAK, which causes the remote systems to cycle through to the next speed. It then waits for the next subexpect ("ogin:" again), which hopefully this time it will get. Usually, only two speeds are supported (300 and 1200 bps), so only a single "ogin:-BREAK-ogin:" would guarantee receipt of a login prompt at the correct speed. However, with 2400-bps modems, an "ogin:-BREAK-ogin:-BREAK-ogin:" sequence might sometimes be necessary.

More Chat

Before we go on to look at some more examples of chat scripts, let's revisit the table of escape sequences we looked at in the last chapter, this time adding the codes that may appear in **uucico**'s debugging output each time one of these escapes is encountered. (Some systems show the escapes in hex. Others display them in octal (\nnn). Still others will use the more familiar DEC notation for control characters, such as ^J for line feed, M for carriage return, or ^D for EOT. (In a few cases, nothing is shown.)

Table 4-1. Chat Script Escape Sequences

Escape Sequence	As Shown By -x Hex	Octal	Description
" "	" "		Expect a null string.
EOT	<0x4>	\004	Send an end-of-transmission character.
BREAK			Cause a BREAK. This is sometimes simulated using line speed changes and null characters. May not work on all systems.
\b	<0x8>	\010	Send a backspace character. On BSD 4.2 systems, send a BREAK.
\c			Suppress newline at the end of the *send* string.
\d			Delay for one second (send only).
\K			Insert a BREAK (BNU only).
\n	<0xa>	\012	Send a newline or linefeed character.
\N	<0x0>	\000	Send a null character.
\p			Pause for a fraction of a second (BNU only).
\r	<0xd>	\015	Send a carriage return.
\s			Send a space character.
\t	<0x9>	\011	Send a tab character.
\\			Send a backslash (\) character.
\ddd			Collapse the octal digits (*ddd*) into a single ASCII character and send that character.

First, some notes on these sequences.

- A BREAK is defined by the RS-232 standard as an extended period of spacing time—that is, a break in the expected sequence of start bits, data bits, and stop bits. On some systems, what UUCP generates as a BREAK is actually a null character and line speed change. According to the documentation, this may not work on all systems. What may show up in the debugging output is <0x0>, that is, ASCII null. Other systems are able to send a true BREAK.

- EOT is (the ASCII character variously known as End-of-Transmission, End-of-File, and CTRL-D).

- Inasmuch as spaces or tabs serve to delimit the expect-send fields in the system file, if you need to include a space or a tab as a part of an expect or send field, you should use the corresponding escape \s or \t. To send a hyphen, use the octal value \055. (This does not work in BNU. In BNU, it is not possible to send a hyphen.)

- Each send string is normally terminated with either a carriage return or a newline. The most portable way to specify chat scripts is to specify explicitly which character you want and suppress the automatic terminator (that is, use \n\c or \r\c to terminate all send strings). However, you generally do not need to worry about this unless a system you are trying to call is not responding properly to your sends.

- BSD UNIX systems support a number of additional keywords, such as ABORT, PAUSE, P_ODD, P_EVEN, and others. See your documentation for details.

Now let's look at some applications of these sequences.

Trouble in the Promised LAN

Many sites nowadays contain a number of machines connected by a local area network (LAN). In most cases, UUCP is no longer used for file transfer between systems, since the local area network supports its own file transfer commands. Nonetheless, UUCP is still used to send mail, files, or news postings over a modem connection to systems outside the local site.

Many sites address this problem by using a device variously called a *port selector*, a *port contender*, or a *data switch*. The contender prompts for the name of the desired network device (such as a modem) and then grants transparent access to the device. We'll talk in a moment about complications in both dialing in and dialing out through a modem attached to a port contender.

At other sites, one machine is designated as the gateway to the outside world. This machine has a complete UUCP setup, complete with modems. Mail or file transfer requests are sent to that machine via the local area network and, from there, are sent on to the outside world via UUCP. Obviously, this can introduce some complications into chat scripts.

There is room for a great deal of variation on this theme, so we'll just discuss the one situation we have worked with and leave further refinements to your imagination.

Calling in through a port contender

As mentioned above, if you are calling in through a modem attached to a port contender, you may have to deal with the prompt put up by the contender before you get to the target system.

For example, to log in through a Develcon switch, you might use the following chat script* (included here by courtesy of Clem Cole of Stellar Computer):

```
"" \d\d quest:-\d-quest: ghost \
   login:-BREAK-login:-BREAK-login:-BREAK-login: uucp word: inaong
```

uucico starts by expecting nothing ("") and then sending two delays (\d\d) followed by a carriage return (which is added to all send strings). Then it waits for the network switch to respond with its "request:" prompt.

Next **uucico** specifies the desired system, in this case *ghost*, and awaits the login prompt from that system. The subexpect-subsend sequence uses a number of BREAKs in case the target system is running at a different speed. Once **uucico** gets the prompt, it will log in and eventually send the password, in this case *inaong* ("I'm not afraid of no ghosts").

BSD 4.2 and 4.3 also support the Develcon switch with automatic baud rate selection. A *gettydefs* entry of type *s* allows the switch to automatically adjust the baud rate to that of the incoming call and allows **getty** to pick up the appropriate baud rate from the switch. If this setup is being used, no BREAKs need be sent by the calling **uucico**.

Calling out through a port contender

BNU makes explicit provision for modems connected to a port contender by allowing for "dialer-token pairs" in the *Devices* file. This allows you to pass arguments to a port contender as part of the device-handling protocol.

In Version 2, you will need to do this as part of your chat script. For example:

```
"" \d\d quest:-\d-quest: hayes "" ATZ OK ATDTphone ...
```

Calling in through a software switch

In setting up a UUCP link with one of our clients, we recently encountered an interesting variation on the "gateway machine" concept. Again, both the problem and the solution are courtesy of Clem Cole.

The company has a network of Sun workstations set up as a temporary development environment until their own hardware is available. Each of the Suns only has two serial ports. As a result, the gateway machine supports one modem for dial-out and one for dial-in, while each of the other machines supports a modem

---

*Remember that the long line here is broken into three, as signified by the backslash at the end of each line. This is to allow printing in this book and will not work in the *L.sys* file. Such interrupted lines are allowed in *Systems*.

for dial-in. (These dial-in modems are used for remote access from home terminals as well as for UUCP.) The dial-in phone lines are on a hunt group, so that
someone dialing in may make the initial connection on any one of the machines.

For dial-out, all machines use Ethernet commands to send mail or file transfer
requests to the gateway, as described earlier. For dial-in, the working UUCP login
account on each system is set up with the following shell script as its login shell:

```
#! /bin/sh
#
# Shunt to the gateway and login there, using the TCP/IP
# rlogin command.  The -8 switch tells rlogin to use an
# 8-bit TCP path.  This is important for UUCP.
#
# On the gateway machine, just relogin.
#
# For System V the hostname call would be replaced by
# a call to ''uname -n.''

GATEWAY=sedalia

echo "switch LOGIN:"
read NEWLOGIN
if [ 'hostname' != $GATEWAY ]
then
        rlogin $GATEWAY -1 $NEWLOGIN -8
else
        login $NEWLOGIN
fi
```

In an ideal world, the chat script we use to call in would look like this:

```
sedalia Any ACU 1200 5555555 ogin:--ogin: uuswitch word: \
    switch_me OGIN: Unewton word: phew!
```

That is, we first log in to whichever machine we arrive at using the login id
uuswitch and the password *switch_me*. This gets us to the switch script shown
above, which puts up a LOGIN: prompt. We reply to this prompt with the real
uucp login we want to use on the gateway machine. The switch script passes this
over the Ethernet, where the login is completed on the gateway machine, which
we are here calling *sedalia*.

Unfortunately, in practice, things did not work quite so simply. Depending on the
system load at the time, the switch sometimes took a while, and **uucico** tended to
time-out before the switch was negotiated. (That is, **uucico** would successfully
log in as *uuswitch* and, after waiting what it thought was a reasonable length of
time for the next login prompt, would decide that nothing was doing and quit.)

So we added some delays, like this:

```
sedalia Any ACU 1200 5555555 ogin:--ogin: uuswitch word: \
    switch_me "" \d\d\d\d\d OGIN: Unewton word: phew!
```

That looked right, but now a curious thing occurred. **uucico** would successfully log in to the destination system, but once it did, the handshake would fail, with the message "Wrong System".

We knew that was not the case. By carefully watching the debugging output, we were able to determine that the delays we were sending were being followed (as are all send strings) by a carriage return. This carriage return was somehow being carried along and passed to the Slave **uucico** as a part of the system name.

The final chat (which worked) looks like this:

```
sedalia Any ACU 1200 5555555 ogin:--ogin: uuswitch word: \
    switch_me "" \d\d\d\d\d\c OGIN: Unewton word: phew!
```

Chat Between uugettys

If two systems running BNU are both using **uugetty** with the **-r** option to allow a single line to be used for both dial-in and dial-out, several carriage returns must be sent before **uugetty** will respond with a login prompt.

The chat script on each system should begin with the following sequence:

```
...    ""   \r\d\r\d\r\d\r in:--in: ...
```

That is, expect nothing; send return, delay, return, delay, return, delay, return before expecting the login prompt.

Calling Over a Public Data Network

In addition to the long-distance telephone network, the United States (and many other countries as well) is crisscrossed by a number of high-speed public data networks. Some of the most well-known data networks are run by GTE Telenet, Tymnet, and GEIS (General Electric Information Services). Most use the X.25 protocol for high-speed data transfer.

Many large corporations have leased lines that connect directly to a public data network. This allows them to connect systems all over the country using a reliable, high-speed data transmission protocol.

In this section, we will be talking less about these direct connections to public data networks, and more about access to these networks by way of the telephone system.

Public data networks have local access telephone numbers in most major cities. You can dial in with a modem, paying only local telephone charges, and be assured of a reliable connection to sites around the country.

The presence of local access numbers begs the question of who is there to call. First of all, there are sites that have a direct connection to a public data network and accept calls through the network from systems calling in to local access telephone numbers. This type of site may be a large corporation that is funding the network connection for its own reasons or a reseller who will charge you for the connection. For example, the UUNET service described in Chapter 8, *Installing Netnews*, provides news feeds via Tymnet and bills you directly for a monthly subscription fee plus connect time fees.

In addition, GTE Telenet runs an economical service called PC Pursuit that acts as a switching service between users who do not have a direct connection. This service allows you to call other systems by telephone number but uses Telenet instead of the telephone system as the long-distance transport medium. This ensures much more reliable communication, even though the speed of the local modem connections on each end keeps you from taking advantage of the higher speed possible with the network.

PC Pursuit

PC Pursuit provides an economical way to use the public data networks to connect to other systems who do not themselves have a direct connection to the network.

To use PC Pursuit, you place a call to the local access number. PC Pursuit routes your call across the network to the station nearest your destination and makes a local telephone call to the system you want to reach. You get a reliable connection; Telenet gets your long-distance revenues.

In more detail, the procedure looks like this:

1. You must call the Telenet local access number. (Local access numbers are available by calling information—telephone information, that is—or Telenet itself.)

2. You must send three carriage returns.

3. You must wait for an at sign (@) (the Telenet prompt).

4. You must send the sequence:

```
C D /area_code/speed,PCP_user-id
```

area code is used to be a real telephone area code. However, PC Pursuit recently adopted mnemonic area code. For example, the Boston area (telephone area code 617) is specified by the code MABOS. Contact PC Pursuit for the correct list of codes. The *speed* is either 3 (300 bps), 12 (1200 bps), or 24 (2400 bps). For example, to dial San Francisco using a 1200-bps connection with user id abcd1234 (you would get this id when you sign up for the PC Pursuit service), you would send:

```
C D/CASFA/12,abcd1234
```

The space between the "C" and the "D" (for "DIAL") is required. (You should encode this in your chat script with the escape sequence \s, or the octal value \040 if your system does not support \s.)

5. PC Pursuit asks for your password, using the prompt PASSWORD = . Again, note the spaces.

6. You must send the password.

7. PC Pursuit responds with "DIAL*area_code* CONNECTED."

8. You must reset the remote modem that PC Pursuit will use to make the call in the remote area code and then dial the actual number (*sans* area code) that you want to reach. PC Pursuit uses modems that recognize both Hayes and Racal-Vadic commands. Because it is not possible to predict whether the modem will be in Hayes or Racal-Vadic mode (it stays in whatever mode the last call left it in), you should send both Racal-Vadic Idle command (I followed by a return) before sending the Hayes reset sequence. For example, this means you send "I\r""ATZ", expect "OK", send "ATDT*phone*", expect "CONNECT", and then go into your standard login chat for the remote system.

An *L.sys* entry (using a Hayes modem) might look something like this:

```
babylon Any ACU 1200 Telenet_phone_no CONNECT \r\r\r \
   @ C\sD/CASFA/12,PCP-userid WORD\s=\s PCP_passwd \
   CONNECTED I\r ATZ OK ATDTbabylon_phone_no CONNECT \r\r \
   ogin: ...
```

This is a real handful! It is somewhat easier to handle this chat script in BNU and BSD 4.3, since the chat with PC Pursuit can all be handled in the *Devices* (*L-devices* in BSD 4.3) file. Steve Howard, of the College of Business Administration at the University of Cincinnati, who sent us the information on PC Pursuit, has created a separate "Dialer" for each area code.

As a result, an entry in his *Systems* file looks like this:

```
babylon Any ACU415 1200 babylon_phone ogin: ...
```

The corresponding entry in *Devices* looks like this:

```
ACU415 tty74 - 1200 415dialer
```

And all of the gobbledygook goes in *Dialers*, like this:

```
415dialer  =,-,  "" \dATZ\r\c OK\r \EATDTTelenet_phone \
    CONNECT \r\r\r @ C\sD/CASFA/12,PCP-userid WORD\s=\s \
    PCP_passwd CONNECTED I\r ATZ OK ATDT\T CONNECT \r\r
```

Trying Multiple Phone Numbers

If your site has multiple devices that can be used for outgoing calls, and one of them is busy, *uucico* will go on to the next one. This can be set up by specifying several devices of the same class (e.g., ACU) in *L-devices* or *Devices*.

But what if the modem is busy on the other end? Again, many sites with multiple modems have them on a "hunt group" so that the telephone company or local PBX automatically shunts the incoming call to the next free line.

However, there are cases in which you want to try several numbers that are not linked in this way. Fortunately, there is a solution.

If you have a Hayes-compatible modem, the modem can be configured to report both dial tone and busy tone in its result codes, using the command AT **X4**. You can either store this setting in the modem's memory (AT **X4** &W), or you can specify it as part of your dialing string (AT **X4** DT **. . .**).

Once your modem reports "BUSY", you can either program the modem to automatically try a series of numbers, or you can test for that string in your chat script.

Here are the two approaches:

1. Store multiple numbers in the modem's memory, and use the modem's shorthand for recalling stored numbers to give several of them in the dialing command. For example:

   ```
   ATX4DT123-4567n1
   ATX4DT234-5678n2
   ATX4DT345-6789n3
   ```

stores the X4 command, plus the dialing command DT123-4567 as n1, with
234-5678 as the corresponding number for n2 and 345-6789 as the number n3.
Now, issuing the command:

```
ATn1n2n3
```

causes the modem to dial n1, and if the line is busy, to try n2. If that's busy, it
tries n3.

2. The approach suggested above works well for *cu* or other interactive dialing,
    but can cause problems with *uucico*, depending on the length of its timeouts.
    For example, on my Sun 3, I found I could dial only two numbers before
    uucico timed out. So instead of letting the modem do all the work, I test for
    the busy condition in my chat script, using the standard subexpect-subsend
    sequence, as follows:

```
ora Any ttya 19200 ttya "" ATZ\r\c OK ATDTfirst_number\r\c \
    CONNECT-ATDTsecond_number\r\c-CONNECT-ATDTthird_number\r\c \
    ogin: ...
```

That is, send ATZ to reset the modem; then expect OK. After that, dial the
first number. Expect CONNECT, and if you don't get it, try another number ... and another. Then go into the real login chat.

Because we're not actually matching the BUSY result code, you'd think we
don't need the Hayes X4 command. However, including it makes a busy call
terminate much more quickly, and so speeds the entire transaction. In the
above example, X4 isn't specified; it is assumed that the modem has been permanently configured to give the extended result codes.

On a related note, BSD 4.3 has added an ABORT keyword, which can be used in
L.sys or *L-devices* to drop a call as soon as the BUSY string appears, freeing you
to make another call without waiting for the normal timeout. The ABORT keyword is followed by a fixed string (not a regular expression). If that string occurs
anywhere later in the interaction, the call will immediately be aborted. In addition, a number following a tilde in an expect string gives a timeout for that expec-
tation.

For example, consider the following *L-devices* example from the Pyramid UCB
universe implementation of 4.3, as posted to the net by Romain Kang (message
141457@pyramid.pyramid.com):

```
ACU ttyi48 - 2400 null "" ATE1Q0V1 OK\r\n~4 ABORT BUSY\r\n \
    ATDT\T CONNECT\s1200\r\n~40
```

In this case, the device chat first sends some configuration settings to the modem.
If an OK isn't received within four seconds, uucico will time out. From that point

on, the call will abort if the string BUSY is received. A forty-second timeout is provided for the CONNECT string to be received.

UUCP Over a Starlan Network

In a recent news posting (*<1642@public.BTR.COM>*), Thad Floryan of BTR Public Access UNIX provided copies of the configuration files he's using on a 3B1 running BNU, with a Starlan network. Thad suggests that the key to getting Starlan working properly was the use of *Sysfiles* to designate separate configuration files for cu and uucp.

Here are the contents of his */usr/lib/uucp/Sysfiles*:

```
service=cu  systems=Systems.cu:Systems   devices=Devices   dialers=Dialers

service=uucico    systems=Systems.uucico:Systems
                  devices=Devices          dialers=Dialers
```

Here's */usr/lib/uucp/Systems.cu*:

```
# StarLAN entries for cu activity
#
amiga Any STARLAN - access0 "" \r\d\r in:--in: nuucp
thadlabs Any STARLAN - thadlabs "" \r\d\r in:--in: nuucp
tlabs3 Any STARLAN - tlabs3 "" \r\d\r in:--in: nuucp
tlabs4 Any STARLAN - tlabs4 "" \r\d\r in:--in: nuucp
tlabs5 Any STARLAN - tlabs5 "" \r\d\r in:--in: nuucp
```

(Note that "access0" is a StarLAN RS-232 NAU.)

Here's */usr/lib/uucp/Systems.uucico*:

```
# StarLAN entries for uucico activity
#
thadlabs Any STARLAN_NAU,eg - thadlabs "" \r\d\r in:--in: nuucp
tlabs3 Any STARLAN_NAU,eg - tlabs3 "" \r\d\r in:--in: nuucp
tlabs4 Any STARLAN_NAU,eg - tlabs4 "" \r\d\r in:--in: nuucp
tlabs5 Any STARLAN_NAU,eg - tlabs5 "" \r\d\r in:--in: nuucp
```

That points out that by using the *e* protocol, he increased throughput from 2 Kbytes/second (with the *g* protocol) to 50 Kbytes/second over the same Starlan network.

Here's his */usr/lib/uucp/Devices*:

```
STARLAN          starlan - Any STARLAN
STARLAN_NAU,eg starlan - Any STARLAN \D.serve pc_uucp
STARLAN_UU,eg  starlan - Any STARLAN \D.serve SLAN_uucico
```

Here's his copy of */usr/lib/uucp/Dialers*:

```
STARLAN_NIU "" "" \r\d\r\d\r DIAL:-\r\d\r\d\r-DIAL: \D "" \d\d\c
pc_uucp "" "" NLPS:000:001:102\N\c
SLAN_uucico ""    "" NLPS:000:001:101\N\c
SLAN_login ""    "" NLPS:000:001:1\N\c
nls    ""    "" NLPS:000:001:1\N\c
```

And finally, the file */usr/net/nls/starlan/dbf* (which contains port definitions for the NLS "Network Listener Service") contains the following entries:

```
1:na:NULL,:/usr/net/servers/sl      #Remote Login
102:n:NULL,:/usr/net/servers/uucplogin   #Mail/File Transfer
```

5

Access and Security Considerations

Creating /etc/passwd Entries
Security in Version 2 UUCP
Security in BNU
Modes and Ownership of UUCP Files

Giving a remote system the ability to copy files and execute commands on your system raises issues of system security. If left unprotected, the UUCP system would allow any remote user to copy in or out any file that has UNIX read/write file permissions. Fortunately, a lot of security measures are already in place.

First of all, like all users, *uucico* must log in to your system. By assigning a password, you can keep unauthorized users from logging in.

Secondly, UUCP's working login in the */etc/passwd* file does not receive a normal shell but instead invokes another copy of **uucico**. The only work that can be done is that allowed by the Slave (receiving) **uucico**.

The system administrator has a few more mechanisms available to increase the level of security of the local site:

- Creating additional *passwd* file entries to grant individual access (with potentially different permissions) to each calling system.

- Restricting local file access by remote systems, or requiring a call-back for certain system logins.

- Controlling the commands that remote systems can execute on the local system.

- Controlling the systems that can forward files through your system and to which other systems they can forward.

- Assigning appropriate file access modes and ownerships to protect the UUCP files (which contain such sensitive data as remote system's telephone numbers and login passwords) from outside users.

Both versions of UUCP allow you to define additional working logins for **uucico**. This allows you to define separate passwords for each remote system that calls you. You can also grant different levels of access on a system-by-system basis. (Some of UUCP's security mechanisms rely on the working login id, while others depend on the calling machine's node name.)

Using separate working logins for each system also makes it easier to track which system has called you, especially in Version 2 UUCP. (BNU keeps better track of this even if you use only one working login.)

In Version 2 UUCP, the file *USERFILE* controls the levels of filesystem access that will be granted to each remote system. It also optionally specifies that a remote system must be called back (this verifies its identity) in order for any work to be performed. The commands that can be executed remotely by **uux** are specified in a file that is usually called *L.cmds*.* In addition, a file called *SQFILE* can be set up to keep a sequence count of conversations between two systems. (This helps to keep other systems from masquerading as a system known to you.)

In SVR1 and SVR2, the files *ORIGFILE* and *FWDFILE* list (respectively) the names of systems that can forward files through your system and the names of systems they can forward to. Check your documentation to see if this feature is supported, and keep in mind that it will only work with other systems that implement forwarding the same way.

BNU has replaced all of these files with a single file called *Permissions* which gives a far greater degree of individual control over the access granted to each system.

This chapter describes each of these mechanisms in detail. It also covers the UNIX file permissions that should be granted to all of the UUCP files in order to maintain a secure system.

---

*In some older implementations of UUCP, the list of allowable commands is compiled directly into **uuxqt**, and *L.cmds* does not exist.

Creating /etc/passwd Entries

On many systems, the */etc/passwd* file one *administrative login* for UUCP maintenance and one *working login*. In BSD, there is only one login, a UUCP working
login.

The administrative login is the owner of all UUCP programs, directories, and files.
It is used by the **cron** program when it runs the UUCP maintenance shell scripts.
The working login is the login id that a remote **uucico** will use to actually log in
to your system. There can be a general access login for all systems, or you can
add a number of system-specific logins.

/etc/passwd

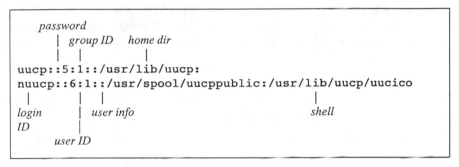

```
        password
            | group ID   home dir
            |   |        |
uucp::5:1::/usr/lib/uucp:
nuucp::6:1:::/usr/spool/uucppublic:/usr/lib/uucp/uucico
    |       |   |                                  |
  login     | user info                           shell
  ID        |
        user ID
```

Field	Function in */etc/passwd*
login id	*uucp* or *uucpadm* for administrative logins; any login name for working logins (for example, *nuucp* or *xuucp*). It can also be a specific system name (for example, *japan*).
password	Initially blank. A password should be assigned with the **passwd** command, after which the encrypted password will appear here.
user id	Usually *5* for **uucp**. You do not need to assign a separate *uid* number for each working login, since **uucico** runs set-userid to **uucp**, the first login with this user id.
group id	Group to which the user belongs; you may use the same group number as your UNIX administrative files.
user info	Optional string describing the login name.

home dir Home directory for this id; */usr/lib/uucp* for the administrative login, */usr/spool/uucppublic* for working logins.

shell Command interpreter the remote system gets when it logs in; use */usr/lib/uucp/uucico* for working logins. The administrative login uses */bin/sh* by default. Specify the pathname of the C shell or Korn shell if you want to use one of these shells instead.

The working login (second entry) in our example above allows *any* remote system linked to yours to log in as *nuucp*.

While BSD systems do not ship */etc/passwd* with both an administrative and a working login, it is recommended that you create one, so that UUCP is set up as described here.

For maximum security, you should not use the general access working login shipped with the system. You should instead create individual UUCP logins for specific systems. This allows greater control over the files that can be accessed by these systems.

For example, assume you want system *japan* to be able to access a larger number of directories than what you would allow a general access login. In this case you might create a separate entry just for that system:

```
uujapan::6:1::/usr/spool/uucppublic:/usr/lib/uucp/uucico
```

This will allow you to set up specific permissions for that system as described below.

Another, intermediate level of security might be provided by using a general login with unlimited access for systems at your own site and a more restrictive login for systems that dial in from outside. This could be either a single external-access login such as *xuucp* or separate system-by-system logins.

If you are communicating with a large number of systems outside of your own company, the use of separate login names makes it much easier to trace security leaks. If you give a different login name and password to each neighbor, you can tell who "leaked" if another system calls up pretending to be that neighbor. Furthermore, if you decide you no longer want a UUCP link with a particular system, you can shut off access by that site without affecting other systems.

NOTE

Be sure to add any additional working UUCP logins after the first one that is already in the file (**uucp**). Even though all the working logins will have the same *uid*, the login *name* is determined by the first entry for a given *uid*. You want to keep that as **uucp**.

Defining UUCP Passwords

As shipped, the two UUCP login accounts may not have passwords. You should assign passwords immediately.

You can assign a password to the administrative login, if it exists, by using **su** to switch to the *uucp* user id, then invoking the **passwd** command. However, since the working login does not have a standard shell, you cannot **su** to it—you will get **uucico** as your shell, and you will not be able to talk to it. You will need to become superuser and use the login id as an argument to the **passwd** command. For example:

```
$ su
Password: akkad
# passwd nuucp
New password: sumer!
Re-enter new password: sumer!
#
```

(The password will not display as you type it in; we have just shown it here to make the example clear.)

Security in Version 2 UUCP

Version 2 provides five files for controlling remote system access to your local files. These are:

USERFILE   Grants access to files and directories.

L.cmds   Specifies commands that can be executed locally by remote sites.

SQFILE   Keeps conversation counts between machines.

FWDFILE   Specifies a list of systems to which your system will forward files. (Not available in all implementations.)

ORIGFILE   Specifies a list of systems (and, optionally, users on those systems) who can forward files through your system. (Not available in all implementations.)

We will now describe the format of these files and how you can vary the level of security by defining certain parameters in these files.

Remote File Access: USERFILE

The text file */usr/lib/uucp/USERFILE* controls local access of files by both remote systems and local users. You should create one *USERFILE* entry for each site or user with a login entry in the */etc/passwd* file.

USERFILE entries specify four constraints on file transfer:

- Which files can be accessed by a local user. A local file is subject to both *USERFILE* and UNIX file permissions.

- Which files can be accessed by remote systems.

- The login name that a remote system must use to talk to the local system.

- Whether a remote system must be called back by the local system to confirm its identity before communication can take place.

You can choose to implement one or all of these constraints in the *USERFILE* entry for the remote system.

The entries are written in the following form:

> *user,system [c] pathname(s)*

An entry in *USERFILE* that uses all four fields might look like this:

USERFILE

Field	Function in *USERFILE*
user	Specifies either the login name of either a local user or the login name that will be used by a remote system. A separate entry must exist in the *passwd* file for this UUCP login name. Each *USERFILE* should include at least one line with a blank *user* field. (See below for details.)
system	Specifies the node name (system name) of a remote system. Each *USERFILE* should include at least one line with a blank *system* field. (See below for details.)
c	An optional *call-back* flag. If you put a "c" in this field, conversation between the two machines stops when the initial login by the remote system is made. **uucico** must call back the remote system in order to establish its identity before the next conversation can occur.
pathname	Consists of a list of absolute pathname prefixes separated by blanks. The remote system can access only those files beginning with these pathnames. A blank field indicates open access to any file in the local system.

USERFILE is probably the most complicated part of UUCP. To make things worse, almost every implementation of UUCP parses it a little differently. And the effect of botching it is almost never visible—it produces only a loss of security. The key rules that apply to all versions are:

- When **uucp** and **uux** are run by users and when **uucico** runs in Master role, only the username part is used.

- When **uucico** runs in Slave role, only the system name part is used. Note that within the course of one conversation, **uucico** can switch between Master and Slave roles an indefinite number of times.

- In any given *USERFILE*, there must be one line that has an empty system name and one that has an empty username. (In BSD 4.2 and BSD 4.3, they can be the same line. Everything else requires two separate lines.) It does not matter where they are in the file relative to lines that have a complete system name and username.

  The line that has no system name is used by **uucico** in Slave role, after it has already searched the entire *USERFILE* and cannot find a matching system name. The line that has no username is used by **uucp**, **uux**, and **uucico** in Master role only when it cannot find a matching username. In addition, the line without a system name is used by the **uuxqt** daemon.

However, there are variations in what happens when you have several lines that are missing the system name or missing the username, as in:

```
xuucp,          /u1
yuucp,          /u2
zuucp,          /u3
,pyramid        /u4
,decwrl         /u5
,hplabs         /u6
```

All versions *except* the 1979 Version 2 UUCP will use the *first* occurrence of an empty system name and/or username, so they would grab "xuucp" and "pyramid" to define the wildcard cases for missing system name and missing username, respectively. Original 1979 Version 2 uses the *last* occurrence, so it would use the "zuucp" and "hplabs" lines.

In SVR2 and in Ultrix, there is a check made when **uucico** starts up in Slave role to see if both the username and the system name are in *USERFILE*. But other UUCP implementations use *USERFILE* for pathname validation and callback only, and the system name and username are never used at the same time.

Given these guidelines, the following sections describe the types of entries you should have in your *USERFILE*.

Username not specified

In order to allow users on your system to request outbound transfer of any file on your system, you must have an entry with the username not specified. For example:

```
,pyramid  /
```

If you did not have an entry with a blank username like this, you would need to have a separate username line for each user on your system!

System name not specified

In order to allow file transfer from any other system while your system's **uucico** is in Slave role and to allow file access by **uuxqt** (even when started from your system), you must have one entry with the system name not specified. For example:

```
nuucp,      /usr/spool/uucppublic
```

Intuitively, you might expect that this line would mean that any system logging in with the name *nuucp* would have access to */usr/spool/uucppublic*. Unfortunately, that intuitive view does not tell the true story.

In SVR2 and Ultrix, UUCP will actually check both the username field and the blank system name field and will allow login by any system using *nuucp*. That is not too far from what you expect.

In other UUCP implementations, however, the fact that *nuucp* appears on this line is completely irrelevant to a system calling in. *Only the system name is used to validate file transfers that occur when the local **uucico** is in Slave role.* If this is the first entry with a missing system name, it will allow access to *uucppublic* by any system for which there is no explicit *USERFILE* entry containing a system name. If it is not the first entry with a blank system name, it will have no effect.

Special permissions

To allow special directory permissions for individual systems, you should make sure systems calling in use a system-specific UUCP login and specify both that login name and the system's node name (hostname) in *USERFILE*. For example:

```
Ujapan,japan  /usr/spool/uucppublic /usr/spool/news /u2/csg
```

This entry will allow system *japan*, logging in as *Ujapan*, to access the directories */usr/spool/uucppublic*, */usr/spool/news*, and */u2/csg*.

You should create a separate entry for each site or user with a login entry in the */etc/passwd* file.*

How entries work together

Note that it does not make sense to have multiple entries with separate login names but missing system names. For example, if you enter:

```
nuucp,      /usr/spool/uucppublic
xuucp,      /usr/spool/uucppublic /usr/open
```

the first line defines the "missing hostname" case, and the permissions on the second line are ignored *except* when **uucico** runs in Master role under login *xuucp*. To give specific permissions to individual systems, you might want entries like this:

```
nuucp,          /usr/spool/uucppublic
nuucp,waltham   /usr/spool/uucppublic /usr/waltham
nuucp,natick    /usr/spool/uucppublic /usr/natick
```

---

*In Version 7 and SVR1, *USERFILE* allows a maximum of 20 entries, and you are out of luck if you have more UUCP connections than that.

Question: What's to keep an intruder from renaming his machine to *waltham* or *natick* and stealing their files? Answer: Not a thing. Even this will not help:

```
nuucp,               /usr/spool/uucppublic
xuucp,waltham        /usr/spool/uucppublic /usr/waltham
xuucp,natick         /usr/spool/uucppublic /usr/natick
```

Why? Because the login name is never used by **uucico** in Slave role; only the system name. And while SVR2 gives you a false sense of security by ensuring that only sites *natick* and *waltham* will be able to log in as *xuucp*, you cannot prevent any remote system logging in as *nuucp* from naming itself *waltham* and reading */usr/waltham*.

Welcome to *USERFILE* security. There are ways around this problem, but they tend to be circular—fixing one hole opens another. And on anything but SVR2 and Ultrix, you cannot validate the login name for a Slave at all.

In short, giving out "public access" UUCP logins is a bad idea. Creating a separate login and password for every remote system (or using callback, as described below) is your best defense.

Requiring callback

If you are extremely concerned about security, you may want to consider requiring callback.

If you put a *c* as the first entry in the path list, when the remote system's **uucico** logs in, no files will be transferred. Instead, your system will call back.

Since your system must dial the remote, you can be sure that you are connecting to the right system, rather than someone masquerading as a system known to you.

What we recommend

So, you may ask, what do you recommend? The latest BSD 4.3 documentation suggests a *USERFILE* like this (modified slightly for non-4.3 systems):

```
,            /usr/spool/uucppublic
# Next line not needed in BSD 4.2 or 4.3
nuucp,       /usr/spool/uucppublic
dan,         /usr/spool/uucppublic      /u1/dan
csg,         /usr/spool/uucppublic      /u1/csg
root,    /
Udecwrl,decwrl   /usr/spool/uucppublic      /usr/spool/news
Upyrnj,pyrnj     /usr/spool/uucppublic      /usr/src
```

In BSD 4.2 and 4.3, the first line defines both the missing username and the missing system name case. In other implementations, two separate lines are required.

The first line will suffice for the missing username, and another line, such as the second one shown here, will account for the missing system name. This line (or lines) will allow any local user, and any remote machine, to transfer files only from the public directory.

If you do not have any particularly trusted sites or users, you may want to stop there. However, you might also want lines like the next three, which give special privileges to particular local users. Users *dan* and *csg* can transfer files to or from their home directories as well as from the public directory. Users logged in as *root* can transfer files to or from any directory.

Finally, there may be specific permissions for known local systems. In the example, *decwrl* is able to transfer files to */usr/spool/news* as well as the public directory. The site *pyrnj* is able to transfer files to and from */usr/src* as well as the public directory.

However, if you do not talk to the outside world and are using UUCP only for communications between UNIX sites internal to your company, you might want the following *USERFILE*:

```
,    /
,    /
```

This will allow any user on your system, and any remote system, to transfer files to or from any directory. (Note that on most systems, two lines are necessary, even though they are identical. One defines the missing username case, and the other the missing system name. In BSD 4.2 and 4.3 (and possibly a few others), a single line will suffice for both cases.)

If you have only slight concern for security, the following *USERFILE* might well suffice:

```
nuucp,      /usr/spool/uucppublic
,    /
```

This will allow remote systems (assuming they all log in as *nuucp*) to transfer files to or from the public directory but will give complete filesystem access to local users.

Remember that even with complete access specified in *USERFILE*, UUCP is still subject to UNIX file permissions. A user requesting outbound transfer of a file must have read access to the file. For a remote system to have access to a file or directory, it usually must be readable and writable by all users. (**uucico** runs set-user-id *uucp*, so any file to be transferred must be readable by *uucp* and any directory to be written into must be writable by *uucp*. Inasmuch as *uucp* is normally a member of a separate group, this means that for a file or directory to be accessible to UUCP, it must have mode 666.)

Remote Command Execution: L.cmds

Most system administrators limit the commands that can be executed by a remote system. This list of valid commands is contained in the directory */usr/lib/uucp* under the filename *L.cmds*, *L-cmds*, or *uuxqtcmds*. Some early UNIX systems (Version 7 or earlier) may not have this file at all.

If a command is not entered in this file, it cannot be executed via **uux**. *L.cmds* should contain the program **rmail** at a minimum. If **rmail** (the remote **mail** program that decides whether mail is to be delivered locally or forwarded on to yet another system) is not listed in *L.cmds*, a local user will not be able to receive mail from remote users.

A typical *L.cmds* file might contain the following list of commands:*

```
PATH=/bin: /usr/bin:
rmail
rnews
lp
who
```

In SVR2 only, you can restrict by system name. For example:

```
rmail newyork, natick, pyramid
lp    natick
```

Add commands to this file carefully, since a sufficiently general command like **cat** may override your security restrictions. You also want to watch out for any command (such as **mail**) that allows shell escapes. Even **who** can be dangerous if you are very concerned about security, since it gives a cracker a list of usernames to try guessing passwords on.

You may also want to *remove* commands from this file. For example, BSD 4.*x* systems include the **ruusend** command, which allows file forwarding. This command is a security hole, since a remote system could ask your system to send otherwise protected files like *L.sys*. (Since this file is owned by uucp, it would be available to **uusend** running set-user-id uucp.)

If the *L.cmds* file exists but is empty, remote commands cannot be executed on your system.

---

*Some systems include a PATH line like the one shown above, but in our experience, it does not always work. On some systems, the commands that can be executed seem to be limited to */bin* and */usr/bin*, despite the presence of a PATH assignment. If you do not seem able to set the path, run **strings** on **uuxqt** (or look at the source code if you have it!) to see if it sets an explicit path.

Conversation Count Checks: SQFILE

As an added identity check for the remote system, you can create the file *SQFILE* in the directory */usr/lib/uucp*. This is an optional file that UUCP uses to keep a record of the conversation count and date/time of the last conversation for particular systems. *SQFILE* must have mode 400 and must be owned by uucp.

SQFILE contains an entry for each system with which you agree to perform conversation count checks. The remote system must also have an entry for your system in its *SQFILE*, so you should ask the remote system administrator to create an entry for your system there.

Let's say you want to keep a count of your conversation with all of the remote systems to which you are linked. The initial entries in *SQFILE* should contain only the remote system name, one on each line:

```
$ cat SQFILE
calif
newyork
japan
$
```

The first conversation between the two systems adds the count and date/time to the entry. The UUCP program **uucico** updates the fields for each subsequent conversation that succeeds. For example, an entry in the *SQFILE* might look like this:

```
calif 9 10/11-10:54
```

There have been nine conversations so far between the local system and *calif*. The last conversation took place on October 11 at 10:54 a.m.

When one system calls another, **uucico** compares the information for the two systems. If they match, further conversation between the two systems takes place. If the entries on the two systems do not match, the login fails. (This protects against someone who gets a hold of your *UUCP* login and password, changing their system node name to masquerade as a system known to you.)

For example, the *SQFILE* entry on the local system for system *calif* looks like this:

```
calif 210 10/15-19:19
```

while that on system *calif* for the local system (*boston*) reads:

```
newton 209 10/15-16:19
```

A call made from *newton* to *calif*, or vice versa, would fail because the conversation counts do not match. If you were on *newton*, the **uulog** command with the -s*system* option would produce a message similar to the one below:

```
$ uulog -scalif
calif!uucp (10/15-19:19:22) (C,648,0) HANDSHAKE FAILED
(BAD SEQ)
                     .
                     .
$
```

The system administrators on both systems have to get in touch and reset the *SQFILE* manually in order for the entries to match. You should change the UUCP login name and password if this occurs.

Forwarding

In some implementations of Version 2 UUCP, it is possible to control the ability of remote systems to forward files through your system to other connected systems. That is, if a user on *boston* types the command:

```
$ uucp myfile newyork!japan!/usr/spool/uucppublic
```

the file will first be sent to *newyork* and from there to *japan*. Forwarding is not usually supported—it may not even be implemented, and even when implemented, it may not be enabled. After all, in the example above, it should be up to the administrator of *newyork* to decide whether the transfer should go through or should be rejected. It is his site that will be footing the telephone bill.

In addition, the three methods of forwarding (System V, BSD, and BNU) are all incompatible. No wonder then that forwarding is usually limited to subnetworks of closely linked systems.

In BSD 4.*x* systems, there is a special command called **uusend** that users can use instead of **uucp** if they want to forward files to a system that does not have a direct link to their own. **uusend** makes use of **uux** rather than **uucp** to do forwarding and requires that **uusend** exist, and be allowed in *L.cmds*, on each system in the forwarding chain.

In System V-derived UNIX systems, there is a mechanism for controlling forwarding that makes use of two files called *ORIGFILE* and *FWDFILE*. Check your documentation to see if this feature is supported, because even when it is present, the files themselves do not exist. You must create them in order to enable forwarding.

ORIGFILE contains a list of systems, one to a line, that are allowed to forward files through your system. You can optionally follow each system name with an exclamation point and an exclamation point-separated list of users on that system who are allowed to originate forwarding requests.* For example:

ORIGFILE

```
japan!yutaka!ayano
newyork
```

FWDFILE contains a list of systems, one to a line, that a remote system can forward to. For example:

FWDFILE

```
waltham
natick
```

Given the two files shown above, users *yutaka* and *ayano* on system *japan* and any user on *newyork* can forward files through *newton*. However, the only systems they can forward to are the (locally connected) systems *waltham* and *natick*.

If a user attempts to forward to a system that is not allowed by *FWDFILE*, the UUCP job will be killed and mail to that effect sent to the user.

If *ORIGFILE* exists but *FWDFILE* does not, systems listed in *ORIGFILE* can forward to any system known to your system. *ORIGFILE* must exist (and contain entries) in order for forwarding to occur.

Remember that if uucp forwarding is not supported by your system, users can still forward files via **mail**. Mail forwarding is supported by all UUCP systems. See the companion handbook, *Using UUCP and Usenet*, for details.

Security in BNU

In Version 2, you can control filesystem access by remote systems as long as they have unique login ids. However, you cannot distinguish between systems in terms of the remote commands they can execute.

---

*This is a poor choice of syntax, since everywhere else an exclamation point is used to separate system names.

BNU provides additional protection and much finer control over which system can do what by introducing a file called *Permissions*. This file replaces the Version 2 *USERFILE* and *L.cmds*. In addition, there is a file called *remote.unknown* that controls whether or not an unknown system (that is, one not listed in your *Systems* file) can log in (as long as they know the login name and password).

The *Permissions* file has two types of entries:

- LOGNAME entries allow you to grant specific permissions for individual login ids that are used *when remote systems call you*. They begin with the word "LOGNAME."

- MACHINE entries allow you to specify permissions for individual systems *when you call them*. They begin with the word "MACHINE."

While it is tempting to think that MACHINE entries set permissions for a remote machine on the basis of its node name, this is not really the case. MACHINE entries give permission *to users on your system* when they call a remote system and do not give general permissions for that system. It is unclear why this somewhat confusing approach was taken, instead of one in which it is simply possible to state the permissions for a remote machine name, regardless of who initiates the call.

You must create separate login ids and write combined MACHINE and LOGNAME entries, as described later in this chapter, if you want complete control over access by each individual machine.

Permissions File Entries

Both types of entries consist of option/value pairs that account for much of the flexibility delivered by the *Permissions* file over the Version 2 security control files. You can have as many of these option-value pairs as you want and can write entries for all or only some of the remote sites.

The options and their allowed values are listed in Table 5-1. In the table, the *Class* column uses the code **M** or **L** to designate whether an option can be used in a MACHINE entry, a LOGNAME entry, or both.

Table 5-1. Allowable Permissions Entries

Option	Class	Description
LOGNAME	L	Specifies the login ids that can be used by remote sites to log into the local system.
MACHINE	M	Specifies machines that the local system can call with the specified conditions in effect.
REQUEST	M, L	Specifies whether the remote system can request to set up file transfers from your computer. Default is "no."
SENDFILES	L	Specifies whether the called site can execute locally queued requests during a session. "Yes" means that your system may send jobs queued for the remote system as long as it is logged in as one of the names in the LOG-NAME option. Default is "call"—the queued files are sent only when the *local* system calls the remote machine.
READ	M, L	Specifies the directories that **uucico** can use for requesting files. Default is the *uucppublic* directory.
WRITE	M, L	Specifies the directories that **uucico** can use for depositing files. Default is the *uucppublic* directory.
NOREAD	M, L	Exceptions to READ options or defaults.
NOWRITE	M, L	Exceptions to WRITE options or defaults.
CALLBACK	L	Specifies whether or not the local system must call back the calling system before transactions can occur. Default is "no."
COMMANDS	M	Commands that the remote system can execute locally. This defaults to the command list in the *parms.h* header file, which is compiled into **uuxqt**. The COMMANDS option overrides the default command list. The keyword ALL grants access to all commands.
VALIDATE	L	Used to verify calling system's identity. Can be used with COMMANDS when specifying commands that may be potentially dangerous to your system's security.
MYNAME	M	Used to link another system name to the local system.
PUBDIR	M, L	Specifies the directory for local access (e.g., */usr/spool/uucppublic/loginA*). Default is the public directory.

Before we show you how to use these options, let's first lay down some ground rules for writing the *Permissions* file entries:

- Each option-value pair has the following format:

  option = *value*

  Blanks are not allowed before or after the equal sign (=).

- Each line corresponds to one entry. A line may be continued on to the next line(s) by a backslash (\) character.

- A blank is used to separate option-value pairs. If an option has one or more values, the values are separated by a colon (:).

- Comment lines begin with a hash mark (#) and end with a newline. Blank lines are ignored.

When writing entries, you should keep in mind the following:

- All login ids used by remote systems must appear in one and *only* one LOG-NAME entry.

- If you do not want to grant permissions to each system by name, the entry MACHINE=OTHER will assign permissions to any system not mentioned by name.

You can combine MACHINE and LOGNAME entries into a single entry if the options are the same. For example, two separate entries like:

```
LOGNAME=xuucp READ=/ WRITE=/ REQUEST=yes SENDFILES=yes

MACHINE=calif:newyork:japan REQUEST=yes SENDFILES=yes \
READ=/ WRITE=/
```

can be combined into the following:

```
MACHINE=calif:newyork:japan LOGNAME=xuucp \
READ=/ WRITE=/ REQUEST=yes SENDFILES=yes
```

We will talk more about this later.

Permissions on Three Systems: An Example

The *Permissions* file can get quite confusing. The best way to explain how the options are used is by example. Figure 5-1 shows the *Permissions* files for three connected systems and discusses the permissions they grant. After the example, the individual options are discussed in more detail.

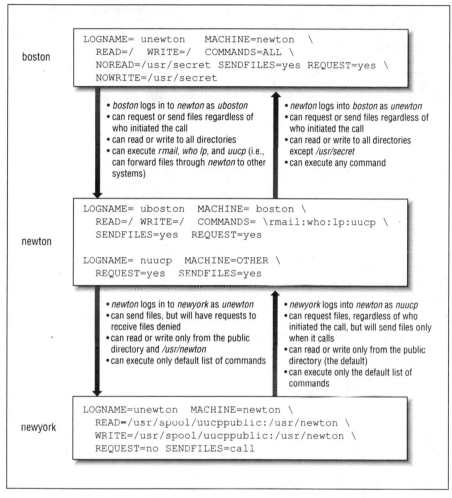

```
                LOGNAME= unewton    MACHINE=newton   \
                 READ=/  WRITE=/   COMMANDS=ALL \
  boston         NOREAD=/usr/secret SENDFILES=yes REQUEST=yes \
                 NOWRITE=/usr/secret
```

• *boston* logs in to *newton* as *uboston* • *newton* logs into *boston* as *unewton*

- *boston* logs in to *newton* as *uboston*
- can request or send files regardless of who initiated the call
- can read or write to all directories
- can execute *rmail*, *who lp*, and *uucp* (i.e., can forward files through *newton* to other systems)

- *newton* logs into *boston* as *unewton*
- can request or send files regardless of who initiated the call
- can read or write to all directories except */usr/secret*
- can execute any command

```
                LOGNAME= uboston  MACHINE= boston \
                 READ=/ WRITE=/   COMMANDS= \rmail:who:lp:uucp \
                 SENDFILES=yes   REQUEST=yes
  newton
                LOGNAME= nuucp  MACHINE=OTHER \
                 REQUEST=yes   SENDFILES=yes
```

- *newton* logs in to *newyork* as *unewton*
- can send files, but will have requests to receive files denied
- can read or write only from the public directory and */usr/newton*
- can execute only default list of commands

- *newyork* logs into *newton* as *nuucp*
- can request files, regardless of who initiated the call, but will send files only when it calls
- can read or write only from the public directory (the default)
- can execute only the default list of commands

```
                LOGNAME=unewton   MACHINE=newton \
                 READ=/usr/spool/uucppublic:/usr/newton \
  newyork        WRITE=/usr/spool/uucppublic:/usr/newton \
                 REQUEST=no SENDFILES=call
```

Figure 5-1. Permissions file on three systems

The Default Permissions

An entry similar to:

```
LOGNAME=nuucp
```

allows any remote system to log in as "nuucp". But since no other options are given, the default conditions hold; these represent the most restrictive access to the local system. Files can only be transferred to */usr/spool/uucppublic* by request of the remote site. This entry is equivalent to:

```
LOGNAME=nuucp\
READ=/usr/spool/uucppublic WRITE= /usr/spool/uucppublic \
SENDFILES=call REQUEST=no COMMANDS=rmail
```

Any site that is called and whose name does not appear in a MACHINE entry has the following default conditions:

- Local send and receive requests will be executed.

- The remote computer can send files to the local */usr/spool/uucppublic* directory.

- The commands sent by the remote computer for execution on the local system must be one of the default commands, usually just **rmail**.

Who's in Charge?

If you are interested in setting up a secure system, the SENDFILES, REQUEST, CALLBACK, and VALIDATE options are your first line of defense (after login and password security, of course).

If you are extremely security-conscious, you may want to use the VALIDATE and/or CALLBACK options.

The VALIDATE option allows you to crosscheck the node name of a calling system against the login name it uses. For example:

```
LOGNAME=domino VALIDATE=tic:tac:toe
```

This specifies that if any systems other than *tic*, *tac*, and *toe* login as *domino*, **uucico** should refuse the connection.

If you set CALLBACK to *yes*, then you can be even more sure of the identity of the caller, since it is much more difficult to appropriate someone's telephone number than it is to discover a login id or password or to temporarily change a node name.

For example, if you set:

```
LOGNAME=domino CALLBACK=yes
```

any system logging in as *domino* must be called back by your system before any transactions can take place.

(In addition to providing additional security, there is one other reason you might want to consider using the CALLBACK option. By specifying a callback for a specific machine or machines, you can choose the machine(s) that will be billed for the call. This is especially important for long data transmissions where costs are a major factor.)

The SENDFILES option describes whether or not your system will send out locally queued work after a system that calls in has finished with its own business. The default value:

```
SENDFILES=call
```

means that your system will only send out work if it has initiated the call. That is, when a remote system calls in, finishes its business, and offers to hang up, your system will accept the offer instead of reversing roles and sending out the locally queued work.

The REQUEST option describes whether or not a remote system can request files from you. The default value:

```
REQUEST=no
```

means that all file transfer requests from your system must *originate* with your system.

If both of these options are set, your system is pretty much in the driver's seat. Regardless of what READ and WRITE options are set (see below), someone on your system must initiate a transfer to the remote system.

There are a number of not-so-obvious implications to these options. For example, if you require CALLBACK, the remainder of the permissions that will be in effect whenever you communicate with the other system are set by the relevant MACHINE entry (and by the remote system's LOGNAME entry for you), not by the LOGNAME entry. This is also true to a lesser extent if you specify SEND-FILES=call.

Furthermore, it is easy to accidentally set things up so no transfers can occur. The most obvious case is when both systems require CALLBACK of each other. Less obviously, if one system requires CALLBACK and the other SENDFILES=call, then the second system will never be able to send out work of its own.

Controlling File Access

The READ and WRITE options define remote access to directories. Consider this entry:

```
LOGNAME=xuucp READ=/ WRITE=/ REQUEST=yes SENDFILES=yes
```

This grants systems that log in as "xuucp" the following permissions:

- Files can be transferred to any directory (WRITE=/). Of course, UUCP is still subject to normal UNIX file permissions. In order for writes to occur in any directory, the directory must have owner of group uucp or must be writable by all.

- Files can be read from any directory (READ=/). Again, standard UNIX file permissions apply.

- Files can be requested from the local site (REQUEST=yes) by the remote system.

- Any locally queued jobs will be executed during the conversation (SEND-FILES=yes).

- The remote system can execute locally only those commands in the default set (COMMANDS not specified).

An entry such as this should be used only with tightly coupled systems that you have complete confidence in. Allowing remote systems this level of access would allow a remote system to read and potentially replace files like *Systems* and *Permissions*. (Since these files are owned by **uucp** and the remote **uucico** is running set-user id **uucp**, the normal UNIX file permissions will pose no obstacle.)

You can modify this example to restrict access to specific directories only. For example, it would not be wise to make the */etc* and */usr/lib/uucp* directories open to writes. Doing this would make your */etc/passwd, Systems*, and *Permissions* files fair game to remote systems. In this case, you can use the NOREAD and NOWRITE options.

```
LOGNAME=uupest NOREAD=/etc:/usr/lib/uucp READ=/ WRITE=/work/rumors:/usr/spool
```

This means that remote machines that log in as *uupest* cannot read */etc* or */usr/lib/uucp* but can read all other directories. They can also put files in those directories.

One of the really nice features of the *Permissions* file is that read and write access are independent. (In Version 2, you had to grant both read and write access, or none at all.) This makes it possible, for instance, to set up a directory for software distribution. Any number of systems can read from this directory, but none of them (or only specially chosen ones) can write to it.

NOTE

When you use the READ and WRITE entries, you should make sure that you leave */usr/spool/uucppublic* readable and writable. This directory is accessible by default only if the READ and WRITE entries are specified, so if you use them, you must explicitly name this directory (or one of its ancestors in the directory tree).

Allowing Command Execution

The commands that remote systems can execute locally are defined by the COMMANDS option. This keyword is an exception to the general rule that MACHINE entries apply to your system when it calls the named remote system. COMMANDS scts up the command list regardless of who originates the call. For example:

```
MACHINE=boston COMMANDS=rmail:lp:views
MACHINE=OTHER COMMANDS=rmail:rnews
```

allows **boston** to execute the **rmail**, **lp**, and **rnews** commands. Other machines can execute only **rmail** and **rnews**.

You should be very careful in selecting commands that can be executed locally by remote sites. A sufficiently general command like **cat** may override your security restrictions.

The entry below uses the "ALL" value:

```
LOGNAME=uupal COMMANDS=ALL READ=/ WRITE=/
```

This is a very "permissive" entry that you might want to give only to a closely coupled system that you allow to offload some of its processes onto your system during peak hours. *Do not do this unless both systems are at the same site.* It is a huge security hole.

Forwarding

In order for your system to forward files to other systems, the COMMANDS option must include the **uucp** command.

This implementation of forwarding is incompatible with the methods used in Version 2 UUCP. It will only work between systems that run BNU. In addition, each system in a forwarding chain must allow **uucp** in the *Permissions* file.

If a user on system *games* types:

```
$ uucp myfile tic!tac!toe!/usr/spool/uucppublic
```

both *tic* and *tac* must allow **uucp** in the COMMANDS option for the calling system. (That is, *tic* must allow *games* to run **uucp** and *tac* must allow *tic* to run **uucp**. Since *toe* is the ultimate destination and is not forwarding the file any further, it need not allow *tac* to run **uucp**.)

Assuming an Alias

There may be situations when you want to be known to other systems by another name. For example, you have named your system *jekyll* only to learn that a central node already goes by that name. Rather than changing your name and calling all systems to which you are connected to update their files, you can use the MYNAME option and give an alias whenever the central node logs in as *cuucp*. This way you can still retain your unique identity within a local network and be known as another to the outside world:

```
LOGNAME=cuucp  MYNAME=hyde
```

Now how will the central node be able to distinguish your system from the other *jekyll*? You can add a line like this:

```
MACHINE=central MYNAME=hyde
```

The MYNAME option can also be used for testing purposes since this allows a system to call itself.

Unfortunately, indiscriminate use of the MYNAME option can lead to some mischief if some machines masquerade as trusted sites. To thwart any such possibility, you can use the VALIDATE option, as described earlier.

Defining Permissions for Individual Machines

As described earlier, MACHINE entries define permissions that are in effect when your system calls a remote system, while LOGNAME entries define permissions when remote systems call you. But what many administrators want is a mechanism to set up permissions for a given system, regardless of who initiated the call.

You can do this by assigning a separate login id for each system with which you communicate and writing a combined LOGNAME and MACHINE entry, such as this:

```
LOGNAME=uboston SENDFILES=yes REQUEST=yes VALIDATE=boston \
MACHINE=boston COMMANDS=rmail:rnews:uucp
```

remote.unknown

In BNU, by default, systems must be listed in each other's *Systems* file in order for communication to successfully take place. The file *remote.unknown* in */usr/lib/uucp* is a shell script* that records attempted calls by foreign systems in the file */usr/spool/uucp/.Admin/Foreign*. (You can modify it so that it sends mail to the *uucp* login instead. Note that the *remote.unknown* script is passed the name of the remote system as an argument, so that you could modify the script to decide on a host-by-host basis whether or not to grant access.)

If this file is found and is executable, foreign systems can log in, but **uucico** will refuse to do any work for them. If you make this file nonexecutable (with **chmod -x**), foreign systems can log in and will be allowed to transfer files, subject to allowable permissions in *Permissions*, just like the default case in Version 2 UUCP.

Modes and Ownership of UUCP Files

The modes and ownership of UUCP programs and data files are designed to provide a fully secure UUCP system. As long as you have put passwords on the UUCP logins, maintaining these permissions will keep unauthorized users from reading or modifying the UUCP files.

Table 5-2 shows the recommended modes and ownership for UUCP system files. The programs **uucp**, **uux**, **uucico**, and **uuxqt** are owned by *uucp* with the *setuid* bit set and only execute permissions. This means that whatever files these programs create will also be owned by the login user *uucp*.

You should be aware that defining mode 777 for the directory */usr/spool/uucp* allows all users to delete files and read mail files spooled in that directory. This is

---

*In SVR3.2, it is a C program.

a potential security leak. However, UUCP will not work correctly if you change these permissions.

Table 5-2. Ownership and Permissions for UUCP Files

Directory	File	Mode	Owner
/usr/bin	uucp	4111	uucp
	cu	4111	bin
	uudecode	755	bin
	uuencode	755	bin
	uuname	4111	uucp
	uusend	755	bin
	uustat	4111	uucp
	uuto	755	bin
	uux	4111	uucp
/usr/lib/uucp		755	uucp
	Devices*	444	uucp
	Dialcodes*	444	uucp
	Dialers*	444	uucp
	L.cmds	444	uucp
	L-devices	444	uucp
	L-dialcodes	444	uucp
	L_stat	644	uucp
	L_sub	644	uucp
	L.sys	400	uucp
	Maxuuscheds*	444	uucp
	Maxuuxqts*	444	uucp
	Permissions*	444	uucp
	Poll*	444	uucp
	remote.unknown*	555	uucp
	SQFILE	400	uucp
	Systems*	444	uucp
	USERFILE	400	uucp
	uucheck	110	uucp
	uucico	4111	uucp
	uuclean	4111	uucp
	uucleanup*	110	uucp
	uudemon.admin*	555	uucp
	uudemon.clean*	555	uucp
	uudemon.day*	500	uucp
	uudemon.hour*	555	uucp
	uudemon.hr	500	uucp
	uudemon.poll*	555	uucp

Table 5-2. Ownership and Permissions for UUCP Files (continued)

Directory	File	Mode	Owner
	uudemon.wk	500	uucp
	uulog	555	uucp
	uupick	555	uucp
	uusched	4111	uucp
	uusub	755	uucp
	uuto	555	uucp
	Uutry	555	uucp
	uuxqt	4111	uucp
	.XQTDIR	755	uucp
/usr/spool/uucppublic		777	uucp
/usr/spool/uucp		777	uucp
	.Admin*	777	uucp
	.Corrupt*	777	uucp
	.Log*	777	uucp
	.Old*	777	uucp
	.Sequence*	777	uucp
	.Status*	777	uucp
	.Workspace*	777	uucp

---

*BNU files.

6

UUCP Administration

Contents of the Spool Directory
Keeping Track of UUCP Activity
Automatic Maintenance
Automatic Maintenance in Xenix
Polling Passive Systems
Troubleshooting

In order for UUCP to run smoothly, the following things must happen on a regular basis:

- **uucico** must be invoked regularly to retry failed calls.

- Jobs that have been queued unsuccessfully for a long time must be deleted, so that **uucico** does not keep trying forever.

- Execution requests that have been pending for a long time must also be deleted, so that **uuxqt** does not keep trying forever.

- Files that have been sitting in the public directory (*/usr/spool/uucppublic*) for more than a certain amount of time need to be deleted.

- The log files created by **uucico** cannot be allowed to grow larger forever. They must be compressed or truncated according to some reasonable scheme.

- Passive systems (if any) in your network must be polled regularly to see if they have any requests pending.

On most systems, these tasks are performed automatically by shell scripts that are invoked by **cron**, the system administrator's reliable assistant.

Before we look at the administrative commands and shell scripts, we ought first to review the scene of the action: the spool directory.

Contents of the Spool Directory

The contents of the spool directory are constantly changing. In addition to log files, which are added to each time a transfer occurs, there are a large number of working files that are dynamically created (and just as dynamically deleted) in the course of communication between systems.

As we discussed in Chapter 1, *How UUCP Works*, when a user issues a **uucp** command, what actually happens is that a *work file* is created in the spool directory. The work file contains the instructions for **uucico** such as the name of the file to be copied, its owner and permissions, its destination, and so on. Appendix Λ, *Working Files*, gives details on the contents of the work file; for the moment, let's just look at its name, which also conveys a great deal of information:

A Work File

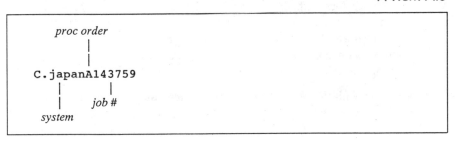

All work file names begin with the characters *C.*. These letters are followed by, in order:

- The remote system name, truncated to the first seven characters.

- A letter indicating the work file *processing order*. In Version 2 UUCP, **uucico** processes files in order from A to Z and then from a to z. The default starting point is A for files created by **uux**, C for files created by **mail**, and *n* for files created by **uucp**. The processing order is incremented as additional work files are created. (In BNU, a separate program called **uusched** periodically randomizes the processing order.)

- The job id. This same job id appears in reports from **uulog** and **uustat**.

Each work file can contain up to 20 file transfer or execution requests for a given system. Additional requests for the same system will result in the creation of a second work file.

If the user specifies **uucp**'s **-C** option, the actual file is copied to the spool directory as well. The copy is kept in a *data file* which has the prefix *D*. and is otherwise named just like the work file with which it is associated. (The name may contain an additional subjob number if there is more than one data file associated with an individual work file.) When a user sends mail, two data files are created—one containing the text of the mail message, the other containing the instructions for execution of **rmail** on the remote system.

When a remote system calls in with a request for command execution, an *execute* file with the prefix *X*. is created. This file contains instructions for **uuxqt**. It is named similarly to work and data files, however, inasmuch as it is created by the **uucico** from the other system, its job number will not match up with any work file on your system. When someone on your system makes an execute request, a data file (*D.xxxx*) is created. It contains the text of what will become the execute file on the remote system.

As execute requests are actually being processed by **uuxqt**, additional temporary files are created in a hidden subdirectory called *.XQTDIR*.

You will also see files with the prefix *TM*. These are temporary files that hold data while a file is being transferred from another system. Once the transfer is complete, **uucico** transfers the contents of the temporary file (which can contain data for more than one transferred file) to the requested destination or to the public directory if the destination is not accessible.

Files beginning with the prefix *LCK*. are *lock files*. **uucico** and **cu** create these files to make sure that no other UUCP process attempts to call the same system or to use the same device while it is in use.

Finally, as we have discussed previously, there are status files whose names begin with the prefix *STST*. .

One of the major improvements of BNU over Version 2 is the introduction of a more organized spool directory. Work files, data files, and execute files are put into subdirectories named for the system that the requests they contain are to or from. Status files are kept in a hidden subdirectory called *.Status*, and temporary (TM) files in a hidden subdirectory called *.Workspace*. Lock files are kept in a separate directory called */usr/spool/locks*.

Table 6-1 shows the directory structure for BNU on the 3B2.

Table 6-1. BNU Directory Structure

File/Directory	Contents
/usr/spool/uucp/	
.Admin	Administrative files.
.Corrupt	Corrupt work and execute files that could not be processed.
.Log	Log files.
.Old	Old log files.
.Sequence	System sequence numbers.
.Status	System status files.
.Workspace	UUCP temporary workspace area.
.Xqtdir	Remote executions.
system1	Directories containing files to/from the specific systems.
system2	
system3	
/usr/spool/uucp/.Log	
uucico	Directory of **uucico** execution logs.
uucp	Directory of **uucp** request logs.
uux	Directory of **uux** request logs.
uuxqt	Directory of **uuxqt** request logs or remote commands executions on the local system.

Because of the revised directory structure, the file names for some of the temporary files have been simplified as well. For example, system status files are simply given the name of the called system, without the STST. prefix. We will continue to use the Version 2 names, but you should be aware that they may be different in a BNU system.

In BSD 4.3 (which has a modified Version 2 UUCP), the spool directory has also been divided into a number of subdirectories. In addition, system status files are kept in a subdirectory and corrupted work or execute files that could not be processed are placed in a subdirectory called *CORRUPT*. When compiling the software, it is possible to set up a subdirectory (called *LCK*) for lock files as well.

If a UUCP request goes through cleanly, all of these temporary files are created and removed in due process. But what happens if you normally exchange a large volume of traffic with a neighboring system and suddenly they stop answering your calls? The spool directory can overflow with backed up job requests. (This is especially true if you are running Netnews, which requires large amounts of regular file transfer.)

Keeping Track of UUCP Activity

UUCP is basically designed to be self-maintaining. Nonetheless, it is worthwhile to learn how to track the progress of UUCP jobs and to determine when there are problems with jobs going through.

For this reason, we are going to cover the general topic of monitoring UUCP activity before we turn to the automatic maintenance facilities and, after that, troubleshooting.

Congestion in the Spool Directory

The biggest bane of UUCP is congestion. Probably the least obvious to the new UUCP administrator, yet perhaps the most important of the administrative functions are those having to do with cleaning out jobs that have been spooled but not completed successfully. In most implementations of UUCP, there are automatic shell scripts to do this cleanup. However, you may need to change the frequency with which they are run or the length of time they allow working files to stay around before they are deleted.

This problem is especially acute in Version 2 UUCP, since it has only a single spool directory. Unless you have a fast disk or your kernel does directory caching, UUCP will slow down dramatically once you get more than a hundred or so requests backed up. (The source of this problem is simply the time it takes UNIX to scan the directory during file opens. If there are a large number of requests for one system, **uucico** may need to keep rescanning the directory. The larger the directory, the longer this takes. If the directory file itself is larger than a single disk block, things will get even slower.) BNU's use of separate spool directories for each remote system alleviates but does not entirely solve this problem. Even if a link does not go down, the volume of traffic can swamp a site.

In general, if the amount of traffic through your system is relatively small, you can pretty well ignore UUCP once you have your links set up. If there is a lot of traffic through your system, you should periodically take a look at the spool directory to see if it looks like things are backing up.

If a listing with **ls** shows a lot of work files, use **ls -lt** to show how old they are. If they are older than they should be (e.g., if you know that you can call a system any time and the work files are many hours old), it may be time to do a little more digging.

UUCP provides two administrative commands that can be used to monitor the transfer attempts made by a local user or a remote system. These are the **uulog** and **uustat** commands. The **uustat** command also allows you to kill UUCP jobs. Instructions on how to use these programs are given in Chapter 4, *Checking on UUCP Requests*, of the companion handbook, *Using UUCP and Usenet*. On BSD 4.3 systems, **uuq** should also prove useful.

In addition, as discussed in Chapter 4 of this book, *Making Sure the Link Works*, you can look directly at the log files (*LOGFILE*, *ERRLOG*, and *SYSLOG* in Version 2; *.Log/uucico/system* in BNU) in the spool directory to get information about what has been going on. We will talk more about this in the section "Troubleshooting" later in this chapter.

Some implementations of Version 2 UUCP also include a program called **uusub** that can be used to gather traffic statistics about the connection between one or more systems. (The list of systems to be monitored is independent of *L.sys*; hence it is sometimes referred to as a subnetwork—hence the name **uusub**.) **uusub** is discussed later in this chapter.

If one of these programs indicates that a link is down, you might want to call the remote system with **uucico** in debugging mode, or with **cu**, to see if the remote system is down or if the problem is on your end.

If the link is down for a while, you might want to call the remote system administrator and ask what he knows. However, the only serious problem you need to worry about is running out of disk space on the filesystem that holds the spool directory. Running out of disk space may paralyze not just UUCP, but the whole system.

Checking Disk Space

To find out if space is a problem, use the **df** and **du** commands. **df** lists the amount of free disk blocks left on your disk(s); **du** shows where the space is being used. Obviously, you need to have a sense of both the amount of disk space on your system and the normal amount of traffic in order for these numbers to make sense. For example:

```
$ df
/usr (/dev/fp003  ): 1410 blocks   2093 i-nodes
/    (/dev/fp001  ): 2800 blocks   2030 i-nodes
$ du /usr/spool/uucp /usr/spool/uucppublic
6045 /usr/spool/uucp
56   /usr/spool/uucppublic
$
```

Since we do not have that much UUCP traffic, it looks like there may be some junk in the spool directory.

Reading uucp's Mail

Some commands (such as **uuclean**) may send mail to the administrative login. Most of it is pretty uninteresting stuff, like:

```
uuclean deleted the file o.SYSLOG.z
```

However, you may occasionally get something that will make you stand up and take notice. You can also have programs such as **uustat** or **uusub** run regularly by **cron**, with the output sent via **mail**.

In BNU, the administrative scripts *uudemon.admin* and *uudemon.clean* send copious amounts of mail to *uucp*. You may want to rewrite these scripts so that they combine the daily multitude of messages into one or two.

In System V, you can have *uucp*'s mail forwarded to you by putting the line "Forward to *yourname*" in the file */usr/mail/uucp*. In BSD systems, you can have *uucp*'s mail forwarded to you by editing the file */usr/lib/aliases*. See *aliases(5)* for details.

uusub (Version 2)

Some implementations of Version 2 UUCP include a nifty command called **uusub**, which collects connection statistics on a list of systems you provide. On our system at least, you must be logged in as *uucp* or *root* (or switched to one of these ids with **su**) to use this command. To tell **uusub** which systems to monitor, use the **-a** option. For example:

```
$ /usr/lib/uucp/uusub -awaltham
$ /usr/lib/uucp/uusub -aboston
```

To delete a system from the list, use **-d***sys*.

The **-c***sys* option exercises the link—in effect, polling the named system. If you give **all** as an argument, all systems will be polled. The **-u***nn* option collects statistics for the last *nn* hours, flushing the data from the previous period. Most systems with **uusub** automatically run it once a day.

To display the amount of data transferred between the two systems, use **-r**:

```
$ /usr/lib/uucp/uusub -r
sysname    sfile    sbyte    rfile    rbyte
waltham    246      256186   99       64348
boston     60       574655   10       18716
```

This listing shows the data transferred between the local system and each monitored system since the system was added or in the period specified by the last **-u** option.

The listing is not quite as obvious as it may appear, though, since the direction of transfer is relative to the system listed in the first column, not to your system. That is, the columns labeled *sfile* and *sbyte* list the number of files and bytes sent to you by the listed system, not the number you have sent to them. The columns labeled *rfile* and *rbyte* list the number of files and bytes they have received from you.

The **-l** option lists connection statistics:

```
sysname    #call #ok latest-oktime #noacu #login #nack #other
waltham    14    14  (5/2-16:18)   0      0      0     0
boston     36    33  (5/2-16:12)   3      0      0     0
```

You can see the total number of calls, the number that succeeded, and the date and time of the last successful call. You can also see the number of failures—the number of times the call-out line was unavailable (*#noacu*), the number of times login failed (*#login*), the number of times there was no response at the other end (*#nack*), and the number of times the call failed for some other unknown reason (*#other*). ("Wrong time to call"—that is, a schedule field that restricts calls to a particular time—will result in a *#other* tally. Do not think of this as an error if you have limited the time for a particular system to be called.)

The data for **uusub -l** is kept in */usr/lib/uucp* under the name *L-sub*; the data for **-r** is in *R_sub*. They are not text files.

Too Many Processes

Besides problems with disk space, a system can experience problems if too many **uucico**s are running at once. Particularly on the receiving end, **uucico** is a resource hog and can really slow a system down.

Fortunately, there is a natural limit on how many **uucico**s can run because of the number of devices that are available for communications. In a local area network environment, though, this limit may be quite large.

For this reason, BNU has added a mechanism for limiting the number of simultaneous **uucico**s and **uuxqt**s that can be running. The limit is kept in the files (respectively) *Maxuuscheds* and *Maxuuxqts* in */usr/lib/uucp*. By default, the limit in each is one. Edit these files if you want a higher limit.

Automatic Maintenance

As mentioned previously, a number of administrative shell scripts are provided to handle routine invocations of **uucico** (or **uusched**) and cleanup of the spool directory.

Let's look briefly at these scripts and what they do before going on to the tasks that you must do manually.

If you look at the file */usr/lib/crontab* on a system running Version 2 UUCP, you should see the following three lines (or something very similar):

```
56 * * * * /usr/lib/uucp/uudemon.hr
0 4 * * * /usr/lib/uucp/uudemon.day
30 5 * * 0 /usr/lib/uucp/uudemon.wk
```

If you look at the file */usr/spool/cron/crontabs/uucp* on a system running BNU, you should see something like the following lines:

```
41,11 * * * * /usr/lib/uucp/uudemon.hour > /dev/null
48, 8,12,16 * * * /usr/lib/uucp/uudemon.admin > /dev/null
45 23 * * * /usr/lib/uucp/uudemon.cleanup > /dev/null 2>&1
```

(In either case, these lines may be commented out with a hash mark (#) at the beginning of each line. If so, remove the hash marks.)

These are shell scripts containing various commands that help to keep a UUCP network running smoothly. **cron** allows you to run them automatically at a regular interval. They can also be run manually if the network needs immediate attention.

Each *crontab* entry consists of six fields separated by spaces or tabs. The first five fields specify the minute (*0-59*), the hour (*0-23*), the day of the month (*1-31*), the month of the year (*1-12*), and the day of the week (*0-6*, with Sunday=0). A star (*) indicates all permissible values for that field. The last field contains the shell command line to be executed at that time. For example, the line:

```
56 * * * * /usr/lib/uucp/uudemon.hr
```

means that the script *uudemon.hr* will be executed in the 56th minute of every hour, day in and day out.

```
0 4 * * * /usr/lib/uucp/uudemon.day
```

means *uudemon.day* will be executed daily at 4 a.m., and:

```
30 5 * * 0 /usr/lib/uucp/uudemon.wk
```

means *uudemon.wk* will be executed at 5:30 a.m. every Sunday.

uudemon.hr

(Version 2)

uudemon.hr attempts completion of UUCP jobs waiting on the local system. **uudemon.hr** usually contains at least the following commands:

```
cd /usr/lib/uucp
uucico -r1
```

It is normally executed by **cron** at least once an hour.

uudemon.day

(Version 2)

uudemon.day cleans the spool directories and merges daily log files with the weekly log files. It is normally run at a fixed time, such as 4 a.m. each day.

It executes the following commands:

```
cd /usr/lib/uucp
uuclean -p -m -n168 >/dev/null 2>/dev/null
uuclean -d.XQTDIR -p -n72 >/dev/null 2>/dev/null
uustat -c168 >/dev/null 2>/dev/null
cd /usr/spool/uucp
mv LOGFILE temp
uniq -c temp >> Log-WEEK
rm temp
cd /usr/spool/uucppublic
find . -type f -mtime +30 -exec rm -f {} \;
```

Let's see what some of these commands mean:

- **uuclean** is a program that can be used to delete UUCP job requests. **uuclean** has four options:

  -n[*hours*]   specifies how old files can be (in hours) before they can be deleted.

  -p[*prefix*]   specifies the prefix (C., D., X., TM., STST., etc.) for the files to be deleted. If *prefix* is not given, all types of working files will be deleted.

-**m**   sends mail to the owner of the file when it is deleted.

-**d***dir* specifies a subdirectory (e.g., *.XQTDIR*) of the spool directory that is to be scanned instead of the spool directory itself.

The first **uuclean** command kills all UUCP jobs that have been waiting on the local system for at least 168 hours (the *-n168* option), or seven days. The second **uuclean** kills **uuxqt** execution requests that have been trying to execute for at least 72 hours (the *-n72* option), or three days.

- **uustat -c** deletes entries from the status files *L_stat* and *R_stat* that are more than 168 hours old.

- The **mv** command moves the contents of today's log records (the file *LOGFILE*) to the end of the weekly log (*Log-WEEK*).

- The **find** command removes all ordinary files from the public directory that are more than 30 days old.

If you find that your spool directory is overflowing, you may need to remove old files and directories from */usr/spool/uucppublic* and */usr/spool/uucp*. You can do this manually using the **rm** command, or you can shorten the time period parameters for the **uuclean** and **find** commands in the *uudemon.day* file. For example, if these commands are currently set as follows:

```
uuclean -p -m -n168 >/dev/null 2>/dev/null
find . -type f -mtime +30 -exec rm -f {} \;
```

you can reset them so that jobs that have been waiting for at least 48 hours (instead of 168) and files in the public directory that have been there for at least 15 days (instead of 30) would be deleted. The modified commands would look like this:

```
uuclean -p -m -n48 >/dev/null 2>/dev/null
find . -type f -mtime +15 -exec rm -f {} \;
```

You might also want to trim the log files.

CAUTION

It was recently pointed out on Usenet that the **rm** commands in the **uudemon.day** script (and in the BNU **uudemon.cleanu**) can cause terrible problems on systems that have replaced the Bourne shell with the Korn shell. Here's the problem: in the Bourne shell, if a built-in command (such as **cd**) used in a script fails for any reason, the script exits. But in the Korn shell, the script continues. Now consider the **uudemon.day** script. If the *cd* command immediately preceding the **find** ... **-exec rm** fails, as it might if the filesystem containing

/usr/spool/uucppublic were not mounted, the script would blindly continue, removing the files in the current directory (probably /usr/lib/uucp) instead.

In the **uudemon.cleanup** script, there are further problems that may lead the script to try to **cd** to a file (which of course fails). Appendix D includes a script that can be used as a replacement for **uudemon.cleanup**.

---

uudemon.wk

(Version 2)

uudemon.wk maintains the weekly log files and gets rid of those more than two weeks old. It is usually executed at a fixed time, such as 5:30 a.m. every Sunday, and may contain something like the following commands:

```
cd /usr/spool/uucp
rm -f o.Log-WEEK* o.SYSLOG*
mv Log-WEEK o.Log-WEEK
(date; echo =^==^==^==^==^==^==^==^==^=) >> o.Log-WEEK
mv SYSLOG o.SYSLOG
>> SYSLOG
pack o.Log-WEEK o.SYSLOG
```

Log files have backup files called *Log-WEEK* and *o.Log-WEEK*. *Log-WEEK* contains log entries for the week to date, while *o.Log-WEEK* contains entries for the previous week. *SYSLOG* is used by the UUCP programs to record the amount of data sent and received by each system within a week. *o.SYSLOG* is a backup file that holds the previous week's *SYSLOG* file.

---

uudemon.hour

(BNU)

This shell script calls the **uusched** program to search the spool directories for work files that have not been processed and schedules them for transfer to the remote site. It also calls **uuxqt** to find execute files that have been transferred but remained unprocessed. This shell script may be run once or twice an hour if the volume of UUCP transactions is high and less frequently for lower volumes.

On the 3B2, **uudemon.hour** is normally executed 9 minutes before and 11 minutes after the hour daily.

---

uudemon.admin

(BNU)

This shell script cleans up jobs that remain undelivered. **uudemon.admin** runs the **uustat** command and reports on the status of work files, data files, and execute files that are queued. It also prints status information for processes listed in the lock files and mails the results to the **uucp** administrative login. As system administrator, you may be particularly interested in the age (in days) of the oldest request in the queue, the number of failed attempts to reach a system, and the reason for the failure.

On the 3B2, this shell script is normally run 12 minutes before the hour every four hours beginning at 8 a.m.

---

uudemon.cleanup

(BNU)

This shell script cleans up the */usr/spool/uucp/.Log* directory by combining all of the log files for particular systems into a single log file that is stored in the directory */usr/spool/uucp/.Old*. This combined log file is named *Old-log-1*. The previous combined log file is moved to *Old.log.2*. It removes work files and data files that are at least seven days old and execute files that are at least two days old from the spool directories. In addition, it returns undelivered mail to the sender and mails daily status information to the UUCP administrative login.

uudemon.cleanup also calls the **find** command to remove "old" files. You may want to shorten the period specified in the **find** command if the spool directory keeps overflowing. Alternatively, you can modify the script to compact the files using the **pack** command.

On the 3B2, this shell script is normally run at 11:45 p.m. daily.

Automatic Maintenance in Xenix

Perhaps because Xenix runs on PCs, which do not expect much traffic (and may not even be turned on continuously), Xenix systems do not include administrative scripts run from **cron**. You must execute cleanup commands manually or add entries to *crontab* yourself.

Merging log files

One major difference between Xenix UUCP and other implementations of Version 2 is that **uucico** does not write directly to the log file. Instead, temporary logfiles are created. These files must be merged into the larger LOGFILE by running **uulog** on a regular basis. To do this, type:

```
$ /usr/lib/uucp/uulog
```

This merges all log files and displays their contents.

To run **uulog** daily from **cron** at 5 a.m., you could enter the following line in
crontab:

```
0 5 * * * /usr/lib/uucp/uulog
```

Cleaning the spool directory

You can remove unwanted files that are more than a given number of hours old by
using the **uuclean** command. For example, to delete TM files that are at least five
hours old and mail a list of each file removed to the owner of the file, you would
enter:

```
$  /usr/lib/uucp/uuclean -pTM -n5 -m
```

The **-p** option causes files with the given prefix to be removed, and the **-n** option
gives the age (in hours) of files to be removed. The default is 72 hours (or three
days). The **-m** option causes mail to be sent to the owner of the file.

You should invoke **uuclean** at least once a day. You can do this by using the system daemon **cron**. For example, to run **uuclean** every day at 4 a.m., you could
add this entry to *crontab*:

```
0 4 * * * /usr/lib/uucp/uuclean -p -m
```

Since the **-n** option is not given, **uuclean** will use the default expiration time of
72 hours for all files.

You can also run **uuclean** manually to remove unwanted files after a system crash
or an aborted UUCP transfer.

Polling Passive Systems

A UUCP network can include one or more *passive systems*—that is, systems that
can be called but cannot make calls of their own. A passive system simply enters
a string that is not recognized by *uucico* such as *Never* or *Polled* into the schedule
field of the *L.sys* (or *Systems*) entry for some other system. (Note that a system
can be passive with respect to some systems but active with respect to others.)

You might set up a passive link for security reasons (one side might want to keep
its telephone number, login id, and password secret or not accept calls at all) or
simply in order to have one side always assume the telephone costs.

Unless the passive link exists only for the benefit of the calling system and there
is no reason for the passive system to originate traffic of its own, arrangements
must be made for *polling* the passive system. That is, it must be called

periodically—even if the active system has no business of its own to transact—to see if there are any jobs waiting.

There are several different ways to poll passive systems:

• Put an explicit **uucico** command in *crontab* to call a passive system at a particular time.

• Add commands to **uudemon.hr** to create dummy work files for a number of passive systems.

• Add a list of systems to be polled, and the frequency, to the file */usr/lib/uucp/Poll* and run the **uudemon.poll** script from *crontab* (BNU only).

Which method to use depends on what software is available on your system, how frequently you want to poll, and who you want to poll.

An Explicit Poll in crontab

We have one semi-passive connection with the system that feeds us news (see Chapter 8, *Installing Netnews*). During the day, we can call them and they can call us at any time, thus allowing mail messages and so on to be transferred immediately. At night, however, they are distributing news to a number of sites and want each of us to call in on a fixed schedule.

They do not allow calls out to us at night. Instead, we call them every hour, on the 20-minute mark, between midnight and 7 a.m.:

```
20 0,1,2,3,4,5,6 * * * /usr/lib/uucp/uucico -sboston -r1
```

If you use this technique, no work file is created, and so there will be no retry of a failed call. If you want to poll only once a day, it is preferable to use the technique described in the section immediately following.

Creating Dummy Work Files (Version 2)

If you want to poll a number of systems on a regular basis, putting individual entries into *crontab* is an inefficient use of system resources. In addition, no work file is created in the spool directory, and so there will be no retry if the call does not go through at exactly the time you specify.

Since **uudemon.hr** calls **uucico** every hour to scan the spool directory and place calls to any systems with unprocessed work files, you can poll a number of systems simply by adding code to **uudemon.hr** that creates dummy work files for each system.

For example, adding the following lines would cause the local system to poll the passive systems named *chicago*, *maine*, and *india*:

```
for i in chicago maine india
do
        touch /usr/spool/uucp/C.${i}nPOLL
done
```

(You should be sure to add these lines before the line that actually invokes **uucico**. Also be sure to check the format of work file names on your system and match it exactly. While most systems have work file names consisting of C.*node* followed by a single letter for the grade, and a four-character sequence number, this is not universal. For example, on one system, there were two letters (unexplained) in the *grade* position. When a name of the form shown above was used, **uucico** swallowed the last letter of the node name in its attempt to interpret the work filename. It then did not recognize which system to call. See Appendix A for more information on work file naming.)

If you want to poll a group of systems once a day, you could add this code to **uudemon.day** instead. Or if you want to poll at some other interval, you can create a separate polling script like the one shown above and run it from *crontab* at any time you like.

You could use a similar script in BNU. However, a separate mechanism for polling is already in place, as we will see in a moment.

uudemon.poll (BNU)

In BNU, passive systems are specified in the file */usr/lib/uucp/Poll*. Each entry contains the name of the system to call, followed by a TAB character and the hours for calling the system. You must specify hour values as integers between 0 and 23.

For example, to poll a passive system called *chicago* every six hours, the entry would be:

```
chicago<TAB>0 6 12 18
```

You then have to make sure that the **uudemon.poll** script is run from *crontab*. This script should be scheduled to run before *uudemon.hr* (as described earlier in this chapter). For example, the default entry on the 3B2 looks like this:

```
1,30 * * * * " /usr/lib/uucp/uudemon.poll > /dev/null
```

This entry schedules **uudemon.poll** to run 11 minutes before **uudemon.hr** runs.

Troubleshooting

At first, many user complaints that "UUCP is not working" are likely to be based on a failure to understand that UUCP is a batch network and that requests are not necessarily executed at the time they are made. Even when you have set up a link to allow communication at any time, communication can fail (dialup lines can be busy, the remote system can be down) and the request will not be retried immediately. However, if any of the following conditions occur, there may be a real problem:

- Mail consistently fails to get through.

- The spool directory contains many old jobs.

- The log files show many failed connections to a given system.

Keep in mind that the problem may be at either end of the link.

You can check the reason why calls are not going through with the **uustat** command, you can look at the log file **uucico** keeps of each transfer or, if you want the most up-to-date information on a transfer in progress, you can look directly at the relevant system status file. The messages in the status file are slightly more current than those in the log files, but they should convey more or less the same information.

There are two types of status messages: ASSERT and STATUS. ASSERT errors are usually due to system problems. STATUS messages provide status information on attempted transactions and whether they were successful. If the message in the log files shows that an ASSERT error occurred, you should look in the error logging file for more details.

Location of Files

Because the spool directory was reorganized in BNU, these files are named differently in the two versions. Table 6-2 shows the location of some of the relevant files. (All pathnames are relative to /usr/spool/uucp.)

Table 6-2. Location of Log and Status Files

File	Version 2	BNU
Error log	*ERRLOG*	*.Admin/errors*
Log file	*LOGFILE*	*.Log/uucico/*system
		*.Log/uucp/*system
		*.Log/uux/*system
		*.Log/uuxqt/*system
Status file	*STST*.system	*.Status/*system
Transfer Statistics	*SYSLOG*	*.Admin/xferstats*

Status File Messages

The list below shows some of the possible status messages that can be contained in the log file or the status file. A complete listing should be available in your UUCP documentation.

If, after looking at the status message, you want **uucico** to try again immediately, you can manually remove the status file and issue a new **uucico** command. For example:

```
$ rm /usr/spool/uucp/STST.waltham
$ /usr/lib/uucp/uucico -r1 &
```

The following messages may appear in the status or log files:*

ALARM *n*

> **uucico** is losing or has lost the connection. Packet acknowledgements are no longer being received. Sometimes caused by ^S or ^P characters in the data stream. Statistically, these characters can occur fairly often in compressed files, so it doesn't necessarily mean that the modem is using XON/XOFF flow control. (However, that can also be a cause of this problem.)

ASSERT ERROR

> ASSERT error occurred. Message is stored in *ERRLOG* (Version 2) or *.Admin/errors* (BNU). See Appendix A, *Working Files*, for a list of messages.

---

*For convenience, we have listed Version 2 and BNU messages together. Those messages that are not marked as either BNU or Version 2 are common to both implementations. Do not be surprised to see variations on these messages.

AUTODIAL (*dev: Interrupted system call*)
> Modem is in use. (Version 2)

BAD LOGIN/MACHINE COMBINATION
> The node name and/or login name used by the calling machine are not permitted in the *Permissions* file. (BNU) Be wary if you see this message: it could mean that someone is trying to crack your security.

BAD LOGIN/PASSWORD
> The login for the given machine failed. It could be a wrong login/password, wrong number, a very slow machine, or failure in getting through the chat script. (Version 2)

BAD READ
> **uucico** could not read/write to a device. (Version 2)

BAD SEQUENCE CHECK
> If an *SQFILE* is used between systems, the sequence numbers do not match. See Chapter 5, *Access and Security Considerations*.

CALLBACK REQUIRED
> The remote system requires callback.

CALLER SCRIPT FAILED
> See DIALER SCRIPT FAILED. (BNU)

CAN NOT CALL (SYSTEM STATUS)
> An unexpired system status file keeps **uucico** from trying again. Check the status file for the reason. (Version 2)

CAN'T ACCESS DEVICE
> Either the device does not exist or the permissions are wrong. (BNU)

CONVERSATION FAILED
> Something went wrong after a successful startup. Either the system on the other side went down, or the line was lost. (BNU)

DEVICE FAILED
> The *open* (2) of the device failed. (BNU)

DEVICE LOCKED
> The requested device is being used. (BNU)

DIAL FAILED

The remote system did not answer. It could be a bad dialer or the wrong telephone number. It could also be that **uucp** has lost ownership of the dial-out device, or that the dial-out device is in use.

DIALER SCRIPT FAILED

The script in the *Dialers* file was not negotiated successfully. (BNU)

FAILED (call to *system*)

uucico was unable to negotiate either the chat script in *L.sys* or the conversation with the modem. (Version 2) BNU replaced this catch-all message with a number of more specific messages.

FAILED (conversation complete)

The conversation failed after successful startup. This usually means one side went down, the program aborted, or the line just hung up.

FAILED (DIRECT LINE OPEN *tty#*)

Opening of the device failed. (Version 2)

HANDSHAKE FAILED (LCK)

Lock file exists for the system or device. Check to see if another **uucico** is already running or if someone is using **tip** or **cu**. (Version 2)

LOGIN FAILED

The login for the given machine failed. It could be a wrong login/password, wrong number, a very slow machine, or failure in getting through the chat script. (BNU)

NO CALL (MAX RECALLS)

The maximum number of call attempts that can be made has been reached but could not complete the call. Remove the *STST* file for further calls. (Version 2)

NO CALL (RETRY TIME NOT REACHED)

Default time for the system status file has not been reached. Remove this file if you want **uucico** to try again soon.

NO DEVICES AVAILABLE

There may be no valid device for calling the system. Check that the device named in *Systems* corresponds to an entry in *Devices*. (BNU)

OK
> Things are working perfectly.

REMOTE DOES NOT KNOW ME
> The remote system does not have the name of your system in its *Systems* file. (BNU)

REMOTE HAS A LCK FILE FOR ME
> The remote file may be trying to call you or may have a lock file left over from a previous attempt. (BNU)

REMOTE REJECT AFTER LOGIN
> Your system logged in but had insufficient permissions on the remote system. (BNU)

REMOTE REJECT, UNKNOWN MESSAGE
> The remote system rejected your call with a nonstandard message. The remote may be running a hacked UUCP implementation. (BNU)

STARTUP FAILED
> Login succeeded, but the initial "shere" handshake failed. (BNU)

SUCCEEDED (call to *system*)
> Self-explanatory.

SYSTEM NOT IN Systems
> One of your users made a request for a system not in your *Systems* file. (BNU)

TALKING
> A conversation is currently in progress.

TIMEOUT (*system*)
> The other system did not answer within a set period of time. Depending on the chat script, **uucico** may keep trying and still get through. (Version 2)

WRONG MACHINE NAME
> The machine we just called is using a different name than the one we called it by. (BNU)

WRONG TIME TO CALL
> The *L.sys* or *Systems* file does not allow a call at this time.

Checking Device Ownership

If you get either of the messages "FAILED (DIRECT LINE OPEN)" or "DIAL FAILED," one possible problem is that the ownership of the callout device has been changed (e.g., by an abnormally terminated **cu** leaving the device with the permissions of the user). UUCP is very picky about ownership and file protection modes, including ownership of the special file(s) used for dial out. You can check (and fix) the ownership and permissions as follows (assuming you are using a dial device called **modem**):

```
$ ls -l /dev/modem
crw--w--w-  2 root  other    0,  6 Jan 28 15:22 /dev/modem
$ su
Password:
# chown uucp /dev/modem
```

On a System V system using the same device for both calling in and calling out, beware of users calling out while **getty** is still active on the communications line. In some cases, the call will work, but the line will not hang up properly.

Out-of-date Control Files

An *L.sys* (Version 2) or *Systems* (BNU) file that contains a large number of entries may be difficult to maintain, and the probability increases that remote systems may have changed the information necessary to call them up without telling you about these changes. After ruling out hardware problems as the cause of failure, you might want to check the information in these files to make sure that they are current. Some things that may be out-of-date for a machine are:

* Phone number

* Login

* Password

It is a good practice to comment your *L.sys* (or *Systems*) file with the name and voice phone number of a person to call at each remote site. This will make it much easier to track down and solve problems when they do occur. (Most versions of UUCP treat a line beginning with a hash mark (#) in column one as a comment.)

If you change login information for your own system, be sure to tell the administrators of other systems on your network, so they don't find out the hard way!

Problems can also occur when a remote site changes its name but not all of your users know it. BSD 4.3 includes an *L-aliases* file that can be used to map old names onto new ones so that users' requests with the old name will still go through.

Notifying Users of Extended Down Times

When your system is down, remote systems on the UUCP network keep trying to make calls even after many failed attempts. When you reboot your system, job requests queued on your system may arrive all at once, possibly creating a jam. You can prevent this by notifying remote systems and local users of extended down times, if you know when they will occur.

If a remote system is scheduled to be down, you can tell local users not to attempt calls to that system. To prevent UUCP traffic, you can temporarily disable the *L.sys* entry for that system by commenting it out (putting a hash mark (#) as the first character of the line) or by changing the *time* field to read "Never".

7

Introduction to Usenet

Newsgroup Categories
Administering Netnews
Overview of the Netnews Software

Usenet is a network of systems that use the freely available* Netnews software to exchange news. Usenet currently includes over 18,000 sites around the world. Many Usenet sites use UUCP as their basic network protocol. However, Usenet is connected through gateway systems to other large computer networks such as the Internet, BITNET, and EASYnet, which use alternative protocols such as NNTP and Notes as well as UUCP.

Netnews software distributions typically include programs that allow users to read and post news messages to the net. Messages are transmitted across the net by what has been described as a "flooding routing algorithm." Each site that receives news forwards the news to one or more other sites; large sites (often referred to as "backbone" sites) forward messages to each other and to several other sites in order to speed transmission.

---

*Current releases of Netnews (B News 2.11, B News 3.0, and C News) are not properly "public domain," since they contain copyright notices by their respective authors. However, they are freely distributed to any and all comers, subject to varying restrictions. The main thrust of these restrictions is to prevent commercial or uncredited use of the code; see the various source distributions for more detail.

Newsgroup Categories

Obviously, some sites have only a single connection. They receive messages and do not forward them. The only messages they post are those created on site. These sites are sometimes called "leaf sites."

Messages are categorized into subject areas called newsgroups. There are nearly 500 different newsgroups, with subjects ranging from UNIX internals to politics to hobbies.

The standard newsgroups are divided into seven major categories, as indicated by the first part of their names:

comp Groups relating to some aspect of computer science (e.g., *comp.ai*).

sci Groups relating to sciences other than computer science (e.g., *sci.physics* or *sci.math.symbolic*).

news Groups relating to the Netnews software (e.g., *news.software.b*) or of general interest to all net users (e.g., *news.announce.important*).

rec Groups relating to recreational activities (e.g., *rec.arts.sf-lovers* or *rec.games.chess*).

soc Groups for social interaction or discussion of social topics (e.g., *soc.singles* or *soc.culture.jewish*).

talk Groups prone to extended and unresolved debate (e.g., *talk.religion.misc* or *talk.politics.guns*).

misc Groups that do not fit into any of the other categories (e.g., *misc.jobs.offered* for job postings).

In addition, there may be one or more local newsgroups that are available only in your local area. There may also be groups found only at your site. One group, called *general*, is fairly likely to exist. It may go under an organizational prefix instead—for example, at the University of California at Berkeley, the group's name is *ucb.general*, while at MIT, it is called *mit.bboard*.

Some groups—those with the prefixes listed above—are broadcast worldwide to all systems on the net. Others are local to a region (for example, *ca* for California, *eunet* for Europe, or *ne* for New England) or even to a particular company (for example, *att* for AT&T).

There are also various hierarchies of newsgroups that have sprung up separately from the standard seven. In general, these groups are not carried in the traditional Usenet hierarchies due to their volume, a restricted sphere of interest, or a different set of administrative rules and concerns.

alt   Groups are here for various reasons. Some (e.g., *alt.drugs*, *alt.sex*) are too controversial to be carried on the traditional Usenet. Others (e.g., *alt.gourmand*, *alt.sys.sun*) are here because it is much easier to create a group on the *alt* hierarchy than in the traditional Usenet hierarchies.

bionet   For topics of interest to biologists (e.g., *bionet.molbio.ageing*).

biz   For commercial postings generally considered unsuitable for the Usenet at large (e.g., *biz.comp.telebit*).

gnu   Groups bidirectionally gatewayed with the Internet mailing lists about the GNU Project of the Free Software Foundation (e.g., *gnu.emacs.bug* or *gnu.gcc*).

inet   Groups with names similar to traditional Usenet names, which are bidirectionally gatewayed with the corresponding Internet mailing lists (e.g., *comp.editors* or *news.software.nntp*).

pubnet   For public access systems (e.g., *pubnet.sysops*).

unix-pc Groups about the AT&T UNIX PC (e.g., *unix-pc.sources*).

u3b   Groups about the AT&T 3B series of computers (everything except the 3B1, which is also known as the UNIX PC) (e.g., *u3b.tech*).

Newsgroup names have one or more parts separated by periods. The first part indicates the category; subsequent parts indicate the topic, which may be broken down into several subtopics. The topic is usually fairly obvious from the newsgroup name—*comp.bugs.4bsd* or *rec.bicycles*—although there are some groups whose names will become apparent only after you become more familiar with the net (for example, the group *alt.flame*, which is used for sounding off about topics that particularly irritate you.)

Some groups are moderated, meaning that submissions must be sent by mail to a moderator, who will post them to the newsgroup if he or she finds them acceptable.* However, most groups are free-form—users can post messages as they like, and those reading the messages are free to respond as they see fit. As you can imagine, freedom can lead to chaos, as many different people respond to the

---

*All modern news software automatically mails postings made to moderated groups directly to the appropriate moderator.

same message. It also can lead to enormous amounts of traffic on the net and a lot of redundant messages if users are not careful.

Administering Netnews

A system need not subscribe to all newsgroups, and likewise, each user need not subscribe to all newsgroups taken by the system. Which newsgroups a site will forward (and receive) is specified in a *sys* file that is somewhat analogous to the UUCP *L.sys* file. In addition, each user has a personal subscription list in a file called *.newsrc* in his or her home directory. As Netnews administrator, you have three responsibilities:

- Installing the software.

- Performing routine administration.

- Informing your users of "net etiquette" (procedures for optimal use of the net), and making sure that it is followed.

In order to join the net, you must find a site willing to feed you news and obtain some version of the Netnews software (generally from that same site). While some UNIX system manufacturers distribute it as a part of a "contributed library," it is most likely that you will get the sources from another user.

Fortunately, Netnews software must run on so many systems that the source code has been made quite portable.

Once the software is installed, there is some routine maintenance that must be performed. Periodically, newsgroups must be added or deleted or system files updated. This is usually done by means of control messages sent out over the net. These control messages are usually executed automatically by the Netnews software, but in some cases, they require manual intervention. In addition, you will need to watch the disk space used by Netnews and "expire" articles if the disk gets full before the automatic time limit for expiration.

In addition, you may want to obtain and install additional software for forwarding mail automatically to Usenet addresses (**pathalias** and **smail**). A database listing all sites on the net is posted monthly to the group *comp.mail.maps*. **pathalias** generates a list of mail paths representing the shortest path from your system to each of the other sites. A mail program such as **smail**, which understands the format of this database, can therefore accept a simple *sysname!username* address, rather than the entire path between your system and the destination.* **smail** also gives your system the ability to use domain addressing, such as *user@host.university.edu*.

Netnews is the collective name for about 20 different programs which comprise the transport and storage functions of a news systems. Programs to read Netnews usually come with the Netnews software distribution. Other readers are available. *Rn* is probably the most widely used of the alternate news readers; others are *nn*, *vn*, *GNUS*, and *Gnews*.†

Currently three different versions of the Netnews software are in use. B News 2.11 is the oldest and most widely used. It comes with the **vnews** and **readnews** news readers. C News is a complete rewrite of the news software, concentrating on simplicity, stability, and speed. It includes one very simple news reader, as its authors recommend using the **rn** program. B News 3.0 (a.k.a. Teenage Mutant Ninja Netnews, or TMNN) is, as of May 1990, still in beta release. Its primary feature is good support for people wishing to write more complex news readers. It comes with re-implementations of **vnews** and **rn**. This handbook supplies full instructions for installing and administering B News 2.11 and C News but does not discuss B News 3.0.

Structure of B News 2.11

In B News 2.11, the basic news program—the one that actually processes all news articles that are received or sent out—is called **inews**. The **readnews** and **vnews** programs provide an interface to **news** for reading news; **postnews** provides an interface for posting news. **inews** is also linked to **rnews** for receiving news.

---

*In B News 2.11 and later versions, the *mailpaths* file allows sites without this software to rely on neighboring sites with more powerful software for mail forwarding.
†*GNUS* and *Gnews* are written in Lisp, to run under the Free Software Foundation's GNU Emacs editor.

Transmission

Transmission from site to site across the net is usually accomplished via UUCP. More specifically, **uux** is used to execute **rnews** on the neighboring system, and articles are passed as standard input to **rnews**. **rnews** screens the incoming messages to see if they have already been received and stores the new ones as separate files in a spool area (usually, but not always, */usr/spool/news*) and also forwards them on to the next system in the net, as shown in Figure 7-1.

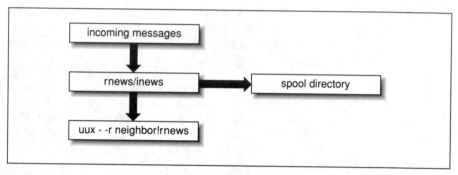

Figure 7-1. News transmission by inews

Messages posted via **postnews** at the local site are passed both to the local **inews** and, via **uux**, to **rnews** at each of the neighboring sites.

Which sites will have messages forwarded to them is controlled by a *sys* file at each site. This file specifies the names of each connected site and the newsgroups that should be passed on to it. In addition, there must be an entry for each site in UUCP's *L.sys* or *Systems* file, so that the basic dialup link is in place.

Batching

Since the volume of traffic is so high, many sites use a batching and compression scheme for forwarding news.

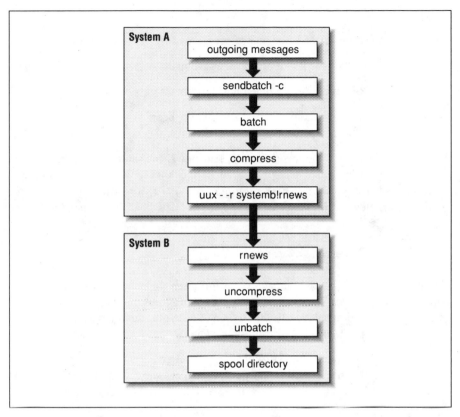

Figure 7-2. News transmission using compressed batching

When batching is used, articles are not spooled separately to **uux** but are instead passed to a shell script called **sendbatch,** which invokes the **batch** program to combine articles into larger files. **sendbatch** then spools the batch file to **uux,** which invokes **rnews** on the remote system (which then invokes **unbatch** to separate the articles out again and pass them to **inews**).

In most cases, if it is desirable to use batching, it is desirable to use compressed batching. The **compress** program uses a Lempel-Ziv algorithm to pack **ascii** data into two 16-bit codes and typically achieves a 50- to 60-percent reduction in the size of the file. Considering the volume of news, this can lead to considerable savings in telephone transmission time and cost. The **sendbatch -c** option is used to handle compressed batching.

Maintenance Scripts

There are also a number of maintenance programs and shell scripts, including:

checkgroups Update the list of active newsgroups.

rmgroup Remove a discontinued newsgroup.

expire Delete messages after they have been around for a predefined length of time.

In addition, there are programs (**recmail, sendnews, recnews,** and **uurec**) that are used to set up news links using **mail** rather than **uux** as the basic transmission mechanism between sites. These programs only work on some systems (those with the Berkeley **sendmail** software) and are not described in this handbook.

Structure of C News

The structure of C News (Figure 7-3) is similar to that of B news. Many of the supplied programs are shell scripts instead of C programs, making the system easier for the local administrator to modify, and some programs have been split into several smaller programs, but overall the system has not changed much.

News is received through **rnews**, which spools received batches with the help of **newsspool**. **newsrun**, which is normally run periodically from *crontab*, calls **relaynews**, which does the work of placing articles into the spool directory.

The **readnews** and **postnews** programs provide *very* simple news reading and posting interfaces; we (and the authors of C News) recommend that you acquire the **rn** program instead. The **inews** program is a front-end processor for **relaynews**, handling local postings.

Batching

The batching script for C news is called **sendbatches**. **Sendbatches** looks up the remote site in the */usr/lib/news/batchparms* file to find the correct batching programs. The builder (normally **batcher**) combines articles into larger batch files, which are passed to the muncher (**compcun** for compressed batches, **nocomp** for uncompressed batches) and finally, to the sender (normally **viauux**), which invokes **rnews** on the remote system. In addition to the maintenance scripts listed in the discussion of B News 2.11, there is an **addgroup** script, which is used to add a group locally, and a **delgroup** script, which is used to delete a group locally.

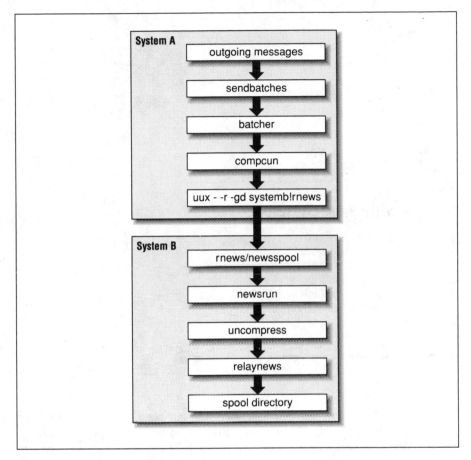

Figure 7-3. C News flow

8

Installing Netnews

Finding a News Feed
Configuring B News 2.11
Configuring C News
The Actual Install
Testing the News Link
Installing Documentation On-line
Registering Your Site

Before you even begin to think about installing **Netnews,** make sure you have enough free disk space. The volume of traffic on the net can be quite substantial (over 4 MByte per day). Since articles are usually left around for a week or two to allow users to read them, you need from 28 to 56 MBytes of free disk space. (This amount can be reduced by subscribing only to a limited set of newsgroups or by expiring articles more frequently.)

Then there are eight steps you need to perform to get the Netnews software up and running.

1. Find a "news feed"—someone willing to forward news to you and send you a copy of the software. Set up a bidirectional UUCP link with your news feed.

2. Configure the software for your site's specific needs. B News 2.11 uses a shell script called *localize.sh*. C News provides a shell script called *build* which creates four shell scripts to do the necessary modifications.

3. Actually install the software.

4. Customize various system data files created by the installation procedure. The *sys* file, analogous to UUCP's *L.sys*, is the most important of these files. It

describes the sites with which you will be exchanging news. The installation procedure will create a dummy file, which you must replace with the real thing. In addition to identifying the system(s) with which you correspond, the *sys* file contains the list of newsgroups to which your site subscribes.

You may also need to modify the *active, aliases, mailpaths,* and *distributions* files, which also contain data needed by the Netnews software.

In addition, you should obtain a list of local groups from your news feed. This lists should include newsgroups that are local to your immediate geographical area, rather than net-wide.

5. Modify UUCP's *L.cmds* file (or *Permissions* in BNU) to allow your news feed to remotely execute the **rnews** command. You should also be sure to set up a communication schedule with your news feed.

6. Test that the link is working. Create a newsgroup to post messages specifically to your news feed, then send a trial message. Have your feed do the same in reverse.

7. Install the on-line Netnews documentation where your users can find it. (There are numerous reference manual pages as well as several articles that should be posted to the local group *general*.)

8. Post a "registration form" to the group *news.newsites*, and mail a copy to the moderator of the *comp.mail.maps* newsgroup.

Finding a News Feed

You may be able to obtain the Netnews software from your system vendor. (For example, it is a standard part of Berkeley UNIX distributions.) Most likely, though, you will get the software from a nearby site that agrees to send you news—your "news feed."

Finding a news feed can present something of a catch-22, since the easiest way to do it is to post a message asking if there is anyone in your immediate area who is already on the net and willing to connect with you. Unfortunately, you already need some kind of connection to take this easy way out.

If you know other UNIX users, ask around to see if anyone you know is already on the net. You want to find someone nearby, since even at local telephone rates, the volume of news can run up a sizeable telephone bill. However, even someone distant can help you by posting an initial message requesting a feed for you.

UUNET

Another way to get on the net is to sign up with UUNET, a nonprofit, commercial UUCP and Usenet hookup, originally funded by Usenix, the UNIX technical user's group. UUNET allows you to access the net via the CompuServe and Tymnet public data networks, which have local access telephone numbers in most major cities.

UUNET modems can also be dialed directly in Mountain View, CA, San Jose, CA, and Boston, MA.

The off-peak (evening and weekend) connect charges for Tymnet are quite reasonable—$5/hour. CompuServe is $5/hour at any time. UUNET estimates that the monthly cost of a full news feed is about $250, in addition to the UUNET membership fee of $35/month. The advantage is that you will be hooked in one hop from a backbone site. UUNET also offers an extensive collection of freely redistributable UNIX source archives.

You don't need to subscribe to UUNET to be able to use their archives via UUCP. By calling 1-900-468-7727 and using the login *uucp* with no password, anyone may **uucp** any of UUNET's on-line source collection. (Start by copying *uunet!/usr/spool/ftp/ls-lR.Z*, which is a compressed index of every file in the archives.) As of this writing, the cost is 40 cents per minute. The charges will appear on your phone bill.

For more information, contact:

UUNET Communications Services
3110 Fairview Park Drive, Suite 570
P. O. Box 2324
Falls Church, VA 22042
Tel: 703-876-5050
e-mail: *info@uunet.uu.net*
        uunet!info

What You Get

Whether you hook up with someone in the next town or with UUNET, your next step is to set up a UUCP link as described in Chapter 3, *Setting Up a UUCP Link*. This will be your basic carrier for mail and news messages.

Once you have the link, your feed can send you the news sources via UUCP—although magtape is preferable, since the sources are large.

NOTE

This handbook discusses B News Version 2.11 and C News. If at all possible, be sure to obtain one of these versions of the software or a later version.

Configuring B News 2.11

The B News 2.11 sources will probably arrive in the form of six compressed **tar** archives, which when unbundled will produce the following six directories:

src   The actual Netnews source code.

doc   Documentation, including an installation manual.

man   Manual pages for each of the Netnews programs.

misc   Miscellaneous accessory programs that you may find useful but are not an essential part of Netnews.

uucp   Various source-code patches to UUCP, designed to optimize it for use with Netnews. You have no use for this if you do not have a UNIX source license.

cvt   Various scripts for conversion of older versions of news.

The sources should be unpacked as follows (file sizes may differ):

```
$ uncompress doc.tar.Z
$ tar xvf doc.tar
x doc/Makefile, 362 bytes, 1 tape blocks
x doc/copyright.mn, 23405 bytes, 46 tape blocks
x doc/howto.mn, 40567 bytes, 80 tape blocks
x doc/install.mn, 84417 bytes, 165 tape blocks
x doc/manner.mn, 39209 bytes, 77 tape blocks
x doc/mn.7, 8687 bytes, 17 tape blocks
x doc/patchlevel.doc, 1 bytes, 1 tape blocks
x doc/standard.mn, 41466 bytes, 81 tape blocks
x doc/tmac.n, 22249 bytes, 44 tape blocks
```

Once you have uncompressed and untarred the Netnews sources, you should print and read the file *doc/install.mn*, which gives detailed installation instructions. You should also pay special attention to the following files in the *man* directory: *checknews.1*, *expire.8*, *inews.1*, *newsrc.5*, *postnews.1*, *readnews.1*, and *sendbatch.8*.

First, though, you should continue on with this chapter, which provides a more colloquial overview of the whole process. Compilation and installation of the software is controlled by a *Makefile*. In earlier releases, there were two *makefiles*: *Makefile.v7* and *Makefile.usg*, for Berkeley and System V-derived systems, respectively. In Version 2.11 of Netnews, there is only one *makefile*; which version you create is determined by variables set in the *makefile*.

You need to edit the *makefile* so that the proper UNIX version is selected. In addition, there are some site- and version-dependent variables that you need to set in the *makefile* and in the header file *defs.h*.

In order to make it easier to upgrade to new releases of the Netnews software, its developers recommend that you make all changes via an editing script. A number of sample scripts are included to get you started:

```
$ ls news2.11/src/localize.*
localize.4.3
localize.7300
localize.clien
localize.mport
localize.nntp
localize.sampl
localize.sh
localize.sun
localize.usg
localize.v.3
localize.v7
localize.vms
localize.xenix
```

The *usg* localize file should be used for System V, *4.3* for Berkeley 4.3, *sun* for a Sun workstation,* *vms* for a VAX running Eunice under VMS, and so on.

The file *localize.sampl* contains a more complete version, as filled in for a particular site (*seismo*, at the Center for Seismic Studies near Washington, DC).

The file *localize.sh* is probably a copy of the localization script used by whomever passed the Netnews software on to you. If you got the sources from someone with a similar machine, this may be the best starting point of all.

You should make a copy of whichever *localize* file most closely matches your system, edit it, and name it *localize.sh*.

---

*Note that this script causes LIBDIR to be */usr/spool/news-lib*, not */usr/lib/news*.

The *localize.sampl* file is shown below:

```
rm -f Makefile
cp Makefile.dst Makefile
chmod u+w Makefile
ed Makefile  <<'EOF'
/^UUXFLAGS/s/-r -z/-r -z -n -gd/
g/^#V7 /s///
g/^#BSD4_3 /s///
g/^#BSD4_1 /d
g/^#USG /d
/^LIBDIR/s;:/usr/lib/news;/usr/new/lib/news;
/^BINDIR/s;:/usr/bin;/usr/new;
w
q
EOF
rm -f defs.h
cp defs.dist defs.h
chmod u+w defs.h
ed - defs.h <<'EOF'
/ROOTID/s/10/352/
/N_UMASK/s/000/002/
/DFTXMIT/s/-z/-z -gd/
/UXMIT/s/-z/-z -gd/
/NONEWGROUPS/s;/ ;;
/INTERNET/s;/ ;;
/MYDOMAIN/s;.UUCP;.CSS.GOV;
/GHNAME/s;/ ;;
/DOXREFS/s;/ ;;
/BSD4_2/s;/ ;;
/ALWAYSALIAS/s;/ ;;
/SENDMAIL/s;/ ;;
/HIDDENNET/s;frooz;seismo;
s;/ ;;
/MYORG/s/Frobozz Inc., St. Louis/Center for Seismic \
Studies, Arlington, VA/
/ORGDISTRIB/s;/ ;;
/ORGDISTRIB/s;froozum;css;
w
q
EOF
```

The distributed software also includes a file called simply *Makefile*, which is probably just the localized version created by whomever passed on the software to you. The interlock between *Makefile* and *localize.sh* is quite clever. Since *Makefile* depends on *localize.sh* and *localize.sh* replaces and edits *Makefile*, simply updating *localize.sh* and typing:

```
% make
```

will cause *Makefile* to execute *localize.sh* as its only act, thereby editing itself before doing anything else. You will have to run *make* again to perform the actual build in this case.

The parameters in the *makefile* and *defs.h* that you may want to change are listed in detail in the *install* document. However, things become clearer when you take a look at the files themselves.

Makefile

The basic *makefile*, before editing, is contained in a file called *Makefile.dst*. If we look just at some of the version-dependent lines in that file, you should get enough of an idea of how it needs to be edited to work through the rest yourself.

```
# '@(#)Makefile.dst      1.17   10/29/86'
# Generic Makefile.
# This is converted to USG/v7/etc by localize.sh
# which should at least be a copy of localize.v7 or
# localize.usg

# definitions

#V7 OSTYPE = v7
#USG OSTYPE = usg

# HOME is the user name whose home dir has all the news
# stuff in it.
HOME= exptools
# Use the -DHOME line if you want dynamic lookup in
# /etc/passwd
#HOMENAME= -DHOME=
HOMENAME=

NEWSUSR = news
NEWSGRP = news
SPOOLDIR = /usr/spool/news
BATCHDIR = /usr/spool/batch
LIBDIR = /usr/lib/news
BINDIR = /usr/bin
DESTDIR =
UUXFLAGS = -r -z

LNRNEWS = ln
#VMS LNRNEWS = cp # No links in Eunice
               .
               .

               .
               .
#USG VFORK=-Dvfork=fork
#V7 VFORK=-Dvfork=fork
```

```
#BSD4_1  VFORK=
#BSD4_2  VFORK=
#BSD4_3  VFORK=
                    .
                    .
                    .
```

You may need to change one or more of the definitions shown here.

As you can see, there are alternate lines for most definitions, all of them commented out. This makes the file very easy to edit. For example, the editing commands in *localize.sh*:

```
g/^#USG /s///
g/^#V7 /d
g/^#VMS /d
g/^#BSD4_[123] /d
```

will uncomment all of the lines for a USG (System V) site and delete the lines for other types. This is 90 percent of the job. The remaining 10 percent takes a little more thought.

NEWSUSR and NEWSGRP are the login id and group that should be used by Netnews. If you can become superuser on your system, you should probably create a new id and group called *news* in the */etc/passwd* and */etc/group* files. For example, in */etc/passwd*:

```
news:NONE:132:10:news:/usr/lib/news:
```

and in */etc/group*:

```
news:NONE:10
```

If you cannot become superuser, see the discussion of this topic later in this chapter.

HOME and HOMENAME are also used if you do not have the ability to become superuser on your system and, therefore, cannot edit the */etc/passwd* file or write to all of the directories where news is usually installed. See below for details if this is true for you; otherwise, you should probably set these to a null string.

SPOOLDIR, BATCHDIR, LIBDIR, and BINDIR tell the *makefile* where to install the software and store the news messages that are transmitted. In general, you do not need to change these assignments unless you do not have space on the */usr/spool* filesystem for news. In this case, you would need to change SPOOLDIR and BATCHDIR.

When received, incoming news messages are stored in SPOOLDIR. Each newsgroup receives its own subdirectory and, in some cases, directory hierarchy. For example, assuming that SPOOLDIR is */usr/spool/news*, the group *comp.bugs.misc* would be stored in the directory */usr/spool/news/comp/bugs/misc*. Within that directory, individual articles are stored in sequentially numbered files.

BATCHDIR contains outgoing news messages if you are using the optional batching mechanism. This directory is usually */usr/spool/batch*.

UUXFLAGS describes flags that will be used with **uux** when it is invoked to receive or transmit news. If the version of **uux** supplied with your system does not support these flags, you may need to change this assignment. Or you may want to add additional flags.

Our system runs System V, so we started with *localize.usg* and added the following commands:

```
/^HOME/s/exptools/""/
/^SPOOLDIR/s/usr/work/
/^BATCHDIR/s/usr/work/
/^UUXFLAGS/s/-r -z/-r/
```

Since we are able to become superuser, we set HOME to a null string.

In addition, since we did not have enough space on the */usr* filesystem, we set up SPOOLDIR and BATCHDIR on another filesystem, called */work* on our system.

Finally, our system's **uux** does not support **-z** (a patch to **uux** to keep it from sending back a flood of "success!" messages to your feed whenever messages are posted to you) and we do not have source code to install the patches, so we have to remove that option from UUXFLAGS. (**-n**, which keeps **uux** from sending back any messages at all, is a somewhat draconian substitute.)

If you can't become superuser

News installation normally includes a couple of steps that can only be carried out by someone who can become superuser. These include creating a login id and group for *news* and installing software in */usr/lib*.

However, the software has been designed to allow people who are not superuser to install Netnews anyway. Here's how:

1. Set NEWSUSR and NEWSGRP to your own login id and group.

2. Change the definition of HOME from *exptools* to your own login id. HOMENAME can be specified directly as a pathname, or your home directory can be looked up dynamically from */etc/passwd* when the **make** command (-DHOME=1=\"($HOME)\") is issued.

Specify BINDIR, LIBDIR, SPOOLDIR, and BATCHDIR with pathnames relative to HOMENAME. For example:

```
SPOOLDIR = spool/news
```

will put incoming news in $HOMENAME/$SPOOLDIR (for example, */usr/tim/spool/news*).

All of this is handled in the source file *pathinit.c*, so if you plan to install news this way, you should look carefully at the comments in that file before running **make**.

defs.h

The file *defs.h* must be created from its template in *defs.dist*. Here, there are more significant edits to be made since they depend on your site configuration. The relevant section of *defs.h* is shown below.

```
/* Things that very well may require local configuration     */
#ifndef HOME
#define ROOTID 10 /* uid of person allowed to cancel anything */
#endif
#define N_UMASK 000 /* mask for umask call, 022 for secure system */
#define DFLTEXP 2*WEEKS /* default no. of seconds to expire in  */
#define HISTEXP 4*WEEKS /* default no. of seconds to forget in  */
#define DFLTSUB "general,all.announce" /* default subscription list */
#define TMAIL "/usr/ucb/Mail" /* Mail program that understands -T   */
#define ADMSUB "general,all.announce" /* Mandatory subscription list */
#define PAGE "/usr/ucb/more" /* Default pager                       */
#define NOTIFY "usenet" /* Tell him about certain ctl messages     */
        /* Default xmit command - remove -z if                     */
#define DFTXMIT "uux - -r -z %s!rnews < %s" /* your uux can't do it */
#define UXMIT "uux -r -z -c %s!rnews '<' %s" /* If uux -c is ok     */
#define DFTEDITOR "vi"   /* Default editor, see also postnews. */
/* #define UUPROG "euuname" /* omit for uuname, put in LIBDIR */
#define MANUALLY  /* Don't execute rmgroups, just notify.    */
/* #define NONEWGROUPS  /* Don't create new groups, just notify.*/
#define BATCH "unbatch"  /* name of unbatcher   */
/* #define SPOOLNEWS  /* Spool incoming news, don't process */
/* #define LOCALNAME   /* There is no full name database.  */
/* #define INTERNET  /* Internet mail works locally  */
#define MYDOMAIN ".UUCP" /* Local domain     */
/* #define CHEAP  /* don't chown files to news  */
/* #define OLD    /* Add extra headers for old neighbors */
/* #define UNAME  /* If uname call returns your nodename */
/* #define GHNAME  /* If gethostname call is available. */
/* #define UUNAME "/etc/uucpname"/*If your nodename is stored in a file*/
#define V7MAIL   /* Local mail format is V7 ("From ") */
#define SORTACTIVE  /* if you want news presented in the order
                    of the .newsrc*/
```

```
#define ZAPNOTES   /* if you want old style notes headers
                       moved into the headers*/
#define DIGPAGE    /* allow digestifying in vnews*/
/*#define DOXREFS   /* Generate xref line for rn to use*/
/*#define MULTICAST  /* If you want to be able to multicast news*/
/*#define BSD4_2   /* If you are running 4.2  or 4.3 BSD */
/*#define BSD4_1C   /* If you are running 4.1C BSD  */
/*#define LOCKF  /* If you have the lockf() sys call*/
/*#define ALWAYSALIAS  /* temporary kludge for conversion*/
/*#define SENDMAIL "/usr/lib/sendmail" /* command line to run "sendmail"*/
/*#define MMDF "/usr/mmdf/submit"/*command line to run mmdf if you have it*/
#define MYORG "Frobozz Inc., St. Louis" /* My organization.  Please */
                            /* include your city (and state, and */
                            /* country, if not obvious) in MYORG, */
                            /* and please keep it short.  */
/*#define HIDDENNET "frooz"    /* if you have a local network and want*/
                            /* The mail address to look like it came*/
                            /* from one machine*/
/*#define NICENESS 4 /* does a nice(NICENESS) in rnews*/
/*#define FASCIST "all,!all.all"/*only permit posting to certain groups*/
                            /* see installation guide for details*/
/*#define SMALL_ADDRESS_SPACE /* If your machine can't address > 32767*/
/*#define ORGDISTRIB "froozum" /* For organization-wide control message
                            handling*/
```

Many of these values are self-evident, and in any case, all are well described in the Netnews *install* documentation. However, there are a couple of points worth emphasizing.

ROOTID is *not* the system root id. It is the user id of the news administrator. If you are the news administrator, look up your user id in */etc/passwd* and set ROOTID to that value. This is only used if you are not using the HOME/HOMENAME construct in *Makefile* and allows you to run various news procedures as yourself, without becoming superuser. (You must still become superuser to do the actual install, as described later in this chapter.)

N_UMASK is the permission mask for the news spool directory. While the comments in *defs.h* seem to suggest that you should change the value to 022 for a secure system, you should be aware that doing so may cause problems in receiving news. Do not make this change without thoroughly reading the documentation.

DFLTEXP specifies the default amount of time news messages will be left around before they "expire" (are deleted). Even if you want to expire news messages sooner, you probably should not change this value, since if you later change your mind, you will have to recompile the news software. Instead, make use of the -e flag to the **expire** program (which is described in the manual page).

DFTXMIT and UXMIT control what command will be used by default for news transmission. (UXMIT is only used if the **U** option is set in the *sys* file; see the *install* documentation. DFTXMIT is more important for most users.) **-z** is the sticker. As discussed in the Makefile, **-z** is a patch to **uux**. If you do not have UUCP source code, you cannot install the patch. Either specify **-n** to prohibit all messages or have your news feed make provision for discarding those messages. **-r** keeps UUCP from posting articles immediately; instead they are spooled for transmission the next time you and your feed make contact. It is advisable to leave this option enabled and to set up a polling schedule via *crontab* (discussed later in this chapter).

ADMSUB specifies a mandatory subscription list for your users. Adding newsgroups to this list (perhaps local, site-specific newsgroups you plan to create) is a way of making sure that users read certain messages. Of course, savvy users can duck this mechanism by simply using a text editor on their *.newsrc* file, but at least you have tried.

NOTIFY specifies the mail id of the Netnews administrator. Certain control messages that need to be acted upon by the administrator are sent to this id. Generally, if you have root privileges on your system, you should not change this value from the default *usenet* but should instead create a mail alias for *usenet* and have the mail forwarded to the administrator. For example, in System V:

```
su# echo "Forward to ambar" > /usr/mail/usenet
su# chown mail /usr/mail/usenet
su# chgrp mail /usr/mail/usenet
```

In Berkeley UNIX systems, this does not work; instead, you must specify the forwarding in the file */usr/lib/aliases*.

INTERNET, if defined, specifies that your site has a mailer that understands Internet addressing (*tim@ora.com* instead of *ora!tim*). (Internet addressing is used not just on the UUCP network but on ARPANET, BITNET, and various other networks that are connected to Usenet. Internet addresses are shown on the "From" header line of news postings, while news paths are shown on the "Path" header line. Internet addresses are much more reliable than the news mail path, because there are many machines which exchange news and not mail.) See the discussion of the *mailpaths* file later in this chapter for more details.

UNAME, GHNAME, and UUNAME are alternate ways that your system can identify its node name when asked. USG (System V) systems need not uncomment any of these lines; a non-USG system that responds to the **uname** system call should uncomment UNAME. Berkeley systems use GHNAME. Use UUNAME and put your node name in a file if your system responds to neither **uname** nor **gethostname**.

Our *localize.sh* file makes the following changes:

```
ed - defs.h <<'EOF'
/ROOTID/s/10/106/
/MYORG/s/".*"/"O'Reilly & Associates, Inc., Cambridge MA"/
/PAGE/s;/usr/ucb/more;/usr/local/bin/more;
/TMAIL/s;^;/* ;
/MANUALLY/s;^;/* ;
/INTERNET/s;^/* ;;
/LINES/s/512/1024/
/SBUFLEN/s/32/128/
w
q
```

This script makes the following edits:

- It changes the id of the news administrator (ROOTID) from 10 to 106; you should look up your own id in */etc/passwd* and substitute it here (assuming you are to be the news administrator).

- It specifies the actual organization name for MYORG.

- It specifies the correct path for the *more* program on our system.

- It comments out the line for TMAIL, since our mail program does not support the **-T** option.

- It comments out the line for MANUALLY, since we are willing to take the risk of someone maliciously removing our newsgroups via a network-wide control message for the added benefit of keeping our active file automatically up to date.

- It uncomments the line for INTERNET, since we are running **smail**.

- It increases the value for LINES, since the number of newsgroups available these days (including regional groups and groups in alternate hierarchies) is rather larger than 512.

- It increases the value for SBUFLEN. This variable sets the size of a buffer used to store host names, which, once two or three levels of subdomains are tacked on, can easily be longer than 32 characters.

You can make other changes as you like. For example, if users at your site generally use **emacs** rather than **vi**, you can change DFTEDITOR. This will cause **postnews** to invoke **emacs** to compose outgoing messages. Or, as mentioned above, you can add additional newsgroups to the mandatory subscription list. See the *install* document for details.

Configuring C News

The C News sources will probably arrive as one giant *shar* file. It may be compressed, in which case the filename will end with *.Z*. Running */bin/sh* on the
uncompressed file will extract the sources, printing the name of each file that is
extracted. The purpose of each of the 25 directories(!) created is documented in
the *ROADMAP* file.

Once you have unpacked the C News sources, you should print and read the file
doc/install.out, which gives detailed installation instructions. You should also
pay special attention to the following files in the *man* directory: *checknews.1*,
expire.8, *inews.1*, *newsrc.5*, *postnews.1*, *relaynews.8*, and *sendbatch.8*.

First, though, you should continue on with this chapter, which provides a more
colloquial overview of the whole process. Compilation and installation of the
software is controlled by four shell scripts, which are generated by *build*, a master
shell script found in the *conf* directory.

You need to *cd* to *conf*, run the *build* shell script, answer the questions it asks, and
follow its instructions about running the shell scripts it creates. (You will probably have to **chmod +x build** before you can run it.)

The build Shell Script

The *build* shell script handles common configuration choices reasonably well.
However, you may want to make some additional changes if your configuration is
unusual.

The script is also remarkably self-documenting, so we have included its complete
output below. We will walk through the script as it is run on our site, *ora.com*, a
386 running Interactive Systems Corporation's 386/ix, Version 2.0.2. Any
answers we typed are shown in **Courier Bold**. If no reply is shown, we
pressed the RETURN key to accept the default. Additional comments on some of
the questions and answers are interspersed in italics.

```
$ ./build
This interactive command will build shell files named
doit.root, doit.bin, doit.news, and again.root to do
all the work.  It will not actually do anything itself,
so feel free to abort and start again.

You probably need your system manuals handy.

When a question is asked in the form "How are you
```

[okay]? ", the answer in brackets is what you will
get if you just press RETURN.

C News wants to keep most of its files under a uid
which preferably should be all its own. Its programs,
however, can and probably should be owned by another
user, typically the same one who owns most of the rest
of the system.
What user id should be used for news files [news]?
What group id should be used for news files [news]?
What user id should be used for news programs [bin]?
What group id should be used for news programs [bin]?
Do the C News sources belong to root [yes]?

C News lives primarily under three directories:
one for articles (and incoming and outgoing spooling),
one for control files, and one for programs.
Where should articles live [/usr/spool/news]?
Where should control files live [/usr/lib/news]?
Where should programs live [/usr/lib/newsbin]?
> *You might need to change these paths if you do not have enough space
> in the /usr filesystem.*

C News by default assumes that all normal UNIX
programs can be found in /bin or /usr/bin. This
is naive, especially on Berkeley-derived systems
where some standard programs inexplicably moved to
/usr/ucb. It would appear that some standard
programs live in /usr/ucb on your system.
Is that right [yes]?
> *This question will be asked only if /usr/ucb exists on your system.
> (The build script checks to see if it is there.)*
Should /usr/ucb go before or after /bin and /usr/bin [after]?
> *It should go before only if there are conflicting programs of the
> same name in these directories. The one found first in the search
> path will be used.*
Is there any other directory which should be searched
to find standard programs on your system [no]?

C News normally uses a umask of 002, turning off only
the others-write bit in the permissions of files used.
(The correspondence between bits and number is:
rwx = 421, so turning off group-write bits and all
others-access bits would be a mask of 027, for example.)
Usually a umask of 002 or 022 is appropriate. What umask
should C News use [002]?

C News wants to mail some forms of trouble reports to
an administrator. You probably want to make this a
system mailbox, rather than that of a specific user,
so you will not have to change the software when you get
a new administrator.

Where should C News mail trouble reports [usenet]?
You should be sure to alias this mailbox to a real person,
as described earlier in this chapter.

The shell files that are everywhere in C News want
to pick up their configuration parameters (mostly,
the last few questions you have answered) from a file
at a known location; this is very hard to avoid unless
you play tricks with environment variables (see
documentation). Where should the shell configuration file
be located [/usr/lib/news/bin/config]? What is the full
pathname of the chown command [/etc/chown]? Can I say
and group id of a file [yes]? no
Check your documentation for this information.
Is there a chgrp command to change the group of a file [yes]?
What is the full pathname of the chgrp command [/etc/chgrp]?

building doit.root...
done
C News has libraries for several kinds of UNIX:
        bsd42 4.2BSD and successors
        usg   AT&T System V
        v7   Version 7 (4.1BSD is pretty close, ditto Xenix)
        v8   Version 8, aka Eighth Edition
Which best describes your system [v7]? usg

C News has libraries for small address spaces (16 bits)
and big ones (preferably 32 bits, but anything rather
bigger than 16).
Which best describes your system [big]?
8086 and 80286 PCs have 16-bit address spaces. Most other systems have 32.

Systems vary in whether certain library functions and
system calls are present. C News contains reasonably-
portable versions of the possibly-missing library
functions, and fake versions of the possibly-missing
system calls, but it needs to know which are missing.
Check Section 2 of your system's UNIX Reference Manual for this information.
Does your system have fsync() [yes]? no
Does your system have getopt() [yes]?
Does your system have memcpy() [yes]?
Does your system have memcmp() [yes]?
Does your system have memchr() [yes]?
Does your system have memset() [yes]?
Does your system have mkdir() [yes]?
Does your system have putenv() [yes]?
Does your system have strchr() [yes]?
Does your system have strrchr() [yes]?
Does your system have strpbrk() [yes]?
Does your system have strspn() [yes]?
Does your system have strcspn() [yes]?
Does your system have strtok() [yes]?
Does your system have symlink() [yes]? no

Does your system have a library function ldiv() as in
ANSI C? [no]?
Does your system have the "dbm" library [yes]? **yes**
> *We do not actually have the dbm library, but we do have dbz, which is a*
> *reasonable facsimile.*

What is the compile option needed to get it [-ldbm]?
/usr/local/src/cnews/contrib/dbz.o
> *We could create libdbz.a, install it in /usr/lib, and answer -ldbz to this*
> *question, but it is simpler just to provide the path to the dbz object file.*

> *The dbm library comes with all BSD-derived systems that we are familiar with, and*
> *may be available on other systems. Using it, if it is available, improves*
> *Netnews performance noticeably.*

> *Unfortunately, some systems, including ours, do not have dbm. C News includes,*
> *in the contrib directory, sources to a library called dbz. Although dbz is*
> *not a fully general replacement for dbm, it has all the functionality required*
> *by Netnews.*
> *We recommend using dbz if you do not have dbm available. Future*
> *releases of C News may use dbz as the default on all systems.*

Many systems, notably older ones, have implementations
of the Standard I/O library ("stdio") in which fgets,
fputs, fread, and fwrite, although correct, are quite
slow. We supply versions of these functions which are
faster than those in any stdio we know; they are
compatible with most AT&T-derived stdios. If they work
on your system, they are a major performance win for C
News. There is a simple compatibility check run after
the library is built. The only system we know of where
the test works but the functions do not is SunOS 4.0.
Do you want to use our fast stdio library [yes]? **no**
> *C News includes a reimplementation of the stdio library which is tuned for*
> *speed. Unfortunately, it does not work on our system. To see if it runs on*
> *your system, first build C News without it. Then, in the libstdio directory,*
> *run **make trials**. If the tests complete without errors, you can use*
> *the library safely. You will have to run the build script again, answering*
> *yes to this question, and rebuild C News.*

Does the store() function in your dbm library return a
value (some old ones did not) [yes]?

A well-tuned strchr() function customized to a particular
machine is usually faster than portable C. Is your
strchr() function indeed fast (okay to guess) [yes]?

Modern UNIXes can generally use the setuid() system call
to set the real and effective user ids to the current
effective user id. In old UNIXes, only "root" can change
the real user id. This causes various problems for C News.

C News provides a small program named "setnewsids" to run
setuserid-root; all it does is change user and group ids
and then execute C News "relaynews". It is needed only in

systems that are too old to do setuid(geteuid()). Relaynews
invokes it automatically if needed (and it then invokes
relaynews in return).
Can this system do setuid(geteuid()) [yes]?
> *Systems with this problem include original Version 7 systems, and*
> *possibly some older Xenix systems.*
Some systems have header files that others lack, and C News
is prepared to fake missing ones.
Does your system have an ANSI-C-conforming <stdlib.h>
            [yes]? no
Does your system have an ANSI-C-conforming <string.h>
            [yes]?
> *If you are not sure whether your system's include files are*
> *ANSI-C-conformant, just answer no.*
Does your system have <sys/timeb.h> [yes]? yes

Some old systems think sprintf() returns a value of type
"char *". The modern standard is that it returns "int".
Does your sprintf() return "char *" [no]?
> *Check your manual or /usr/include/stdio.h for this question.*

Very old UNIX systems needed the order of object modules
in a library chosen very carefully. V7 introduced
"ranlib" which removes the need for this. Recent
System Vs have had the same facility built into "ar"
(look for "symdef" in the "ar" manual page) so "ranlib"
is not needed.
Does your system have a 'ranlib' command [no]?
Does your "ar" have a "symdef" feature [yes]?

Historically the C compiler is named "cc", but this is
not true on some systems, and on others there are
several different C compilers.
What is the name of the C compiler to be used [cc]?

Historically the only normal compilation option needed
for most programs is -O, but again compilers, especially
newer ones, differ. What options should be given to the
compiler [-O]?

The final linking ("ld") step of compiling might need
an option, such as -n or -i, to produce the preferred
form of executable file. On many modern systems the
preferred form is the default. What options, if any,
should be given for linking [none]?

On unusual systems it may be necessary to link C News
programs with libraries other than the usual C library.
These can be specified as either full pathnames or
-l... options. What libraries, in addition to the one(s)
picked up automatically by the compiler, should be used
when linking C News [none]?

Does your system have a "hostname" command [yes]?

C News tries to limit the backlog of news batches
spooled up for transmission to a site, to control
use of disk space. To do this, it needs to be able
to determine the length of the queue of news batches
for a particular site. This is UUCP-version-dependent.
There is a good chance that you will have to customize
the "queuelen" program. C News knows about several versions:

    hdb   Honey DanBer, aka Basic Networking Utilities
    sub   old uucp with subdirectories
          (e.g., /usr/spool/uucp/C.)
    null don't run uucp or don't care about queue
          lengths
Which one is most appropriate [hdb]?

*If your system has a Version 2 UUCP, which does not use
subdirectories, you are going to have to customize the queuelen
program. Answer sub here, and modify the queuelen script after you
have built C News.*

C News often wants to ask how much disk space is available.
The format of output from the "df" command unfortunately
varies a lot. C News knows about several different
versions:

    bsd   4.2BSD and later
    sysv   most System Vs
    sgi   Silicon Graphics Iris systems
    ultrix DEC Ultrix 3.0 (and later) (and earlier??)
    v7   plain old style: no headers or fluff, just
           name and number
    null   don't know or don't care how much space is
           available
Which one is most appropriate [bsd]? **sysv**
Beware—test "spacefor" to make sure it works.
System V "df" formats vary widely, indeed wildly.
"Consider it standard". Sure.

*spacefor takes a size and a type, and returns the number of
"type" things ("type" can be incoming, articles, control, "outbound
for-host-name", or archive) of "size" (interpreted in bytes) that can
fit onto your disk. More documentation can be found in the newsaux
manual page.*

Some "df" commands, especially on old systems, must be
given the name of a device. Modern ones can be given
any directory name and the system handles the details
of figuring out what device is meant. Does your "df"
accept a directory name as an argument [yes]? **no**
You are going to have to customize "spacefor" for your
system. It will be generated assuming that directory
names do work.

Are you planning to use expire to archive news on disk [no]?

Are you particularly short of disk space [no]?
You may want to inspect "spacefor" to make sure its
defaults for things like desired free space are
appropriate for your system, although the defaults
are fairly conservative.

Are you running C News on a group of machines hooked
together with NFS, with articles filed on only one
"server" machine [no]?

Several programs need to know an overall name for the
system news is being run on, where "system" may include
multiple machines if they share a common set of control
files and articles; this is used in article headers and
related places. For uucp sites, this usually should be
the uucp name. What is the name of the overall system
for news purposes? ora

> *We assume here that you have followed the procedure given in*
> *Chapter 3, Setting Up a UUCP Link, to ensure that your uucp name*
> *is unique on the Usenet. Since uucp names are relative and not absolute,*
> *duplicated uucp names will cause misdirected mail and lost news.*

The "From:" lines of news postings, on the other hand,
should carry a mailing address, which in particular
should be a domain address for sites that have one.
What is the mailing-address name of this system,
preferably a domain address [ora.uucp]? ora.com

> *A domain address is a name assigned by a source of authority* and*
> *guaranteed to be unique. Acquiring a domain name is a good way to*
> *guarantee that you have a unambiguous name that can be used from many*
> *networks other than the Usenet.*

> *While the .uucp domain is not, technically, a real domain, it is*
> *generally used to specify a unique name found in the UUCP maps. It*
> *will do until you acquire a domain name from the NIC.*

What is the name of the organization, for insertion into
articles posted from here? O'Reilly and Associates, Inc.

Manual pages are normally stored in a tree structure
under /usr/man. Local practices vary a great deal,
however, and System V has also introduced some bizarre
distortions into this once-simple structure.
What is the top-level manual-page directory [/usr/man]?

C News adds manual pages to Chapters 1 (programs), 5
(files), and 8 (administrative programs). These chapter
numbers have changed in some variants of UNIX. Also,
originally pages from Chapter 5 (for example) were stored
in /usr/man/man5. This has also changed in some

---

*In this case, the Network Information Center at SRI International in Menlo Park, CA.

variants. Has your system made either of these
changes [no]? **yes**

> *Our System V system supplies no manual page sources at all, and the
> few formatted manual pages that are supplied come in pack format and
> live in strangely-named directories under /usr/catman/man1.*

You will have to hand-edit the last few lines of
doit.bin to install the manual pages where they belong
on your system.

The "rnews" and "cunbatch" commands (which are identical,
the latter being purely for backward compatibility with
seriously-old systems) have to be installed somewhere
where uucp can find them to execute them. It is not
normally necessary for users to be able to run them, so
they need not go in the directories searched for normal
commands... although uucp often searches only those
directories. What directory should "rnews" and
"cunbatch" go in [/bin]?

Our "postnews", "readnews", and "checknews" are included
mostly for completeness. They are very simple and crude
compared to the user interface many users are accustomed
to. As far as we know, B News (or other) versions should
run fine with C News. If you are already running such
user-interface software, you may not want to change.
Do you want to install our user-interface programs [yes]? **no**

The "inews" command(s) should go in one of the directories
searched for normal commands, so users can run them without
special arrangements. What directory should these
commands go in [/bin]?

For replies to control messages, C News invokes
"mail" (typically /bin/mail unless you make special
arrangements) with either an Internet-style "@"
address or a uucp-style "!" address. Internet style
is probably better... if your mailer supports it at all.
Will "mail" handle "@" addresses [no]? **yes**

The ihave/sendme protocol, although marginally useful
in some cases, is a security hole—it lets another
site ask for any article by Message-id, and if your
Message-ids are predictable enough (which C News's
generally are not, mind you), that site can get any article
currently on your system. Do you have any newsgroups
containing confidential or proprietary material [no]?

building doit.bin...
done

building doit.news...
done

```
building again.root...
done
```

```
You should now run doit.root as root, doit.bin as
root, doit.news as news, and again.root as root, in
that order.  (This assumes that the source directories
are owned by root.  If you need to do installation work
by hand, run 'doit.bin -i' as the owner; this will create
the programs but will not install them.)  Finally, you will
want to add the contents of 'cron', or something similar,
to your cron's work-to-be-done file(s), and the contents
of 'rc', or something similar, to /etc/rc or whatever your
system executes when booting.
```

```
"make gclean" will clean up everything afterwards.
"make lclean" does a less drastic cleanup affecting
only the library directories.  "make spotless" does
"make gclean" and also removes the doit files.
```

```
Good luck and happy news reading.
```

The Actual Install

Installing B News 2.11

As described earlier, simply creating *localize.sh* and typing: **make**; **make** will compile the software. (You should be sure, of course, that you have not made any errors in your editing script, and that the resulting *Makefile* and *defs.h* do in fact have the required definitions. This may save you from unnecessary worries about difficulty in porting the programs. According to the *install* document, if you get any question marks when running *localize.sh*, that probably means that the script did not work correctly.)

Once the make has completed successfully, become superuser and type:

```
# make install
```

The first part of the install procedure, run directly out of *Makefile*, actually installs the software in BINDIR and LIBDIR, as you have defined them. Generally, programs that either the user or **uux** need to invoke directly are put into BINDIR (usually */usr/bin*), while those that are invoked by other news programs are put in LIBDIR (usually */usr/lib/news*). It also changes the ownership and permissions to the values specified by NEWSUSR and NEWSGRP in the *makefile*.

Then type:

```
# make update
```

Makefile then invokes a shell script called *install.sh*, which creates various system files needed by Netnews. These files include:

- */usr/lib/news/sys*

- */usr/lib/news/active*

- */usr/lib/news/newsgroups*

- */usr/lib/news/aliases*

- */usr/lib/news/mailpaths*

- */usr/lib/news/distributions*

You may be prompted to take various actions to manually customize these files before they can be used. See the sections on these files for more information. In addition, you are warned to add the **rnews** command to */usr/lib/uucp/L.cmds* (*Permissions* in BNU).

Installing C News

The *build* shell script creates four shell scripts, which take care of building and installing the news software. The first shell script, *doit.root*, makes directories required by the news software, such as */usr/spool/news*. It should be run by root. The second one, *doit.bin*, does the actual build. Before running this script, you should **su** to the userid that will own the news programs (*bin* by default). The third script, *doit.news*, installs the news software and various system files it needs. It should be run as the news user. The last, *again.root*, corrects the permissions on some of the newly installed programs. It too should be run as root.

The system files installed by *doit.news* include:

- */usr/lib/news/active*

- */usr/lib/news/localgroups*

- */usr/lib/news/mailname*

- */usr/lib/news/mailpaths*

- */usr/lib/news/sys*

- */usr/lib/news/explist*

- */usr/lib/news/batchparms*

You may be prompted to take various actions to manually customize these files before they can be used. In addition, you are warned to add the **rnews** command to */usr/lib/uucp/L.cmds* (*Permissions* in BNU).

Let's take a look at what you need to do.

The sys File

The *sys* file should contain a line for every system to which you forward news. It should also contain a line for your own system.

Each line contains four fields:

- A system name. It can be followed by a slash and a comma-separated list of system names. If this optional subfield exists, articles which would otherwise be queued for this system will not be sent if they have already passed through one of the hosts in the subfield.

- The newsgroups to be forwarded to that system. In C News, it can be followed by a slash and a comma-separated lists of distributions, which are matched against the Distribution: header, if any, in each article. This subfield only affects article transmission, not article reception. If this subfield is not present, it defaults to the list of newsgroups.

- Flags describing the connection.

- The command to run to send news to the remote site. If left blank, this will default to the value specified for DFTXMIT in *defs.h* for B News 2.11, or **uux -****-z -r** *sysname***!rnews** for C News.

As created by *install.sh*, the B News 2.11 *sys* file should look something like this:

```
yoursys:world,comp,sci,news,rec,soc,talk,misc,na,usa,to::
oopsvax:world,comp,sci,news,rec,soc,talk, misc,na,usa,to.oopsvax::
```

The first line describes what newsgroups your site expects to receive. *yoursys* will be the actual UUCP site name of your system. The special name *ME* can be used instead; it is automatically interpreted as your local system name. The second line lists groups you expect to send back through your news feed. *oopsvax* is a dummy name that must be replaced with the actual name of your news feed. If you plan to exchange news with more than one system, there should be a line for each system.

Your news feed should also add a line describing your system to its own *sys* file. This will allow your sites to exchange all newsgroups with the prefixes shown in the second field. (As shown, this includes the seven major categories described earlier, as well as the regional distributions *na*, *usa*, and *to*.

The sample *sys* file provided by C News is somewhat more complex, though its syntax is similar. The one difference is that it allows you to specify distributions as a subfield of the newsgroups field, rather than (confusingly) mingling distribution and hierarchy names. If present, the subfield is separated by a slash, followed by the comma-separated list of distributions. If absent, the list of distributions defaults to the list of newsgroups.

As in B News 2.11, the first line describes newsgroups to be received by your site. Subsequent lines contain several possible entries for a number of different possible configurations. You should choose which one is appropriate for (each of) your news connections and comment out the rest. The sample file will look something like this:

```
# line indicating what we are willing to receive; note local groups on end
ME:comp,news,sci,rec,misc,soc,talk,to,can,ont,tor,ut

# sample insignificant feed not using batching
huey:news.config,to.huey/all::uux - -r -gd huey!rnews

# sample of mailing newsgroups to someone
# (note distribution)
daisy:soc.women,soc.couples/all::mail daisy@duck

# sample major batched feed, including (unnecessary)
# explicit file name
dewey:comp,news,sci,rec,misc,soc,talk,to.dewey,can,ont,\
tor,ut/all:f:dewey/togo

# sample long-haul feed; note no local groups
donald:comp,news,sci,rec,misc,soc,talk,to.donald/all:f:
# sample local-postings-only feed direct to major site
# (gets them out fast)
scrooge:comp,news,sci,rec,misc,soc,talk,to.scrooge/all:Lf:

# sample ihave/sendme link
# Send ihave telling louie what we have -- batcher turns
# the batch into a # giant control message and posts it to
# "to.louie".  (#1)
louie:rec.music.synth,!to/all,!sendme,!ihave:I: louie.ihave/togo
# Send sendme in response to ihave from louie --
# again, turned by batcher
# into giant control message posted to "to.louie".  (#3)
```

```
louie-send-ids:to.louie/ihave:I:louie.sendme/togo
# Transmit said giant control messages by normal
# batching.  (#2,#4)
louie-ctl:to.louie/all,!sendme,!ihave:f:louie/togo
# Send articles in response to sendme messages from
# louie. (#5)
louie-real:to.louie/sendme:f:louie/togo
# Actually the last two could be combined.
# and send local postings to louie without waiting
# (beware ihave/sendme)
louie-local:comp,news,sci,rec,misc,soc,talk/all, !sendme,!ihave:L:
```

The third line in the above example demonstrates how to mail newsgroups to someone. The distribution line is needed to make sure that all articles received at this site will be sent.

The fourth line demonstrates a usual full feed, including *all* local groups and distributions. To exclude postings to local distributions, you would have to edit the distribution field to read *all,!localdist.**

The fifth and sixth lines demonstrate two more restricted batched feeds. The rest of the sample file provides an example of *ihave/sendme* transmission. ihave/sendme is a mechanism intended to optimize news transmission by only sending articles that the remote site does not already have. The conversation between sites *daffy* and *louie* might look like this:

- *daffy: ihave <message-id1> <message-id2> <message-id3>*

- *louie: sendme <message-id1> <message-id3>*

- *daffy: batch and send to louie the requested messages.*

Further documentation can be found in *notebook/ihave*.

Limiting the number of newsgroups

Because of the volume of news, smaller sites may want to subscribe only to certain newsgroups. If you do not want your feed to pass you every newsgroup, you should ask them to modify the line describing your system in their *sys* file, placing an exclamation point before the name of each newsgroup or hierarchy that you do not want. (You can look up the names and descriptions of available newsgroups in the file *LIBDIR/newsgroups*.)

---

*We strongly recommend that you exclude the distribution *local*, and any other distributions that are local to your site. For example, the distributions subfield that we use for non-local sites is: *all,!local,!ora*

A sample "unsubscription" list is shown below (ellipses at the end indicate that the list goes on for some time):

```
ora:world,comp,sci,news,!rec,!talk,!soc,misc,ne,\
na,usa,to.ora,!comp.lang,!comp.protocols...::
```

You can also put an unsubscription list in your own *sys* file to filter out newsgroups that your news feed insists on sending you.

News transmission flags

You may also want to specify certain flags in the third field. All of the available flags are described in the *install* documentation. Those you might be most concerned with include:

- The **L** flag, which allows forwarding only of messages created at your site. This is used to ensure that you do not forward messages you receive back to a site that already has them. For example, if you are fed by a major site, you might want to set up an L feed back to them, so that messages your users post get sent to it but your system does not waste time trying to transmit messages the large site already knows about.

- The **F** flag, which is used if you plan to batch articles (see below). This flag specifies that the fourth field contains a pathname for batched articles, rather than a transmission command.

- The **f** flag in C News, which is preferred over **F**, as it allows C News to calculate the size of outgoing batches more precisely. This flag specifies that the fourth field contains a pathname for batched articles, rather than a transmission command.

You may instead want to specify an explicit transmission command in the fourth field. As mentioned above, the default command is **uux - -r -z** *sysname***!rnews,** which causes **uux** to pass its standard input to the **rnews** command on the remote system.*

The **-z** option is a patch to **uux** that causes it not to send the user mail when a job has been completed. If you are not a UNIX source licensee and cannot install this patch, you may need to specify an explicit command line here.

---

*B News 2.11 and C News allow you to use a form of **mail** to transmit news articles; however, this does not work on all systems. How to set up a mail link is described in the *install* document of B News 2.11, or the *newsmail*(8) manual page of C News.

The **-r** option specifies that outgoing new messages will not start a UUCP daemon (**uucico**) right away but instead should wait until UUCP is invoked for some other reason. Many sites wait until a specified time to transmit news and do it all at once.

You can control the frequency with which news is transmitted by UUCP by specifying in the *schedule* field of *L.sys* that **uucico** can only run at a particular time, as described in Chapter 2, *The Physical Connection*. You can also set the *schedule* field to *Any* and run **uucico** from */usr/lib/crontab* at some regular interval.

For example, to run **uucico** every hour on the hour, the *crontab* entry would read:

```
0 * * * * /usr/lib/uucp/uucico -r1
```

In some cases, you may need to poll your news feed at a particular time. Particularly if a site is feeding news to more than one other site, they may have strict time constraints on when they want to transmit to your system. So, for example, your news feed may set up UUCP so that it cannot call you between midnight and 7:30 a.m. (His dial-out line may be devoted to polling his own news feeds at that time.) In this case, you might want to poll hourly for news starting at 12:40 a.m. through 7:40.

To do this, you would put the following entry in */usr/lib/crontab*:

```
40 0,1,2,3,4,5,6,7 * * * /usr/lib/uucp/uucico -r1 feedsite
```

It is also possible to "batch" articles using the **sendbatch** script that is supplied as part of the B News 2.11 distribution. (The C News equivalent is called **sendbatches** but is otherwise similar.) When you use batching, individual articles are not spooled to **uux** for transmission. Instead a file is created in BATCHDIR (*/usr/spool/news/out.going* in C News) which contains the pathnames of files which are to be sent out to a particular system. These files are then put together into a single large message that is optionally compressed before being sent out.

To use batching, specify **F** in the third field of the *sys* file (use **f** instead for C News), and then, instead of specifying a command in the fourth field, specify the name of a file in BATCHDIR that will contain the names of files to be batched. By default, this file has the name of the system to which the batched articles will be sent.

For example, to send batched articles to a system called *venture*, you would put the following line in your *sys* file:

```
venture:world,na,usa,comp,sci,news,misc,rec,soc,talk,to.
venture:F:/usr/spool/batch/venture
```

Then you would need to run the **sendbatch** shell script from */usr/lib/crontab* in order to actually send out the articles.

In B News 2.11, this script invokes the **batch** program to create large batch files (usually 100,000 bytes) and then invokes **uux** to do the actual transmission.

sendbatch with the **-c** option compresses the files before transmission, using the **compress** program included in the Netnews distribution. (**compress** is worth the price of admission even if you do not want news. It achieves 50 to 60 percent space saving on most ASCII files.)

The syntax for **sendbatch -c** is:

```
/usr/lib/news/sendbatch -c sitename
```

To run this script from *crontab* on the hour to send batched articles to system *venture*, you could make the entry:

```
0 * * * * /usr/lib/news/sendbatch -c venture
```

Batching is probably not appropriate for a "leaf site" that mainly receives news and forwards only news that is created on site. However, for sites that pass on a large body of news, batching (especially with compression) is highly recommended.

C News has a more general and flexible mechanism for controlling news transmission. The *batchparms* file defines what programs are run to create news batches on a per-site basis. The builder (normally **batcher**) combines articles into larger batch files, which are passed to the muncher (**compcun** for compressed batches, **nocomp** for uncompressed) and finally to the sender (normally **viauux**).

The active File

The *active* file contains a list of all currently active net-wide newsgroups. It is used by **inews** to check for valid newsgroup names and to keep track of local article numbers for each article received at your site.

The contents of the *active* file should look something like this:*

```
general 0000000001 0000000001 y
misc.consumers 0000000032 0000000030 y
misc.consumers.house 0000000022 0000000021 y
misc.forsale 0000000086 0000000085 y
           .
           .
           .
```

Each line has four fields, separated by spaces. The first field is the name of the newsgroup. The second and third fields are dynamically updated as news

---

*The newsgroups shown here will likely change from time to time.

messages are received and contain, respectively, the highest local article number in that newsgroup and the lowest. (These numbers are assigned sequentially as articles are received; the highest number is therefore the most recently received article, and the lowest is the earliest article that has not yet been expired.) In B News 2.11, the fourth field contains either "y", "n", or "m" and indicates whether local users are allowed to post messages to that newsgroup. C News adds two flags: "x", which means that the group has been locally disabled, and "=*some.other.group*", which causes all articles bound for the listed group to be filed under *some.other.group* instead.

As created, most newsgroups are marked "y". No one may post to groups marked "n".* Moderated groups (see below) are marked "m".

Newsgroups are normally listed in alphabetical order. When a user invokes **read-news**, articles will be presented, newsgroup by newsgroup, in the order that they appear in *active*. For this reason, you may want to rearrange the file to put the most important newsgroups first.

If you have specified SORTACTIVE in *defs.h* (this is the default), the B News 2.11 **readnews** will actually present newsgroups in the order in which they are specified in the *.newsrc* file in each user's home directory. (The C News **readnews** does not have this feature.) However, since *.newsrc* is initially created from *active*, you can save your users a lot of trouble by doing some rearranging for them.

The problem with the B News 2.11 install procedure is that it will only bring the *active* file up to date as of the date of the Netnews software release. This may be quite out of date by the time you are doing the install. In true minimalist fashion, C News provides you with a four-line active file which defines only the *general*, *control*, *junk*, and *news.announce.newusers* newsgroups. In either case, you need to run a special script called *checkgroups* that will bring the active file into closer accord with current reality.

After typing *make update* in B News 2.11, you may get a message like this:

```
Subject: Problems with your active file

The following newsgroups are moderated and not marked so.
     misc.handicap
     news.lists
        .
        .
        .
     comp.unix
```

---

*If you have enabled the FASCIST option in B News 2.11, you can allow posting access on a per-user basis: see *doc/install.mn*. C News lacks this feature.

```
You can correct this by executing the command(s):
/usr/lib/news/inews -C misc.handicap moderated </dev/null
/usr/lib/news/inews -C news.lists moderated </dev/null
        .
        .
        .
/usr/lib/news/inews -C comp.unix moderated </dev/null
```

The output of *checkgroups* (the above message) is copied into the file */tmp/check-groups.out.* You can edit out the first part of the message, save the list of **inews** commands, and execute it as a shell script to bring your active file up to date.

However, even the *checkgroups* script included with your distribution is not completely up to date. Every month an updated list of active groups is posted to the newsgroups *news.admin.* You should get a copy of this list from your news feed or you should look for it as soon as you get up on the net.

This list is in the form of a message to system administrators and looks something like this:

```
From uunet!gatech!purdue!spaf Wed Feb  3 18:20:56 1988
Path: ora!uunet!gatech!purdue!spaf
From: spaf@cs.purdue.EDU (Gene Spafford)
Newsgroups: news.admin
Subject: Checkgroups message (without INET groups)
Message-ID: <3132@arthur.cs.purdue.edu>
Date: 3 Feb 88 23:20:56 GMT
Expires: 24 Feb 88 23:20:53 GMT
Distribution: na
Organization: Dept. of Computer Sciences, Purdue Univ.
Lines: 338
Supersedes: <2964@arthur.cs.purdue.edu>


Recent versions of news support a checkgroups control
message that can be used to help keep your active file in
sync with the "standard" Usenet groups.  What follows is
a skeleton checkgroups control message that you can
customize and run locally to check your active file.

** This version does NOT contain entries for the      **
** "inet" groups. If your site receives the inet      **
** distribution, you should receive a version of      **
** this message with all the inet groups included.    **

To run this message you must:

1) Edit this message.  Remove everything before (and includ-
ing) the first line marked with equal signs ("="), and every-
thing after (and including) the last line marked with equal
signs.
```

2) Add in lines representing any groups you receive in alternate distributions such as "alt", "bionet", or "unix-pc".
You can also add in lines for local groups, if you want.
Entries should be one per line with the newsgroup name starting in column 1. The newsgroup names should be separated from
the description (if any) by tabs. The keyword "Moderated"
should appear in any line describing a moderated group.

3) Edit the "Distribution:" header line to reflect an organizational distribution, if appropriate. DO NOT remove this
line, or change the distribution to something wider than your
organization.

4) "su" to root or your news user, and provide this
as input to the inews program with the -h option; e.g.,
"/usr/lib/news/inews -h <thisfile"

```
=^==^==^==^==^==^==^==^==^==^==^== cut to this line =^==^==^==^==^==^==^==
Newsgroups: news.admin.ctl,control
Distribution: local
Approved: spaf@cs.purdue.edu
Subject: cmsg checkgroups
Control: checkgroups

!mod
comp.ai                 Artificial Intelligence discussions.
comp.ai.digest          Artificial Intelligence discussions.\
                          (Moderated)
comp.ai.neural-nets     All aspects of neural networks.
              .
              .
              .
talk.politics.theory    Theory of politics & political systems.
talk.religion.misc      Religious, ethical, & moral implications.
talk.religion.newage    Esoteric & minority religions & philosophies.
talk.rumors       For the posting of rumors.
=^==^==^==^==^==^==^==^==^==^==^== cut from this line =^==^==^==^==^==^==^==
--
Gene Spafford
Dept. of Comp. Sciences, Purdue Univ., W. Lafayette IN 47907-2004
Internet: spaf@cs.purdue.edu uucp: ...!{decwrl,gatech,ucbvax}\
          !purdue!spaf
```

You should do as the message says: save the message in a file, clip off the header
and footer, and provide the remainder of the file as input to **inews**. This will
cause **inews** to issue a series of "newgroup" or "rmgroup" control messages at
your site. Note that the *checkgroups* message suggests that you add lines for
local groups before running it. In C News, you should add the lines for local
groups to NEWSLIB/*localgroups* instead. C News will automatically check this
file when processing a *checkgroups* message.

The control message will automatically be executed by **inews**. You will receive mail (assuming you have set up mail to "usenet" to be forwarded to yourself) that looks something like this:

```
From tim Fri Jan 17 11:11 EST 1988
Subject: Problems with your active file
Status: RO

The following newsgroups are not valid and were removed.
      rec.food.recipes
         .
         .
         .

The following newsgroups were missing and were added.
      comp.ivideodisc
      rec.games.moria
         .
         .
         .
      talk.politics.soviet
```

If you have the MANUALLY variable set in *defs.h*, the control messages will not be executed, but you will instead get mail that looks something like this:

```
From tim Mon Feb 22 16:11 EST 1988
Subject: Problems with your active file
Status: R

The following newsgroups are not valid and should be removed.
      rec.food.recipes

You can do this by executing the command:
      /work/lib/news/rmgroup rec.food.recipes

The following newsgroups were missing and should be added.
      comp.ivideodisc
      rec.games.moria
         .
         .
         .

You can do this by executing the command(s):
/work/lib/news/inews -C comp.ivideodisc </dev/null
/work/lib/news/inews -C rec.games.moria </dev/null
         .
         .
         .
```

```
The following newsgroups are moderated and not marked so.
      news.lists
      rec.guns
         .
         .
         .

You can correct this by executing the command(s):
/work/lib/news/inews -C news.lists moderated </dev/null
/work/lib/news/inews -C rec.guns moderated </dev/null
         .
         .
         .
```

You might also see these messages if the version of the *checkgroups* shell script included in your distribution is set up only to notify you rather than actually to add the groups. Look at this script (in LIBDIR for B News 2.11, in NEWSBIN/*ctl* for C News) if you have problems running the *checkgroups* control message.

It is fairly easy to save this message in a file, then edit it so that it contains only the necessary commands. The resulting script can then be run with *sh*. (Be sure to redirect *stderr* to */dev/null* so you will not have to read all the verbose messages that result.):

```
% sh savedfile >& /dev/null&      (C shell)
```

or:

```
$ sh savedfile 2> /dev/null&      (Bourne shell)
```

The newsgroups File

The *checkgroups* control message described in the last section will also update a second file in LIBDIR called *newsgroups*. This file contains a brief description of each group and is printed by **postnews** if users ask for a list of valid groups when they are trying to post a message.

The aliases File

Sometimes users make errors in posting to newsgroups. They misspell the name or make some other trivial error. In addition, when newsgroups are renamed, it takes time for the transition to spread across the entire net. The *aliases* file simply provides a mapping of bad names to the correct ones. The file should look something like this:

```
comp.os.fidonet        comp.org.fidonet
net.sources            comp.sources.misc
misc.jobs              misc.jobs.misc
rec.skydive            rec.skydiving
talk.philosophy.tech   sci.philosophy.tech
talk.religion          talk.religion.misc
talk.rumor             talk.rumors
```

Each line has two fields, separated by a tab. The first field is the incorrect newsgroup name; the second is the correct one. You may want to add aliases to this file if you find that your users are making posting errors.

This file is only used in B News 2.11. You can provide similar functionality in C News with the following command:

```
$ addgroup bad.group =good.group
```

The mailpaths File

Certain newsgroups are moderated. That is, you cannot post to them directly but must send the message to the moderator, who will post the message if it is approved. Both B News 2.11 and C News will automatically mail postings to moderated newsgroups to the moderator; earlier versions may reject the posting or just post it locally.

The *mailpaths* file should contain the address of the nearest "backbone" site. (For this purpose, it is any site which maintains an up-to-date list of moderators. The monthly postings in *news.admin* contain a list of sites which provide this service.) Earlier versions of Netnews used a local *moderators* file to list mail paths to each of the moderators. This file was almost always out of date at many sites.

When someone posts to a moderated group, the article will be forwarded to the "backbone" site, from which it will be mailed to the current moderator of the group.

The *mailpaths* file also contains the address of the nearest site that understand Internet mail addressing syntax. This is used by B News 2.11 if INTERNET is defined in *defs.h*, and by C News if you told **build** that your system cannot handle Internet mail. It allows the news software to use the "From:" line in an article for forwarding mail replies instead of the "Path:" line. (The Path header is really a list of sites through which that message passed. Though these sites (may) exchange Netnews, they do not necessarily exchange mail! Using Internet addressing gives you a much better chance that a reply will make it to the poster.)

As created by the installation procedure, the addresses found in *mailpaths* are not likely to be correct for your system:

```
backbone    %s
internet    %s
```

If your own system supports Internet addressing, leave the second line as it is. Otherwise, you should precede the *%s* on each line with the uucp address of the appropriate system. (We are assuming you are not a backbone site, or you would not be reading this!)

You can probably get the information that you need to update these addresses from your news feed. For example, on our system, the edited file looks like this:

```
backbone bloom-beacon!%s
internet %s
```

The distributions File

Not all newsgroups are net-wide. There are also a number of more local distributions. (These allow users to post messages that are only appropriate to a particular geographical area. For example, "for sale" postings are generally of limited interest to remote users.)

In B News 2.11, the *distributions* file contains the list of "local" distributions and what they mean. (This file is only used by the B News 2.11 news readers and posters; hence, C News does not create or depend upon this file.) These lines will be used to prompt the user posting news to certain groups to limit distribution of the message. As installed, the file contains:

```
local          Local to this site
regional       Everywhere in this general area
usa            Everywhere in the USA
na             Everywhere in North America
world          Everywhere on Usenet in the world
```

You should add lines describing any additional local distribution groups to which you belong. For example, a system in Massachusetts might want to add the *ne* (New England) distribution.

Again, consult with your local news feed to find out what distribution groups are appropriate for your area.

Modifications to L.cmds

The last step in the installation procedure is to add **rnews** to the list of allowable commands in the UUCP *L.cmds* file. (If you are using BNU, you need to edit the *Permissions* file; see Chapter 5, *Access and Security Considerations*, for more information.)

The file should look something like this:

```
#      @(#)L.cmds  1.3

rmail
rnews
```

Testing the News Link

You should now create a special newsgroup for posting messages directly to your news feed. This newsgroup should be called *to.system*, where *system* is the name of the news feed system.

Use **inews -C** to create the newsgroup if you are running B News 2.11. You should be running as the news user. For example:

```
$ /usr/lib/news/inews -C to.venture
```

Use **addgroup** to create the newsgroup if you are running C News. You should be running as the news user. For example:

```
$ /usr/lib/newsbin/maint/addgroup to.venture y
```

After you get a message back saying that the newsgroup has been created successfully, you should post a message to this group (using **postnews** or **Pnews**).

Your news feed should post a similar message back to you. If all goes well, you are ready to receive news.

Installing Documentation On-line

There are two types of on-line Netnews documentation that you should provide to your users:

- The manual pages provided in the *man* subdirectory of the news distribution.

- The articles on reading and posting to the net which were provided in the *doc* subdirectory of B News 2.11. If you are using C News, don't despair; a series of messages about the Usenet and how to make best use of it are posted monthly to the newsgroup *news.announce.newusers*, and you should be able to ask your upstream feed to send you copies.

There is a *makefile* in the *man* directory that will install the on-line manual pages; you can modify this file to install them in whatever location you keep manual pages on your system.

The three files in the B News 2.11 *doc* directory called *howto.mn*, *manner.mn*, and *copyright.mn* should be formatted using **nroff** and the "mn" macro package included with the distribution then posted to the group *general*:

```
$ nroff tmac.n howto.mn > howto
$ nroff tmac.n manner.mn > manners
$ postnews -e 365 days
```

Here, post the articles as described in the companion handbook, Using UUCP and Usenet. *You may want to post an initial article describing what follows. Then read each of the formatted files into separate articles using the editor's "read" command (:r in vi).*

The **-e** option to **postnews** specifies the length of time that the article should remain on the system. This overrules the default expiration period specified in *defs.h* by DFLTEXP for B News 2.11, or in NEWSLIB/*explist* for C News. This value can be specified in many ways—either as a number of days, as shown here (hours, weeks, or months can also be used), or as an explicit expiration date (e.g., January 5, 1990).

Registering Your Site

The final step in Netnews installation is to register your site by posting information about your site to the newsgroup *news.newsites*. This information needs to be in a very specific form, so that it can be added directly to the database of UUCP sites that is posted monthly in *comp.mail.maps*.

You should also post a copy to the moderator of the *comp.mail.maps* group. If you need to contact the UUCP map administrators, you can reach them at *uucpmap@rutgers.edu* or *uunet!rutgers!uucpmap*.

Your news feed should be able to supply you with detailed instructions on filling out the registration form. However, here is the general idea.

The form is as follows:

```
#N    UUCP name of site
#F    name of site's Internet mail forwarder, if any
#S    manufacturer machine model; operating system
#     & version
#O    organization name
#C    contact person's name
#E    contact person's electronic mail address
#T    contact person's telephone number
#P    organization's address
#L    latitude / longitude
#R    remarks
#U    netnews neighbors
#W    who last edited the entry ; date edited
#
sitenameremote1(FREQUENCY), remote2(FREQUENCY),
      remote3(FREQUENCY)
```

Here is an example of a completed entry for our site:

```
#N    ora
#S    Zenith 386; ISC Sys V Rel 3.2
#O    O'Reilly & Associates, Inc.
#C    Bill Love
#E    love@ora.com
#T    +1 617 354 5800
#P    90 Sherman Street, Cambridge MA 02140
#L    42 22 N / 071 06 W city
#U    bloom-beacon ccavax
#W    love@ora.com (Bill Love); Wed Aug 7 10:55:45 EDT 1991
#
ora   .ora.com(LOCAL)
ora   bloom-beacon(HOURLY+FAST), esegue(HOURLY), minya(DAILY),
      wtp(DAILY), uunet(DEMAND+FAST), z-code(DEMAND)
#
zipcode = z-code
```

Most of the comment entries are fairly straightforward, though you must be careful to follow the format exactly, since various editing scripts are used to manipulate the database. Each comment line begins with a hash mark (#) and a key letter, followed by a tab and then the comment data.

You should also be careful to enter the data in the format shown. For example, the date the entry was created should be marked by reading in the output of the system **date** command, rather than in any manually entered form.

You may have a little trouble with the latitude and longitude. If you have a news feed in your immediate geographic area, you can probably ask them. Otherwise, try calling the local library's reference desk.

The critical part of the entry is the uncommented lines at the end, which are the actual description of your UUCP connections to other sites on the net. Your system name should be in the first field, followed by a comma-separated list of all other systems with which you are connected. (This includes sites that you do not exchange news with directly but only have a UUCP link. If they are not already registered on the net, *please* make sure that their name does not conflict with that of an already registered site before placing them in your map entry. Your upstream feed should be able to help you out with this. Accidental name conflicts are one of the most common causes of lost and misdirected mail on the Usenet.)

Note the line:

```
ora    .ora.com(LOCAL)
```

This line (along with the #F line) exist to support our domain name. The first line says that the cost of passing mail to any of our internal hosts is LOCAL. If this line did not exist, **pathalias** would assume a default cost of 4000, which is too high.

The keywords in parentheses indicate a hypothetical cost of connection, calculated according to Table 8-1.

Table 8-1. Hypothetical Cost of Keyword Calculation

Keyword	Cost Factor	Description
LOCAL	25	Local area network
DEDICATED	95	High-speed dedicated
DIRECT	200	Local call
DEMAND	300	Normal call (long distance, anytime)
HOURLY	500	Hourly poll
EVENING	1800	Time-restricted call
DAILY	5000	Daily poll
WEEKLY	30000	Irregular poll
DEAD	very high	Not a usable path

Additionally, HIGH and LOW (used like DAILY+HIGH) are -5 and +5, respectively, for baud-rate or quality bonuses/penalties. FAST is -80, for adjusting costs of links which use high-speed modems (9.6Kbps or more). Arithmetic expressions can be used; however, you should be aware that the results can be counter-intuitive (e.g., (DAILY*4) means every four days, not four times a day). This is because the numbers represent "cost of connection" rather than "frequency of connection."

The line describing your connections should be followed by a single blank line, which terminates the entry.

You should update your map entry whenever you establish a new connection to another uucp site. In addition, you should update at least the date on your map entry at least once a year to show that it is still a current map entry. Failure to do so may cause your entry to be deleted.

Note that UUCP map registration is not the same as domain name registration. See Appendix F, *Frequently Asked Questions*, for more information on the Internet Domain Naming System.

9

Administering Netnews

Administering Netnews on a regular basis is not a major job, but there are some things that you will need to do. These include:

- Maintaining the list of active groups.

- Dealing with UUCP congestion.

- Creating new newsgroups.

- Setting a schedule for removing articles after their expiration date.

- Trimming *history* and *log* files.

Maintaining the List of Active Groups

Every month an updated list of active groups is posted to the newsgroup
news.admin. As described in the last chapter, in the section on setting up newsgroups, this list is in the form of a "checkgroups" message that, when executed,
will automatically update your *active* file.

You should execute the latest version of this script on a regular basis in order to
keep your *active* and *newsgroups* files up to date.

If you set the MANUALLY variable or the NONEWGROUPS variable in *defs.h*
when compiling B News 2.11, the control messages to **inews** issued by this script
will not be executed. Instead, you will simply receive mail telling you to add or
delete the specified group.

By default, C News will create any groups for which it received an additional
request but will simply notify you about any requested group deletions. If you
want to modify its behavior, you need to edit the *rmgroup* and *newgroup* scripts
found in NEWSBIN/*ctl*.

You may also periodically receive mail to *usenet* requesting that a group be
added, deleted, or renamed.

In either case, you will be given instructions on what to do.

UUCP Congestion

If you are forwarding news on to other sites, a neighboring system that is down
can cause a major UUCP bottleneck, since outgoing articles will still be spooled to
UUCP but will not be transmitted until the down system comes back on line.

This is a good argument for using batching, since you can simply disable **sendbatch** (called **sendbatches** in C News) in *crontab*. The list of articles to be
batched (in BATCHDIR for 2.11, or in NEWSSPOOL/*out.going* for C News) will
continue to grow, but the actual batching and spooling to UUCP will not occur
until you re-enable **sendbatch**. Of course, if the other site is down for so long
that you begin to expire articles that have not been batched for them yet, they will
never see those articles.

Suggested *crontab* entries for **sendbatch** and **sendbatches** follow. Choose the appropriate one.

```
40 * * * *    su news -c '/usr/lib/news/sendbatch'
40 * * * *    su news -c '/usr/lib/newsbin/batch/sendbatches'
```

Creating Newsgroups

As system administrator, you have the power to create new newsgroups. However, with the exception of local groups which you control, *do not do it without asking*. The proper procedure for creating a new newsgroup is detailed in a posting titled *How to Create a New Newsgroup*, which is posted monthly to the groups *news.admin*, *news.announce.newusers*, and *news.groups*.

Of course, you can create newsgroups with local distribution that will be read only at your site. To do this in B News 2.11, use the -C option of **inews**. (Depending on your configuration, you may need to **su** to *news* or *root* in order to execute this command.) For example:

```
$ su news
$ /usr/lib/news/inews -C ora

Please type in a paragraph describing the new newsgroup.
End with control D as usual.

/usr/lib/ncws/inews -n ora.ctl -d local -t cmsg newgroup ora

Messages of interest only to users at O'Reilly & Associates.
^D
$
```

This newsgroup will not be forwarded to other sites, since the default distribution is local. (The -**d** option to **inews** can be used to request broader distribution.)

To create a local newsgroup in C News, use the **addgroup** command. (You will need to **su** to *news* in order to execute this command.) For example:

```
# su news
$ /usr/lib/newsbin/maint/addgroup ora y
$
```

Expiring Articles

Unless you have gigabytes of optical storage, it is a certainty that your disk will shortly overflow with incoming news articles. For this reason, you need to periodically "expire" outdated articles.

Expiring Articles in B News 2.11

To expire news in B News 2.11, you should put an entry in *usr/lib/crontab* to run the program **expire** each night. The following *crontab* entry runs **expire** at 11:15 every evening:

```
15 23 * * * /usr/lib/news/expire
```

By default, articles will be expired after they have been on your system two weeks (unless you set a different value for DFLTEXP when you were installing the software). To change the aging, add the **-e** *days* option to the **expire** entry in *crontab*. For example:

```
15 23 * * * /usr/lib/news/expire -e 7
```

to expire articles after they have been around for a week.

You can also use the **-n** *newsgroups* option to expire articles in particular newsgroups. You might find it useful to run **expire** manually for a particular newsgroup if your disk is overflowing, but you do not want to change the overall expiration date.

There is even a **-f** option to expire all messages posted by a particular user. While this option is designed for those cases in which a batch of duplicate news is inadvertently posted to the net, it can be used to clear out voluminous postings by certain verbose users of the net.

Certain articles (such as those in *news.announce.newusers*) are posted with an artificially long expiration date associated with them. These articles are exempt from the normal expiration process but can be expired by using either of the **-i** or **-I** options, which force expiration.* There are also options to archive expired articles and for debugging expiration. See the *expire*(8) manual page for details.

---

*We don't suggest you do this, as the reason for the expiration dates is to ensure that information is always available to new users on your system. Another mechanism, known as the Supersedes mechanism, ensures that there is never more than one copy of each article on your system at any given time. B News 2.11 automatically takes care of this for you, unlike C News.

With news versions earlier than 2.11, it is not a good idea to run **expire** while news is coming in, since the *active* file will get corrupted by two processes trying to access it at the same time. If you are using an older version, be sure to set up the timing of your news feeds so that they do not conflict with **expire**. This problem has been fixed in B News 2.11.

Expiring Articles in C News

To expire articles in C News, you should put an entry in */usr/lib/crontab* to run the script **doexpire** (a wrapper for the **expire** program) each night. The following *crontab* entry runs **doexpire** at 12:59 every morning:

```
59 0 * * * su news -c '/usr/lib/newsbin/expire/doexpire'
```

How long articles in each group are kept and how long lines in the *history* file are kept are controlled by NEWSLIB/*explist*. Our system's *explist* file is reproduced below.

```
# hold onto history lines 28 days, nobody gets >90 days
/expired/               x     28      -
/bounds/                x     0-1-90      -

# override later defaults for some groups
rec.equestrian,rec.food.veg  x     10      -

# most groups held for a week
sci,rec,talk,soc,misc,alt    u     7       -

# real noise gets thrown away fast
junk                    x     2     -

# default: 10 days
all                     x     10    -
```

The first field contains comma-separated newsgroup names. The second field is one letter, *m*, *u*, or *x*, indicating whether the line applies only to moderated groups, only to unmoderated groups, or to both, respectively.

Certain articles (such as those in *news.announce.newusers* and *comp.mail.maps*) are posted with an artificially long expiration date associated with them. **Netnews** makes use of a mechanism known as *Supersedes* to get rid of these articles as their updates arrive, so that there is one, and only one, copy of the article on your system at any one time. To implement this mechanism in C News, you will have to add the following line to your *crontab* file:

```
45 3 * * *  su news -c '/usr/lib/newsbin/expire/super\
    kludge comp.mail.maps news.announce.newusers'
```

A future release of C News (due in early 1990) will handle this mechanism automatically (like B News 2.11), eliminating the need for this script.

Trimming History and Log Files

Three files in LIBDIR, *history*, *log*, and *errlog*, are used to keep track of **Netnews** activity. These files rapidly grow quite large and may need to be trimmed. *DON'T FORGET THIS!*

history contains a record of every article that has been received by your system. This is used by the news system to decide which articles have already been received and should be rejected. (This is especially important when your system has multiple news feeds.) **expire** cleans out this file when articles are deleted; however, it may be wise to check it occasionally to make sure that it is in fact being trimmed. Lines in a B News 2.11 *history* file look like this:

```
<2587@hub.UUCP> 624784558   comp.sys.mac.programmer/1005
```

Each line contains the message id, followed by the date and time received (in UNIX *ctime*() format), and then the newsgroup name and local message number.

The C News version would look like:

```
<2587@hub.UUCP> 624784558-¯  comp.sys.mac.programmer/1005
```

Older news versions would look like:

```
<2587@hub.UUCP> 89/10/25 21:38:14   comp.sys.mac.programmer/1005
```

log is a log of actual news activity. It may be helpful for you to scan it when there are problems with news. (Before looking in *log*, look in *errlog*, which lists the most important error messages; you can go to *log* for additional details if necessary.) Messages in a B News 2.11 *log* file look something like this:

```
Oct 25 21:38      bloom-beacon      received <6109@portia.\
   Stanford.EDU> ng comp.unix.i386 subj 'Re: Cache \
   performance on 386 boards running Unix' from dhinds\
   @portia.Stanford.EDU (David Hinds)
Oct 25 21:38      bloom-beacon      received <6779@sybase.\
   sybase.com> ng comp.databases subj 'Re: Sybase\
   Questions' from rhoda@mercury.sybase.com (Rhoda Neimand)
Oct 25 21:38      bloom-beacon      received <2398@convex.UUCP>\
   ng comp.sys.amiga.tech subj 'Re: Flick-Off Flicker\
   Fixer' from swarren@eugene.uucp (Steve Warren)
```

The C News variant looks like this:

```
Oct 18 08:11:17.071 bloom-beacon + <964@maxim.erbe.se>\
    mit-eddie tut.cis.ohio-state.edu think bu-cs apple uunet usc
Oct 18 08:11:18.039 mit-eddie - <964@maxim.erbe.se> duplicate
Oct 18 08:13:59.219 tut.cis.ohio-state.edu + <11969@\
    eerie.acsu.Buffalo.EDU> bloom-beacon mit-eddie think apple usc
Oct 18 08:15:51.765 bloom-beacon + <15213@bloom-beacon.\
    MIT.EDU> mit-eddie tut.cis.ohio-state.edu think apple uunet usc
```

In B News 2.11, the *log* and *errlog* files do not get trimmed automatically, and can grow quite large very quickly. You may want to truncate these files weekly from *crontab*. B News 2.11 provides a script called *trimlib*, which can be found in the *misc* directory.

For example (assuming that you have moved *trimlib* to */usr/lib/news*), the line:

```
15 2 * * 0  /usr/lib/news/trimlib
```

will trim the logfile at 2:15 every Sunday morning. (*trimlib* does not just empty the logfile; this you could do by copying */dev/null* to it. Instead it saves a portion of the old entries to maintain continuity.)

In C News, the *log* and *errlog* files and various other files, are managed by the *newsdaily* and *newswatch* scripts. Suggested *crontab* entries are below.

```
10 8 * * *        su news -c '/usr/lib/newsbin/maint/ newsdaily'
00 5,13,21 * * *  su news -c '/usr/lib/newsbin/maint/ newswatch'
```

Creating Recordings

B News 2.11 includes a facility for specifying warning messages that will be displayed to users whenever they try to post to a particular newsgroup.

The file *recordings*, if present in LIBDIR, is searched for a list of such recording messages. Each line in this file has two fields separated by a space: the name of a newsgroup and the name of a file containing a recording for that newsgroup. If the filename does not begin with a slash, it is searched for in LIBDIR. For example:

```
unix% cat /usr/lib/news/recordings
comp.ai ai.r
```

This line tells **inews** to display the message contained in the file *ai.r* whenever someone tries to post to the newsgroup *comp.ai*. The file *ai.r* might contain the following message:

```
Be sure not to give away any company trade secrets when
posting to this group!
```

The file *recordings* does not exist by default. You must create it.

The presence of a recording does not prevent a user from posting to a group; it simply displays the warning. The user can go on simply by pressing RETURN or can quit **postnews** if the recording has raised second thoughts.

Unbatching News Articles

C News allows you to delay the actual unpacking of news articles until any time you find convenient. The following *crontab* entries will unpack news articles every 15 minutes between 5 p.m. and 8 a.m. on weekdays and around the clock on weekends.

```
15 * * * *       su news -c '/usr/lib/newsbin/input/newsrun'
30 8 * * 1-5     su news -c '/usr/lib/newsbin/input/newsrunning off'
00 17 * * 1-5    su news -c '/usr/lib/newsbin/input/newsrunning on'
```

Obtaining Additional Software

There are a number of additional software packages that you may want to add to your system. These include:

- **rn, vn, nn**, *GNUS*, *Gnews*, and **notesfiles**, all alternate interfaces for reading news. (We highly recommend **rn** and *GNUS*, but each of these programs has its own group of fans.)

- **pathalias,** a program for processing the database of UUCP sites that is posted monthly to *comp.mail.maps*.

- **smail,** a program that allows users to address mail to remote sites using abbreviated pathnames (*site!user*) or Internet addresses (*user@site.do.main*). **smail** automatically looks up the proper address in the database processed by **pathalias**.

- **arbitron** and **inpaths** are two small programs that collect news statistics. They are posted monthly in *comp.sources.d*. The results are posted monthly in *news.lists*.

Read the newsgroup *comp.sources.unix*, and talk to your news feed about getting access to these programs.

Keeping Up to Date

Helpful hints on news administration are posted in the group *news.admin*. You should read this newsgroup (and other subgroups in the *news* group) regularly in order to keep up to date. In particular, comments on, discussion about, and patches for the news software are found in the group *news.software.b*.

10

NNTP: Transferring News Over the Network

What Is NNTP and Why Do We Care?
Configuring, Compiling, and Installing
   NNTP
Administering NNTP
For More Information

What Is NNTP and Why Do We Care?

NNTP stands for Network News Transfer Protocol. It defines the way that machines connected by high-speed networks such as TCP/IP or DECNet exchange news, much as SMTP (Simple Mail Transfer Protocol) defines how such machines exchange mail. NNTP makes more efficient use of the capabilities of a TCP/IP network than kludges like running UUCP over TCP (although the latter has been done!).

NNTP can be used for machine-to-machine transfer of news between two news servers (defining a news server as a machine that is running the B or C News software). In this function, it acts as a replacement for UUCP. NNTP can also be used to allow users on other TCP/IP connected machines to read news directly from a remote news server, without transferring the articles to their machine's disk. This allows organizations to consolidate news onto one machine without having to give every user who wants to read news an account on the news machine.

NNTP over the Internet has drastically reduced the amount of time needed to propagate an article over the Usenet. Five years ago, it was not unusual for an article to take weeks to propagate to leaf nodes on the net. Now, an article can be spread across the Internet-connected Usenet sites in less than an hour, and most leaf sites will receive it in less than three days.

NNTP also allows sites to "screen" news being offered to them by their neighbors. It checks to see if a message has already been recieved by the local site before accepting it from a remote site. This reduces the amount of news processing done by sites with multiple feeds, and the amount of network bandwidth used to send news.

A further benefit is that NNTP is not limited to UNIX systems. While this chapter focuses on the UNIX implementation, NNTP can also be used to provide Usenet news services on DEC VMS machines, or on IBM mainframes running VM. Because NNTP is a protocol, not a piece of software, it could conceivably be implemented for just about any operating system.

A Walk Through an NNTP System

The NNTP software for UNIX consists of several C programs and a couple of shell scripts. The two most important are **nntpd**, the NNTP daemon (also referred to as "the NNTP server") and **nntpsend**. Let's trace the flow of news through an NNTP system and see how they're used. Figure 10-1 shows the flow using B News. Figure 10-2 shows the same flow for C News.

The NNTP daemon, **nntpd**, is the workhorse of the NNTP suite. It handles incoming connections, allowing remote users to read and post news and other sites to send news. News comes in through the NNTP daemon, which sends it through *rnews* (for B News systems), or writes it into appropriately-sized batch files (for C News systems).

nntpsend and its auxiliary program **nntpxmit** are equivalent to the **sendbatch** and **sendbatches** programs (B and C News respectively); they process the batch files created by the news system into articles that are ready to be sent to neighboring sites. **nntpsend** is intended to be run periodically by *cron*. The **nntpsend** script is distributed in C shell and Bourne shell versions. A Perl version has also been posted to the net. While it's not included in the NNTP distribution, you may be able to find it at some archive sites.

The method of news transmission we have just described—where each site contacts its neighbors periodically and offers articles to them—is sometimes called the "push" method of news transmission, since the sender is the one initiating the transaction. **nntpxfer,** another program provided with the NNTP suite, instead implements the "pull" method of transfer; your site runs it periodically, telling it what remote site to connect to and what articles you would like it to transfer to your site.

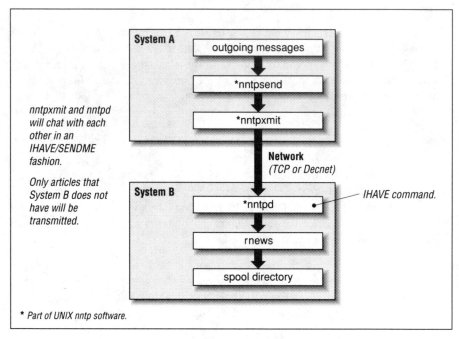

Figure 10-1. News flow using NNTP and B News

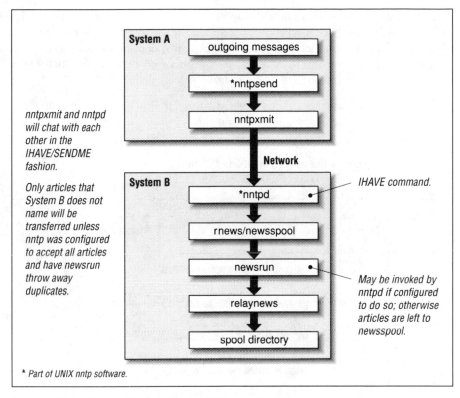

Figure 10-2. News flow using NNTP and C News

The pull method demonstrates the transaction-oriented nature of NNTP, which is somewhat concealed by the batching in the push method. NNTP provides a list of interactive commands that can be exchanged between news clients and news servers. For example:

NEWNEWS   Send me a list of new news articles.

HEAD   Send me the header for an article.

ARTICLE   Send me the article I just asked for by number.

NEXT   Send me the next article in the current newsgroup.

LIST   Send me a list of valid newsgroups.

POST   Post the following article according to its headers.

IHAVE   I have a particular article; do you want it?

When **nntpxfer** connects to an NNTP server, it first asks for a list of new articles in any newsgroups that are typically received at the local site. After receiving the list, it asks, article by article, for those articles that it doesn't already have. (This is very different from the standard news transmission method, in which entire batches of news are transmitted, and duplicate articles discarded.)

nntpxmit also implements an interactive session, but it is a simpler one, in which **nntpxmit** says "IHAVE <article_id>" and the receiving **nntpd** says either "OK send it" or "No, I have that one."

Figure 10-3 illustrates the news flow using the pull model.

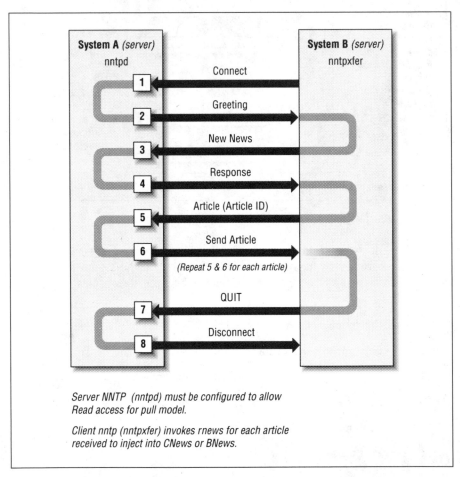

Figure 10-3. The pull model of netnews transfer

While the pull method sounds as though it might be more efficient, **nntpxfer** tends to be very hard on the remote sites that feed news. Many heavily-loaded sites would rather feed you five hundred newsgroups in the conventional fashion than ten via **nntpxfer**.

The pull method of transfer is also used by news reader programs that support NNTP, but because they don't typically transfer many articles at one time, they don't cause anything like the same system load. This is where NNTP really shines.

Configuring, Compiling, and Installing NNTP

The version of NNTP that is current as of this writing (November, 1991) is 1.5.11. NNTP 2.0 is expected in the second quarter of 1992, and will be a complete rewrite based on Version 2 of the NNTP protocol.

Getting and Unpacking the NNTP Sources

The current sources can be picked up by anonymous uucp (or ftp) to uunet. They are in the form of a compressed *tar* file:

```
$ uucp uunet!~ftp/news/nntp.1.5.11.tar.Z /usr/spool/uucppublic
```

If you are planning to run NNTP on a machine running Interactive System Corporation's 386/ix Version 2.2, you will want to pick up this set of patches as well:

```
$ uucp uunet!~ftp/news/nntp.isc.shar.Z /usr/spool/uucppublic
```

(These patches are probably useful for other versions of 386/ix, and may be useful for other System V systems as well.)

First, copy the file to the place where you want to keep the sources. Then uncompress and untar them:

```
$ mkdir /src/nntp
$ cp /usr/spool/uucppublic/nntp.1.5.11.tar.Z /src/nntp
$ cd /src/nntp
$ uncompress nntp.1.5.11.tar.Z
$ tar xovf nntp.1.5.11.tar
x common/Makefile, 222 bytes, 1 tape blocks
x common/README.IRIX, 833 bytes, 2 tape blocks
x common/conf.h.dist, 11155 bytes, 22 tape blocks
  .
  .
```

This will produce seven directories, a *Makefile*, and a handful of *README* files.

The directories are:

- *common*. Contains the configuration file and routines that are common to all the programs in the NNTP suite.

- *doc*. Contains man pages for various NNTP programs, and RFC977, the paper that defines the NNTP protocol.

- *inews*. Contains sources for the mini-inews that is needed to allow NNTP clients to post.

- *server*. Contains the sources for the NNTP daemon, *nntpd*.

- *support*. Contains sources for support programs and scripts.

- *xfer*. Contains sources for the "news-pulling" transfer program.

- *xmit*. Contains sources for the "news-pushing" transfer program.

If you're using the ISC patches, you'll need to uncompress them and then delete the top six lines from the file with your favorite text editor. Then do the following:

```
$ mv nntp.isc.shar /src/nntp (or wherever you've put the NNTP sources)
$ cd /src/nntp
$ /bin/sh nntp.isc.shar
Entering directory 'server'
shar: extracting 'timer.c' (4008 characters)
shar: extracting 'subnet.c' (6645 characters)
   .
   .
```

This patch updates five files: *server/timer.c*, *server/subnet.c*, *xmit/nntpxmit.c*, *xmit/remote.c*, and *xfer/nntpxfer.c*.

Configuring NNTP

Once you've unpacked the sources (and the ISC patch if you need it), read the top-level *README* file, which will give you an overview of the installation process that we will be detailing in this section.

Installing NNTP is a five-step process:

1. Edit *common/conf.h*.

2. Run **make server** or **make client**, as appropriate. (We'll explain which you want, and when, later.)

3. Run **make install_server** or **make install_client**, as appropriate.

4. Add NNTP to the */etc/services* and */etc/inetd.conf* network configuration files.

5. Install the *nntp_access* file, which allows you to control the level of access granted to various systems and networks.

Editing common/conf.h

The *conf.h* file gives you control over various compile-time options for NNTP. Edit this file before starting the build. The various options in *conf.h* are documented in *common/README*.

You should probably print the README file out (or keep it in a separate window if you're on a workstation) and edit *conf.h* as you read through it. You should also see README.SYSV if you are compiling NNTP on a System V machine, as there is some extra stuff you need to do. There are also separate README files for MTXINU, IRIX, XENIX, and HP/UX systems.

While the README file is quite thorough, there are a number of possible gotchas, and a few areas that deserve a bit of expansion:

*   According to Stan Barber, the most frequent configuration questions have to do with the NDIR parameter, and System V support. (NDIR is automatically defined if USG is defined.) The README file announces that if your system doesn't support the *readdir()* system call, NNTP will use the ndir compatibility library . . . but it neglects to mention where you can obtain that library. It is available via anonymous ftp from *bcm.tmc.edu* in the */unisys* directory under the filename *ndir.shar*. It can also be retrieved via the archive server. Send mail to *archive-server@bcm.tmc.edu* and place the following text in the "Subject:" line:

    ```
    send unisys ndir.shar
    ```

    For more information on anonymous ftp, see Appendix F, *Frequently Asked Questions*.

*   You must build NNTP with the same news history file format as you built your original B or C News software. The default is USGHIST, which uses the USG (System V) history file format. If you want to use a DBM, NDBM, or DBZ-style database for the history file, you must make the appropriate define.* If it is not the same one you chose when building news, NNTP will not work.

---

*DBM is a database file format supplied with BSD 4.2. It was replaced by the more efficient NDBM format in BSD 4.3. DBZ is a format supplied with C News.

This portion of our configuration file looks like this:

```
#define NDBM    /* Use new-style (4.3) ndbm(3x) library */
#undef  DBM     /* don't use the old dbm(3x) library */
#undef  DBZ     /* don't use the dbz library */
#undef  USGHIST /* we don't want a USG-style history file */
```

- The current implementation of NNTP has not been ported to SVR4. The necessary fixes *may* be in the next interim release (1.6).

- The configuration file allows you to specify the location in the filesystem of various NNTP and news files (usually in */usr/lib/news*). You should generally not need to relocate the files—but if you changed the locations during news installation, be sure to change them here as well.

- If you wish to use the authorization feature of NNTP, see the section, *Requiring Authentication*, later in this chapter.

Building NNTP

As we mentioned earlier, the compilation and installation of NNTP is divided into two parts—one for a "server" and one for a "client". What's the difference? A server (for the purposes of this software) is a machine that has the NNTP version of the news software (either B News 2.11 or C News) installed on it. A client is any machine that someone may use to read and post news remotely.

A single machine may be both a server and client, and many sites configure their machines this way deliberately, so that the newsreading software can be consistent across all machines.

Everyone installing NNTP will need to build the server portion for their news machine. If you intend to use remote news readers, then you will need to compile the client software for your remote systems. Because there are so many news readers that now support NNTP, we won't describe how to compile them all here; see the documentation distributed with each news reader. Be aware that you may need to recompile them with NNTP support if you are just adding NNTP to your news site.

Before you start building the software, check the top-level *Makefile*. Depending on choices you made in *conf.h*, you may also need to make changes here. (Necessary changes are documented in *conf.h*, where appropriate.) For example, if you defined DBZ in *common/conf.h*, in order to use the DBZ news history file format provided with C News, you will need to add *-lcnews* (or the pathname to the compiled C News library) to the LIBS define. That is, change:

```
LIBS=-ldbm
```

to:

```
LIBS=-lcnews
```

Also, some System V machines may keep networking functions in a separate library, which will also have to be added to that line of the *Makefile*. For example, our Interactive 386/ix machine needs to add *-linet* to LIBS so that the daemon can compile.

Running a **make server** builds the programs in the *server, support, doc, xmit,* and *xfer* subdirectories. Running a **make client** will build the *inews* and *doc* subdirectories. If everything is built cleanly, do a **make install_server** or **make install_client**.

Installing the nntp_access file

When the software installation has been completed, copy *support/access_file* to */usr/lib/news/nntp_access*. As distributed, the file will allow any site to transfer news, but not read or post. You must edit the file to add appropriate permissions for the hosts and networks you support. Details of how to do this are given below, in the section *Administering NNTP*.

Adding NNTP to the list of network services

TCP sites (that is, most NNTP users) must remember to add a line to their */etc/ services* file which looks like this:

```
nntp      119/tcp   readnews    # Network News Transfer Protocol
```

If your system uses **inetd**, you must also add a line to */etc/inetd.conf*. The entry looks like this for BSD 4.3:

```
nntp    stream  tcp    nowait  root    /etc/nntpd    nntpd
```

and like this for 4.2 BSD machines:

```
nntp    stream  tcp    nowait /etc/nntpd    nntpd
```

Don't forget to restart **inetd**. Use **kill -HUP** (or kill it outright, and restart it on SunOS versions prior to 4.1).

If you aren't running *inetd*, you must be sure to define ALONE in *common/conf.h* before building the software. It is also recommended that you define FASTFORK to improve the performance of a standalone server. In addition, if you are using a standalone server (i.e., one not started by *inetd*), you will need to edit */etc/rc.local* to start */etc/nntpd* directly.

See *server/README* for details if you are running DECnet.

Testing the News Server

Once the **nntpd** daemon is installed and running, you can test the new news server by telnetting to it:

```
% telnet ora nntp
Trying...
Connected to ora.ora.com.
Escape character is '^]'.
201 ora NNTP[auth] server version 1.5.11 (10 February 1991) \
ready at Sun Apr  707:21:42 1991 (no posting).
help
100 This server accepts the following commands:
ARTICLE     BODY         GROUP
HEAD        LAST         LIST
NEXT        POST         QUIT
STAT        NEWGROUPS    HELP
IHAVE       NEWNEWS      SLAVE

Additionally, the following extension is supported:

XHDR        Retrieve a single header line from a range of articles.

Bugs to Stan Barber (Internet: nntp@tmc.edu; UUCP: ...!bcm!nntp)
.
quit
205 ora closing connection.  Goodbye.
Connection closed by foreign host.
%
```

If that works, try firing up an NNTP news reader and testing it some more. Also, if you have already lined up someone who is willing to feed you news via NNTP, ask them to send some articles to you to test the link. Pay attention to the **nntplog** (if you defined LOG when configuring NNTP) as well as the news logs. This should let you know whether news is being transferred successfully.

Administering NNTP

The final stage of setting up NNTP is also the first stage of administering it: using the *nntp_access* file to specify the level and type of access to be granted to each system. Depending on how restrictively you use this file, you may need to update it whenever your network changes.

Granting Access to Systems and Networks

The *nntp_access* file contains a table of host or network names, together with the type of access granted to each host or network. There are four whitespace-separated fields:

```
host/network    read/xfer/no    post/no   newsgroup_mask
```

- The first field contains the host or network name. For individual hosts, you can use a fully-qualified domain name, like *isla.oraca.ora.com*, or you can use * as a wildcard to indicate any host in the specified domain. For example, *.ora.com* would mean any host in the *ora.com* domain. A wildcarded hostname is, in effect, a name for a network of hosts. However, you can also use any network names defined in the local host's network alias database, */etc/networks*. You can also use an IP number for a host or a network; however, due to a bug in NNTP release 1.5.11, you can't use both host/network names and numbers in the same file. (This may be fixed in release 1.6.)

- The second field contains one of the three keywords **read, xfer,** or **no.** This defines the set of NNTP commands that the specified network or host will be allowed to execute. Specifying **read** grants the broadest permission; it means that the host in question can execute commands to transfer or read news. If you specify **xfer,** the host in question can issue only commands having to do with the transfer of news, such as NEWNEWS, IHAVE, and ARTICLE. Specifying **no** refuses all NNTP commands from the host in question.

- The third field defines whether a host has permission to post news. The possible values are **post** and **no.** You must specify **read** permission in the second field in order to specify **post** in the third. Specifying:

```
bogus.com    no    post
```

is the same as specifying:

```
bogus.com    no    no
```

- The fourth field is an optional, comma-separated list of newsgroup names, preceded by an exclamation point. The host in question cannot read or transfer articles in any of the newsgroups specified in the list. (By default, if a host has read or xfer access, it can read all newsgroups.)

For example, the following line says that system *undergrad.bogus.edu* will be unable to read or post to groups *alt.sex* or *alt.drugs*.

```
undergrad.bogus.edu    read    post !alt.sex,alt.drugs
```

Any text following a hash mark (#) is interpreted as a comment, and is ignored.

The first entry in the *nntp_access* file must always specify the keyword **default** in the host/network field. This entry specifies the permissions for any system that doesn't match any other line in the file.

As distributed, the first entry looks like this:

```
# by default, let anyone transfer news, but not read or post
default                 xfer          no
```

The order of the remaining entries is significant. The more specific the host/network matching, the earlier the entry should appear. For example, if you were giving specific permissions to the host *widgets.acme.com*, you would put that entry before the generic entry for **.acme.com*.

A more specific entry will take precedence over a general one. For example, an entry for a particular host will take precedence over an entry for the network to which the host belongs.

The NNTP daemon reads the file at the start of each session with a client, so there is no need to restart the daemon after editing the file.

Requiring authentication

The NNTP 2.0 specification (still under development) includes an authentication facility, which is available on an experimental basis in the current release. When this facility is used, clients connecting to the NNTP server must provide an id and password before they can execute certain classes of commands.

Currently, only **nntpxmit** and **inews** support authentication. Therefore, you should not plan to use this facility with sites fed with **nntpxfer** or sites using only NNTP-compliant news readers to read and post news remotely.

To use authentication, you must take the following five steps:

1. Make sure the AUTH variable is defined in the *conf.h* file before building the software. (It is defined by default.)

2. In *nntp_access*, capitalize the access keywords for any services for which authentication will be required. For example, the following entry allows

anyone in the domain *roadrunner.edu* to read or post news, but only after supplying their id and password:

```
*.roadrunner.edu          Read           Post
```

The following entry requires authentication only for posting:

```
*.roadrunner.edu          read           Post
```

There is one other change in the semantics of the *nntp_access* file if authentication is used. Without authentication, **read** access is considered a superset of **xfer**. However, with authorization, you must use the keyword **Both** in order to grant both read and xfer access.

3. Create */etc/passwd* entries for each NNTP client host, assigning them a user id and password that you agree on with the remote system's administrator (assuming you don't control both systems). **nntpd** will read the password file when it first starts up a session with a host for whom authentication is required in *nntp_access*.

    The shell field of the */etc/passwd* entry is not used by **nntpd** when it reads the file. However, for additional security, you should probably supply some innocuous command, such as */bin/sync*. That way, even if the password is compromised, no harm will be done.

4. Create an **nntp** group in the */etc/group* file, listing each system that will be using the authentication mechanism when connecting to your NNTP news server. For example:

```
nntp:*:75:
```

5. Set up an authentication file on each *client* system that will be connecting to a server requiring authentication. This file should contain an entry for each server to which the client will connect with the format:

```
nntp_server userid password
```

That is, if one of your NNTP-based news feeds requires authorization, you will need to set up this file on your system. If you require it of someone to whom you feed news, they will have to set it up there.

For example, the authentication file on system *ora*, describing its connection to NNTP servers *ccavax.camb.com* and *bloom-beacon.mit.edu* might look like this:

```
cca.camb.com  oranntp givemenews
bloom-beacon.mit.edu  oranntp iwantitnow
```

The location of the authentication file is defined in *common/conf.h* as PASSFILE. By default, the file is */etc/nntp.sys*.

Because the user id and password are given in plain text, you should protect this file using mode 600, just as you do the UUCP files *L.sys* or *Systems*. The file should be owned by *usenet* or whatever user id you use for news:

```
# chown usenet /etc/nntp.sys
# chmod 600 /etc/nntp.sys
```

Sample nntp_access file

The example below provides an example of an *nntp_access* file that demonstrates many of the considerations described in the previous sections.

```
#
# host/net        read/xfer/no     post/no      newsgroup mask
#
# by default, don't let anyone do anything
default                  no          no
# allow anyone in your local domain (e.g. acme.com) to read and post
# without authentication.
*.acme.com          read        post
# allow anyone in another domain (e.g. roadrunner.edu) to read and post
# but authentication must be used (assumes that you have compiled it into
# the server). Notice that the first letter is capitalized.
*.roadrunner.edu Read        Post
# allow an nntp partner to xfer, but nothing else. In this case,
# authentication is not used.
nntp.friend.com        xfer         no
# Prevent another site from reading certain newsgroups. In this case,
# this site will be unable to read groups alt.sex or alt.drugs.
abernathy.chronical.com read      post         !alt.sex,alt.drugs
# Due to a bug in the current server (1.5.11), you can't mix addresses
# and names in the same access file, so the next line will not currently
# work, but this does show the format.  The bug will be fixed in 1.6.
128.42                  read        no
# The line above matches on the basis of IP address and not the domain
# name.  This is useful when the DNS for that network is not set up to do
# reverse lookups.
```

Log Files

If logging is enabled in *common/conf.h**, *nntpd* will keep a log file describing the news transfers it executes. Defining SYSLOG will log error messages only; if you define LOG as well, *nntpd* will also log a variety of status messages (up to 100K/day on a busy system); defining IHAVE_DEBUG in addition will produce even more voluminous messges. (It is useful only if you suspect a site is repeatedly offering the same article to your site after you have rejected it.)

SYSLOG is defined by default in *common/conf.h*; LOG is not. For both types of logging, your *common/conf.h* file ought to include the following lines:

```
#define SYSLOG   LOG_NEWS

#ifdef SYSLOG   /* Define LOG if you want copious info */
#define   LOG /* undef it if you don't; but you can */
#endif          /* only have LOG if you have SYSLOG */
```

If you don't want any logging, undef SYSLOG.

Normally, error and status logging is handled via the UNIX *syslog* facility; the location of the log file is specified via the standard syslog configuration file */etc/syslog.conf*.

The *syslog* facility allows you to write messages of varying severity into different log files, to forward the messages to another host, to write them to a list of administrators, and so on. (See *syslog.conf*(5) in your system's UNIX reference manual for details.)

For typical usage, simply put the following line in */etc/syslog.conf*.

```
news.debug              /usr/lib/news/nntplog
```

If your system doesn't support the *syslog* facility, define SYSLOG (and optionally LOG) as described above when configuring NNTP, but also define FAKESYSLOG as the name of a file to which *nntpd* will write its logs directly. For example:

```
#define FAKESYSLOG      "/usr/lib/news/nntplog"
```

If LOG is enabled as well as SYSLOG, the log file includes the time and date of each session, the number of articles transferred, and the number rejected, and the elapsed time. Here's a small section from a representative log file:

```
Nov 12 14:35:31 localhost nntpd[11442]: snorkelwacker.mit.edu \
   ihave_stats accepted 0 rejected 41 failed 0
Nov 12 14:35:31 localhost nntpd[11442]: snorkelwacker.mit.edu \
   times user 0.310 system 0.650 elapsed 41.000
Nov 12 14:37:16 localhost nntpxmit[11461]: cca.camb.com stats \
   38 offered 38accepted 0 rejected 0 failed
Nov 12 14:37:17 localhost nntpxmit[11461]: cca.camb.com xmit \
   user 1.867 system 2.383 elapsed 132.000
Nov 12 14:37:46 localhost nntpd[11487]: bloom-beacon.mit.edu \
   connect
Nov 12 14:40:55 localhost nntpd[11487]: bloom-beacon.mit.edu \
   ihave_stats accepted 90 rejected 0 failed 0
Nov 12 14:40:55 localhost nntpd[11487]: bloom-beacon.mit.edu \
   times user 4.590 system 7.090 elapsed 189.000
Nov 12 14:44:42 localhost nntpd[11658]: snorkelwacker.mit.edu \
   connect
Nov 12 14:45:23 localhost nntpd[11658]: snorkelwacker.mit.edu \
   ihave_stats accepted 0 rejected 57 failed 0
```

```
Nov 12 14:45:23 localhost nntpd[11658]: snorkelwacker.mit.edu \
    times user 0.370 system 1.090 elapsed 42.000
```

As with all log files, you should make arrangements to truncate the nntp logs on a
regular basis, perhaps with an entry in a *crontab* file.

Note that there is a useful *awk* script in the *support* directory, called *nntp_awk*,
that can be used to produce a summary report from the log file.

Here's an example of how to use the script, and the resulting output:

```
% awk -f nntp_awk /usr/lib/news/syslog

NNTP peer article transfers

Article Reception (they contact us)
System                 Offered  Took  Toss  Fail Toss    Elapsed        CPU  Pct
cca.camb.com                11     0     0     0   0%    0:00:10    0:00:05  51%
bloom-beacon.mit.edu      1632  1501   131     0   8%    0:45:20    0:03:58   9%
snorkelwacker.mit.edu     2456   367  2089     0  85%    0:44:21    0:02:25   5%

TOTALS                    4099  1868  2220     0  54%    1:29:51    0:06:29   7%

Article Transmission (we contact them)
System                 Offrd   Took  Toss  Fail  Pct    Elapsed        CPU  Pct
cca.camb.com            1813   1733    80     0   4%    1:21:34    0:03:02   4%
news.uu.net                6      2     4     0  67%    0:00:17    0:00:01   9%

TOTALS                  1819   1735    84     0   5%    1:21:51    0:03:04   4%

Transmission Connection Attempts       ------errors-------
System                 Conn     OK    NS   Net   Rmt  Pct
cca.camb.com             76     76     0     0     0   0%
news.uu.net               5      5     0     0     0   0%

TOTALS                   81     81     0     0     0   0%

NNTP readership statistics
System                 Conn Articles Groups Post    Elapsed        CPU  Pct

TOTALS                    0        0      0    0   0:00:00    0:00:00   0%

Unknown NNTP server explorers
System                 Conn
opal.ora.com              1

Newsgroup Request Counts (by category)
ne                          10
rec                         59
soc                          3
misc                       120
comp                       649
news                         1
```

```
Newsgroup Request Counts (by newsgroup)
comp.sys.mac.games          2
comp.sources.mac            1
comp.sys.next.program      13
comp.os.xinu               47
misc.books.technical      113
rec.arts.startrek.info      1
            .
            .
            .
comp.sources.unix           1
```

For More Information

For more information on NNTP, see RFC977, "A Proposed Standard for the Stream-Based Transmission of News" by Brian Kantor and Phil Lapsley, available in the file *doc/rfc977.txt* in the NNTP distribution.

A

Working Files

Work Files
Data Files
Execute Files
Temporary Receive Files
Lock Files
System Status Files
Log Files
Statistics Files
Sequence File
Audit File

When a user sends a job request to UUCP, a number of system files are created and used by the **uucico** program in the directory */usr/spool/uucp* (referred to in this appendix as the *spool directory*). Some contain instructions for **uucico** and some are used to reserve devices and hold data during file transfers. Others contain log, status, and error records. We refer to them as *working files*. They are listed in the table below.

In Table A-1, we have shown the filenames and locations as used in Version 2 UUCP. These files may be named or located differently in BNU and 4.3 BSD. Throughout the appendix, we have tried to indicate differences between Version 2 and BNU wherever possible.

Table A-1. Format and Use of Working Files

File	Filename Format	Use
Work files	C.*xxxx*	Contain instructions for **uucico** on which system to contact, the type of transfer, and where the file will be sent.
Data files	D.*xxxx*	Contain copies of source files for **uucico** to transfer. Created when you use the -**C** option (default in Version 7 and other UUCPs) or when you send mail to another system.
Execute files	X.*xxxx*	Contain work orders for commands to be executed locally by **uuxqt** on behalf of a remote system.
Temporary receive files	TM.*xxxx*	Hold data during file transfers.
Lock files	LCK..*dev*, LCK..*sys*, LCK.*file*	Prevent multiple attempts to use the same device, system, and files.
System status files	STST.*xxxxx*	Contain information about the status of conversation between two systems.
Log files	LOGFILE, LTMP.*xxxx*, SYSLOG, ERRLOG	Contain record of calls to remote systems, requests queued, execution of **uux** commands, and file transfer results.
Statistics files	L_stat, R_stat, L_sub, R_sub	Contain connection and traffic statistics for use by **uustat** or **uusub**.
Sequence files	SEQF	Contain four-digit sequence numbers that UUCP programs use in work and data filenames.
Audit files	AUDIT	Contain debug error messages.

This appendix contains the format of the working files which might be useful to you in monitoring UUCP activity and in determining the cause of a UUCP failure.

Work Files

Work files contain instructions for **uucico** on which remote system to contact, the type of transfer request, and where the file will be sent. They are created in */usr/spool/uucp* by **uucp** and **uux**. In BNU, they are found in a subdirectory for each called system.

A work file for a file transfer between the local system and system *japan* would be named as follows:

Work File Naming

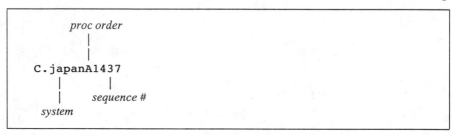

Field	Function in Work Filename
system	Name of remote system for which work is queued; truncated to the first seven (or, in some implementations, six) characters.
proc order	Work file processing order, or *grade*. **uucico** processes files in order from *A* to *Z* and then *a* to *z*. Default is *A* for files created by **uux** and *n* for files created by **uucp**. In BNU and 4.3 BSD, you can change the grade with the **-g** option to **uucp** and **uux**.
sequence #	Sequence number (also sometimes referred to in this book as the job id) for the work file assigned by *uucico*. Used to ensure a unique filename. The latest sequence is stored in the file */usr/lib/uucp/SEQF*.

Each work file can have up to 20 entries, with one entry for each request. Each entry has seven fields and an optional eighth field. An entry in a work file may look like this:

Inside a Work File

Field	Function in Work Filename
type	Type of request, which can be one of the following: *S* Send a file from the local system to a remote system. *R* Copy a file from the remote system to the local system. *X* Send an execution request to the remote system.
source	Source file pathname.
dest	Destination file pathname.
sender	Login name of the user that requested the work.
options	List of command options that the user specified for the **uucp** or **uux** commands.
data	Name of data file for **uucico** to copy. It is "D.0" with the default **-c** option to copy the source file directly to the data file at the time of transfer. The data filename is given if the **-C** option (to copy the source file to the spool directory) is used. This field is only used with the **S** request.
mode	UNIX permissions of the source file in octal format. This field is only used with the **S** request.
notify	Login name of the user who should be notified upon completion of the job request. It is used only when the **-n** or **-m** option of **uucp** and **uux** is given. This field is only used with the **S** request.

Our example above thus tells **uucico** to send the file */usr/john/sales* to the file *mktg* in the login directory of *jean* and to send mail to *jean* (the **-n** option) when the transfer is complete. The request was made by user *john* on the local system. The file *sales* has read/write (*666*) UNIX permissions.

Data Files

Data files are named similarly to work files, except that their names begin with the prefix *D.*, and the system name is followed only with job sequence numbers. They contain data to be transferred, if any, and are created when the user invokes **uucp** with the -C option, or when the user invokes **uux** or sends **mail** to a remote system. In the case of **uux**, the data file contains the instructions for the remote **uuxqt**. It will be copied to an *X.* file (see below) on the remote system. In the case of **mail**, two data files are created, one containing remote execution commands for **rmail**, the other containing the text of the mail message.

A data filename looks like this:

Data File Naming

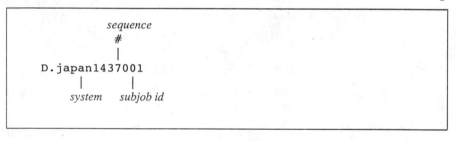

Field	Function in Work Filename
system	Name of local system for files waiting to be transferred to another system; name of remote system for files received from another system. Truncated to the first seven characters (six in some implementations).
sequence #	A four-digit sequence number (also sometimes referred to in this book as the job id) for the work file assigned by *uucico*. This should be the same as the corresponding field in the work file.
subjob id #	A three-digit number identifying additional data files associated with the same work file. (Not used in all implementations.)

Execute Files

Execute files are work orders created by **uux** in the spool directory. They contain the command for execution, information about standard input and output, and files needed for executing the command.

An execute file would be named something like this:

An Execute Filename

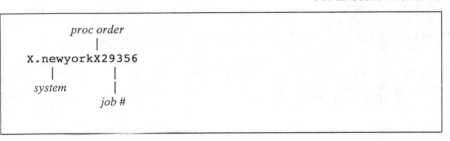

An execute file is always prefixed with an *X.*. The above example is the execute filename for the remote system *newyork*; its execute file job number is "29356". The processing order number for any execute file is always "X".

An execute file may contain lines with the following prefixes:

Prefix   Function

U   User line; identifies the requester's login name and system.

F   Required file line; identifies the filename for transmission.

I   Standard input line; specifies the standard input.

O   Standard output line; specifies the standard output.

N   Status return line; if present, inhibits mailing of acknowledgement message of **uuxqt** command completion. Generated by **-n** option to **uux**.

Z   Error status return line; indicates that acknowledgement should be mailed only if command failed. Generated by **-z** option to **uux**. (This option not available in all versions of UUCP.)

R   Requestor line; identifies complete return address of requestor. Generated by **-a** option of **uux** to override the mail return address derived from the user line. Used by mailers that know how to forward mail more than one hop.

C   Command line; identifies the UNIX command for **uuxqt** to execute.

Each execute file contains at least one *U* line and one *C* line. The *F*, *I*, and *O* lines are present only if files are needed for command execution. An execute file can have multiple *F* lines.

The following is an example of an execute file:

```
U root ora
F D.babelB0024
I D.babelB0024
C rmail ira
```

Temporary Receive Files

uucico creates temporary files in the receiving system's spool directory to hold data during file transfers. These files are moved to a destination file if the transfer is successful. If the transfer fails, temporary files remain in the spool directory but do not prevent future transfer attempts. The **uuclean** program automatically removes leftover temporary files.

A temporary filename may look like this:

TM Filename

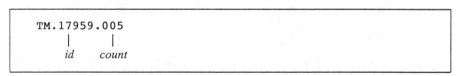

Field	Function in Work Filename
ID	Job sequence number assigned by **uucico**.
count	A sequential three-digit number starting at zero. It shows the number of files received.

Lock Files

Lock files are created by **uucico** in the spool directory for each device, each system, and each file in use. These files prevent multiple attempts to use the same device, duplicate conversations, and overwriting of files.

In BNU, lock files are found in */usr/spool/locks*.

uucico deletes lock files when a process ends normally. When a process or conversation ends abnormally (usually only in a system crash), lock files may remain in the spool directory and *prevent further UUCP transactions*. They are then reused after 90 minutes. When runs abort and calls are desired before the time limit, you should delete the lock file before setting up a transfer.

Lock files have the following format:

Name   Function

LCK..sys   where *sys* is a system name (for example, *LCK..japan*).

LCK..dev   where *dev* is a device name (for example, *LCK..cua0*).

LCK.file   where *file* is an abbreviation for the following filenames: *LOG* for *LOGFILE*, *SQ* for *SQFILE*, and *SEQ* for *SEQF* file. For example, a locked *LOGFILE* would be named as *LCK.LOG*.

Lock files usually contain the process id of the process requesting the lock. In BSD 4.3, you can print out the process id with the **od** (octaldump) command. In BNU, they are stored in ASCII form, so you can use **cat**. For example:

```
$ cat /usr/spool/locks/LCK..tty008
3686
```

You can then use **ps** to find out who is running that process:

```
$ ps -fp 3686
  UID  PID   PPID  C  STIME     TTY  TIME  COMMAND
  tim  3686  1549  9  11:28:49  008  0:07  cu
```

In this case, *tim* is running **cu**. If **ps -fp** does not turn up any active processes, then it is likely that the lock file is stale and can be deleted. (Note that in BNU this should not normally be a problem, since **uusched** periodically makes this check anyway, and cleans up the lock files accordingly.)

System Status Files

In Version 2, status files have the name *STST*.system. In BNU, they have the name
.Status/system. An entry in the status file consists of six fields separated by
blanks:

Inside a Status File

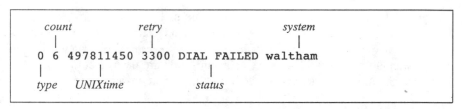

Field	Function in Status Files
type	A code from zero to five indicating the status of the job. The code is also explained in the *status* field.
count	The number of call attempts made by the local system; it is incremented each time **uucico** tries to call a remote system. After 26 retries, **uucico** will give up.
UNIXtime	Time of the last connection attempt expressed in UNIX internal time format. (The number of seconds since January 1, 1970, GMT.)
retry	Number of seconds that *uucico* must wait before it tries calling the remote system again.
status	Status of the conversation.
system	The remote system name.

Remember to remove the status file when you are debugging a faulty link to a
remote system. If you forget to remove this file before invoking the **uucico** program, **uucico** will fail with a "RETRY TIME NOT REACHED" message. A list of
the status file messages is given in Chapter 6, *UUCP Administration*.

Log Files

Log files are created by UUCP programs in the spool directory. They contain records of calls to remote systems, requests queued, execution of **uux** commands, and file transfer results. In Version 2, the log files are *LOGFILE*, *LTMP*, *SYSLOG*, and *ERRLOG*. The UUCP programs append information to the log files and do not overwrite them.

LOGFILE

In Version 2, *LOGFILE* contains information about transfer requests and the status of calls to remote systems. In BNU, there are four separate log files for each system you communicate with: *.Log/uucico/*system, and *.Log/uuxqt/*system, where system is the name of each system you communicate with. A portion of the log file is displayed when you use the command **uulog**. An entry in a log file may look like this:

A LOGFILE Entry

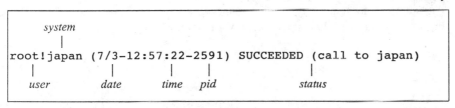

Field	Function in *LOGFILE*
user	The login name of the user who made the request.
system	The name of the system where the request originated.
date	When the request was made.
time	What time the request was made.
pid	The process id of the program writing to the log file.
status	Message describing the status of the call and the type of request. The status messages are listed in Chapter 6.

In BNU, the *pid* field is followed by a sequence number identifying successive log entries pertaining to the same UUCP job. There also may be a final field that lists the actual UUCP command that is being performed.

In Version 2, log files have backup files called *Log-WEEK* and *o.Log-WEEK*. *Log-WEEK* contains log entries for the week to date, while *o.Log-WEEK* contains *LOG-FILE* for the previous week. *LOGFILE* is automatically moved to the end of *Log-WEEK*, and *Log-WEEK* to the end of *o.Log-WEEK*. Refer to Chapter 6 for a partial listing of *LOGFILE* status messages.

In BNU, the individual system log files are combined into a single log file, typically once a day. This file is stored under the name *.Old/Old_log_1*. (The previous combined log file is moved to *Old_Log_2*. If you want to keep more than two combined log files, you can modify the section in **uudemon.clean** that saves them.)

LTMP

The UUCP programs write directly to the *LOGFILE* unless it is locked by *LCK.LOG*. When a lock file exists, other programs create and write to temporary log files called *LTMP*. The **uulog** program automatically moves *LTMP* files to the end of *LOGFILE*.

The name of a temporary log file consists of the prefix *LTMP.* and a process id. An example of a temporary log filename is *LTMP.6987*. Temporary log files have been done away with in many implementations of UUCP.

SYSLOG and .Admin/xferstats

In Version 2, *SYSLOG* is used by the UUCP programs to record the amount of data sent and received by each system. *o.SYSLOG* is a backup file that holds the previous week's *SYSLOG* file. *SYSLOG* is automatically moved to the backup file.

In BNU, this file is called *.Admin/xferstats*.

An entry in *SYSLOG* appears as follows and shows the following information:

A SYSLOG Entry

Field	Function in *SYSLOG*
sys	Remote system name.
user	Name of sender.
status	*S* for "sent data," *R* for "received data," and *M* for "sent mail."
date-time	When the request was made.
pid	The process id of the **uucico** that make the transfer.
seqno	The sequence number of successive parts of the same UUCP job.
bytes	Number of bytes sent or received.
secs	Processing time, in seconds, that the transfer used.
device	The device over which the connection was made.

The BNU *xferstats* file is substantially similar in format.

Note that you can calculate the effective data transfer rate by dividing the number of bytes transferred by the time.

If you consistently get a much lower data rate than you expect from the nominal speed of the line, this implies that there are probably a lot of errors (and hence, retried packets) on the line.

ERRLOG

In Version 2, the file *ERRLOG* contains records of **uucico** system errors. The entries contain *ASSERT* messages generated by local UUCP programs that indicate the cause of a file transfer failure. The ASSERT errors do not go to the *ERRLOG* file if you invoke the debugging option (**-x**n) of the **uucico** program.

In BNU, this file is called *.Admin/errors*.

ASSERT messages reflect conditions that do not fix themselves; the system manager must correct the condition himself. An entry in the error file looks something like this:

An ERRLOG Entry

Field	Function in *ERRLOG*
prog	The name of the program that generated the error.
pid	The program's process id.
date-time	When the error was made.
error	A message giving the nature of the error. This field contains a numeric code in parentheses that gives more information about the message. A zero indicates the code is not relevant to the message.

In BNU, an entry in *.Admin/errors* also includes a final field giving the SCCS id of the program that caused the error, the name of the source file, and the line in that file.

This entry shows that the **uucico** program failed on September 30 at 12:53 p.m. because **uucico** cannot open the directory */usr/spool/uucp*. Table A-2 shows the ASSERT messages for Version 2. See your documentation for BNU ASSERT messages.

Table A-2. ASSERT Messages for Version 2

ASSERT Message	Probable Cause
ARG COUNT (*num*)	One of the system files has too few fields. The actual number of fields is *num*.
BAD DEVICE ENTRY *entry* (0)	An entry in *L-devices* is incorrect.
BAD DIRECTORY *dir* (0)	**uucico** cannot open directory *dir*.
BAD UID (0)	The user id is not defined in */etc/passwd*. The filesystem is in trouble, or the */etc/passwd* file is inconsistent.
BAD WRITE (0)	**uucico** cannot write to a remote line or device.

Table A-2. ASSERT Messages for Version 2 (continued)

ASSERT Message	Probable Cause
CAN NOT GET SEQLOCK (0)	**uucico** cannot create *LCK.SEQF*.
CAN'T OPEN *file* (0)	**uucico** cannot open *file*.
LINK ERROR (-1)	**uuxqt** cannot link an execute file to */usr/spool/. uucp/.XQTDIR*
STAT FAILED *file* (0)	**uucico** could not access *file*.
STAT FAILED (0)	**uucico** cannot change the *stty* modes of the active port.
SYSTAT OPEN FAIL (0)	**uucico** cannot open an *STST* file. The modes may be wrong, or there is a file with bad modes in the directory.
TOO FEW LOG FIELDS (*num*)	*L.sys* has too few fields. The actual number of fields is *num*.
TOO MANY LOCKS (*max*)	There is some internal problem! **uucico** cannot create another lock file. The limit is *max*.

Statistics Files

The **uustat** and **uusub** programs create four files in */usr/lib/uucp* to record statistics: L_stat, R_stat, L_sub, and R_sub.

Use the **uustat** program to view the contents of L_stat and R_stat, and the **uusub** program for L_sub and R_sub. L_sub and R_sub are binary statistics files that contain connection statistics. L_sub holds connection statistics, while R_sub contains traffic statistics.

Sequence File

The sequence file *SEQF* is used by **uucico** or **uux** to record the general sequence numbers that the programs use in the work and data filenames. The *SEQF* file entry contains a four-digit sequence number.

Audit File

The audit file, called *AUDIT*, contains debug error messages when the **-x***n* option is used in the *SLAVE* mode. It is created in the spool directory by **uucico**.

B

Talking to Modems

Know Your Modem
modemcap
acucap
Dialers
The Telebit TrailBlazer Plus

As discussed earlier in this handbook, UUCP originally was designed to support the Bell 801 dialer, which was used with dumb modems. As smart modems with built-in dialers became available, individual UNIX system manufacturers added support for some of those dialers.

In many cases, instructions for certain types of modems were compiled in to the software and could not be changed by the users. In other cases, users were given the option of writing their own dialer programs and interfacing them to UUCP.

One approach that was used with a number of systems was to develop a *termcap*-like database describing the dialing sequence for different types of modems. There are two different implementations. One is called */usr/lib/uucp/modemcap*, and the other */etc/acucap*. Either file is better than nothing, although the number of modems already defined is limited, and the syntax makes it difficult for a novice to add an entry. Few systems offer either file.

In BNU, a still more general mechanism was developed. The *Dialers* file contains dialing instructions for modems, using a syntax similar to the chat-script sequence used in the system file *L.sys* or *Systems*. Many of the most common modems are already described in *Dialers*, and it is relatively easy to add new descriptions.

This appendix describes the syntax of *modemcap*, *acucap*, and *Dialers*. After reading this appendix, you should be able to write an entry for a modem that is not already supported in one of these files.

If your system supports none of these mechanisms, remember that you can tell UUCP that you are using a direct connection and then embed the dialing sequence for the modem in the chat-script portion of the system file. You will have to repeat the sequence for each system to be called, but this is a small price to pay for a solution that on the whole works fairly well.

Know Your Modem

Before attempting to write a description for any modem, you should carefully read your modem documentation for details such as modem DIP switch settings or other factors that may influence the activity of your modem. You also need to learn the modem's command language, so you can tell UUCP how to issue dialing instructions.

To give you a sense of the kinds of complexities that can arise, we are going to consider the case of a Hayes-compatible modem. First, we will look at the modem switches and command language. Then we will discuss what an entry for the modem looks like in *modemcap*, *acucap*, and *Dialers*.

Hayes-compatible modems have become quite common, so you may already have an entry for a Hayes. Nonetheless, a close analysis of the entries should give you a good feel for how to write an entry for a different modem as well.

We also include a discussion of the Telebit TrailBlazer Plus modem. Its speed (up to 19,200 bps when talking to another TrailBlazer) and features such as UUCP protocol support and data compression have made it very popular with Usenet sites, particularly those that must communicate with far-away sites.

It is said that TrailBlazers can be configured to do everything but empty the trash. All this flexibility can make it difficult to configure; we provide a guide to some of the major decisions at the end of this appendix.

DIP Switches

Hayes modems (and many, but not all, Hayes-compatibles) include an eight-position DIP switch that controls, among other things, the way the modem uses certain RS-232 signals. The switch settings are shown in Table B-1.

Table B-1. Hayes Switch Settings

Switch	Position	Function
1	up	Modem responds to DTR from computer.
	down	Modem forces DTR high, so no signal is required from computer.
2	up	Result codes in English.
	down	Numeric result codes.
3	up	No result codes.
	down	Result codes are sent in response to each modem command.
4	up	Commands are echoed.
	down	Commands are not echoed.
5	up	Modem will answer telephone.
	down	Modem will not answer telephone.
6	up	CD asserted when carrier is actually present.
	down	CD and DSR forced high.
7	up	Modem attached to single-line telephone.
	down	Modem attached to multi-line telephone.
8	up	Modem recognizes dialing commands.
	down	Modem is a dumb modem.

As shipped, Hayes modems usually have the switches set as follows: *duduudud* (where *u* represents up and *d* represents down). This may be ideal for a PC, but it is a disaster for many a UNIX system.

Switch 6 is down, supposedly to force the computer to accept locally echoed commands and result codes from the modem. This will work for a dial-out-only line, but it may cause a lot of trouble for a dial-in line (one with a **getty**) or one used for both dialing in and dialing out. When CD and DSR are asserted, the UNIX system will respond with a login prompt. The modem will echo back the prompt, which the system will interpret as an attempt to log in.

After a few iterations of this deadly embrace, the **getty** will die, leaving the line unavailable for dial in. Either that, or the cycle will continue, putting an unpleasant drain on your system's response time *and* leaving the line unavailable for dial in. And if you are using the line only for dial out, if the modem forces CD high, the system will never know when the call is done and, as a result, may not properly terminate processes associated with that line.

Switch 6 should be placed in the up position to allow normal use of CD and DSR. You may also think to set switch 1 in the up position to allow normal use of DSR. However, on our old Convergent Technologies Miniframe, we found that the system only asserts DTR when it is trying to open the line (e.g., for dial out) and that the modem would not assert CD and DSR unless it received DTR. The net effect was that the modem would answer when someone dialed in, but the system would never put up a login prompt. (This may be a peculiarity of the Miniframe. Most systems will put up a **getty** when the line is enabled in *inittab* or *ttys*. The *tty* driver will just sleep until carrier is detected.)

As a result, we needed to keep switch 1 in the down position, forcing the modem's DTR permanently high (or at least making the modem act as though it were forced high!). When a call comes in, the modem feels free to assert CD, which causes the system to put up a login prompt. Note that many modems will hold the phone "off hook" when DTR is asserted, and hang up the phone when it is deasserted.

Other users have reported a different set of problems with other systems. For example, a note in *Digital Review*'s "Tech Talk" column in early 1986 discussed problems with Hayes modems on the VAX. (We repeat those comments here both to give you a feel for what kinds of issues may arise and for the benefit of VAX users among our readership. However, we have not tested the following information ourselves.)

The editors at *Digital Review* suggested setting the switches to *uxuxuuuu* for incoming-only use (where *x* means don't care and *u*, as before, means up). This allows normal use of the modem control signals but disables command recognition, result codes, and command echo from the modem. They had found that if they did not disable command recognition on incoming calls, the modem hung up in response to carriage returns in their login prompt.

For outgoing-only use, they recommended setting the switches to *uududuud*. This turns on command echo and result codes so that users can get feedback from the modem but turns off autoanswer.

For both incoming and outgoing use, they recommended switch settings *uuuduuud*. Result codes and command echo are disabled because of the problems encountered with the login prompt (mentioned above). The user has the option of dialing blind or of sending Hayes commands to re-enable command echo (ATE1) and result codes (ATQ0) and then resetting the modem to its original state (+++ followed by a brief pause for the modem to switch to command mode and then the ATZ). Or the able system administrator could build these commands right into the *modemcap, acucap,* or *Dialers* entry . . . .

Unfortunately, if you are using *modemcap* or *Dialers,* it is easy enough to send the commands to re-enable command echo and result codes; however, there is no provision for sending commands to the modem when **uucico, cu,** or **tip** exits or is aborted. Only **acucap** provides this capability.

It is doubtless possible to work around this problem using other UNIX facilities. However, we will not go so far, since the problem was reported on the VAX, and Ultrix at least supports *acucap.* Even if result codes are disabled, you can still use the modem for UUCP—all that you will be missing is the modem's report of why the call failed.

We will look at how to talk to the modem both with and without result codes in the discussion that follows.

Learning the Command Set

This, of course, brings us to the main point of knowing your modem: its command language. Each modem tends to have its own command language (apart from the growing number of Hayes-compatible modems that share the Hayes command set).

In order to write an *acucap, modemcap,* or *Dialers* description, you first need to understand those commands, so that you can give UUCP the instructions it needs to make the modem do its bidding.

We will not look at the entire Hayes command set here, but let's summarize the commands that we expect to use. In cases where the command includes a choice of values, the choices are shown in brackets and separated by a vertical bar:

Command	Explanation
AT	Attention! Must precede all other modem commands.
D[P|T]	Dial, using *P*ulse or *T*ouchtone dialing. This command should be followed immediately by the number to be dialed.
Q[0|1]	Enable (0) or disable (1) result codes (status messages) from the modem. Default state is set by DIP switches.
E[0|1]	Enable (1) or disable (0) command echo from the modem. Default state is set by DIP switches.
Z	Reset the modem to its default state, as defined by the DIP switches.

Command	Explanation
S[*reg=val*]	Set register *reg* to value *val*.
,	Pause for 2 seconds.
+++	Place modem in command mode, without dropping the connection.

With the exception of +++, all commands must be preceded by AT and followed by a carriage return. Multiple commands can be put on the same line.

Thus armed, let's look at the first of our dialing languages.

modemcap

modemcap definitions consist of a modem name, followed by a list of capabilities that define the characteristics of the modem. For example, if result codes were disabled or ignored, the following very simple description could be used with a Hayes-compatible modem such as the Qubie:

```
# Qubie modem -- DIP switch settings dudduuud
# No result codes or command echo; could also be used with
# result codes and command echo but would ignore them.
qb|qubie|Qubie\
        :pa=,:sa=AT :ph=DT:eh=\r:\
        :pl=saph:
```

modemcap Syntax

The first three lines of the definition shown above are comments, as indicated by the hash mark (#) in the first column.

The fourth line defines names that can be used in *L-devices* for referring to the modem. Three names are given here, in a convention similar to that used for the *termcap* terminal database. Multiple names are separated by a vertical bar (|). The middle name is usually the one to be referenced in *L-devices*.

You should notice that each line in the definition ends with a backslash. This "hides the newline," effectively making the definition into one long line. The location of the actual line breaks is therefore arbitrary.

The following lines contain capability definitions, delimited by colons. The first capability on a line must begin with a colon. Tabs and spaces at the start of the line are ignored.

Capability definitions have three parts:

- A two-character capability name.

- An assignment operator (# for numeric capabilities, = for string capabilities).

- The actual value to be assigned to the capability.

For example, the **pa** capability might be defined as follows:

```
pa=,
```

to specify that a comma (,) is used in the telephone number when you want the modem to pause while dialing.

In addition to characters or character strings, the value given to string capabilities can include the following escape sequences:

Escape	Function
\xxx	An octal value equivalent to a character (where *xxx* is one to three octal digits). In particular, you may need to use \072 for a colon (:) since colon is used as the capability delimiter. \200 is used to send a null (\000 does not work).
\E	escape (\033)
\n	newline (\012)
\r	return (\015)
\t	tab (\011)
\b	backspace (\010)
\f	formfeed (\014)

Placing the Call

pl (**pl**ace call) is the one essential capability. It is the actual executable procedure that defines the interaction between the system and the modem. The value of the string assigned to the capability is a sequence made up of the other capabilities.

You might say that the other capabilities define the language in which the system and the modem will converse. **pl** defines the actual conversation. The communication program works its way through the sequence, using each capability in the order in which it appears in the **pl** string.

The next most important capability is probably **ph**, the telephone number capability. It is defined as follows:

:ph=*string*:   Send (*string*,phone#,eh), where *string* is a prefix that should be sent before the actual telephone number and **eh** is a string defined by the **eh** capability described below.

Basic Capabilities

The next group of capabilities describe basic features of the modem. They do not appear directly in the place call string but are implied or used indirectly by other capabilities. They include:

:ps=*char*:   Primary command start character; used to precede modem commands issued with the *sx* capability, if necessary. This is used when modem commands must be prefixed with a special character to distinguish them from normal data. (For example, the Bizcomp 1012 modem requires that commands to the modem be prefixed with the special character STX (\002).)

:es=*char*:   Primary command end character; used to terminate modem commands issued with the *sx* capability. (For example, the Bizcomp 1012 requires that commands be terminated with a carriage return (\r).)

:eh=*string*:   End-of-telephone string; sent after the telephone number by the *ph* capability. For example, in the Qubie definition given above, this is defined simply as \r (carriage return).

:pa=*char*:   Character used to indicate a pause when dialing (replaces default -).

:pw=*char*:   Character used to indicate that the modem should pause and wait for a dial tone.

The remaining basic capabilities that you may need to use are send capabilities that can be used to send particular character sequences required by the modem. The first character in the names of these capabilities identifies the general capability type; the second character allows you to define multiple capabilities of that type.

For example, if your place call conversation with the modem requires you at one point to send a control code such as STX (\002) and at another, a carriage return (\r), you might define two **s** capabilities, as follows:

```
:sr=\r:
:sx=\002:
```

The second character used in these two examples was chosen to be vaguely mnemonic, but you can use any character in the set (a-z,0-9).

These capabilities are the low-level language of the *modemcap* entry.

:s[a-z,0-9]=*string*:   Send **ps**,*string*,**es** (if ps,es are not defined, only *string* is sent).

:t[a-z,0-9]=*string*:   Send *string*.

:d[a-z,0-9]#*num*:   Delay *num* seconds.

Probably the best way to understand the interaction of these basic capabilities is to dissect the place call string from the *modemcap* definition shown above:

```
:pl=saph:
```

The Qubie modem is a Hayes-compatible modem. In a normal interactive dialogue (say, on a PC) directly with the modem, the place call sequence is:

```
AT DT phone number<CR>
```

The **pl** capability must recreate this dialogue.

The following capabilities can be used to do this:

:sa=at :   Send the Hayes **AT** (**AT**tention!) command to the modem.

:eh=\r: Send a carriage return after the telephone number.

:ph=dt: Send the Hayes **DT** command (Dial Touchtone) followed by the telephone number. This will itself be followed by the *eh* string defined above.

The resulting **pl** capability looks like this:

```
:pl=saph:
```

In addition, since the Hayes command sequence recognizes the comma rather than the hyphen as a pause character, the *modemcap* entry should also include a redefinition of the **pa** capability:

:pa=,:   Use the comma rather than the hyphen as the pause character.

Control Flow and Error Trapping

There are also low-level capabilities that allow you to trap for various conditions, skip other parts of the place call string, and abort with error messages to the user. The simple description above ignores result codes from the modem and so does not use these capabilities. However, if we wanted to enable result codes, we could use these capabilities to trap for them and print error messages.

:w[a-z,0-9]=*char*:   Watch for a character. Read characters from the modem into a buffer. Characters up to but not including the watched-for character are saved. (NULLS are squashed.)

:c[a-z,0-9]=*string*:   Compare *string* to previous results of "w" (not including the last character). Set the comparison flag to EQUAL if they match and to NOT_EQUAL if they do not.

:a[a-z,0-9]=*string*:   Abort if the comparison flag has been set (by a previous c*x*) to EQUAL. Print *string* as an error message.

:b[a-z,0-9]=*string*:   Abort if the comparison flag has been set (by a previous c*x*) to NOT_EQUAL. Print *string* as an error message.

:m[a-z,0-9]#*num*:   Skip *num* instructions if the comparison flag has been set (by a previous c*x*) to EQUAL.

:n[a-z,0-9]#*num*:   Skip *num* instructions if the comparison flag has been set (by a previous c*x*) to NOT_EQUAL.

We have not found a need for these capabilities, since we use our Hayes-compatible modem in verbose mode and can simply read the modem's messages if we are using **cu**. And we are quite content to have **uucico** fail on its own if the modem is not working, without needing to capture the exact messages the modem prints out.

However, using a brief, hypothetical example, one can see how these commands could be used to get more information from a modem that used obscure numeric result codes.

Assuming that the modem returns a code of 1 when the connection is made, and 2 when there is no answer, and that returned codes are followed by a carriage return, you could define the following capabilities:

:wr=\r: Watch for a carriage return.

:c2=2:   Compare the input from the modem with the string "2". Set the comparison flag to EQUAL or NOT_EQUAL.

:a2=NO ANSWER: If the comparison flag has been set to EQUAL, abort with
the message "NO ANSWER."

These capabilities would be used in the **pl** capability in the following sequence:

```
:pl=...wrc2a2...:
```

Additional Examples

The following examples are considerably more complex than the Qubie entry
given above. They are included more for the benefit of extending the contents of
your *modemcap* database than for pedagogical purposes. (That is, we do not take
the time to explain them!)

```
# bizcomp 1012 - option switch 9 down
bz|bizcomp|bizcomp 1012\
    :ps=\02:sa=A:sz=Z:sv=V:sx=X:ph=\02D:pw=\072:\
    :a1=NO ANSWER:b1=NO DIAL TONE:b2=NO ANSWER:\
    :wp=\r:eh=\r:sq=Q:c1=1:c2=2:c7=7:d1#1:d5#5:\
    :pl=szd5wpd1svwpsqwpsxwpd1phwpc7b1wpc2a1c1b2d1:
#
# Racal-Vadic VA212
va|vadic|racal vadic VA212\
    :d1#1:d5#5:es=\r:se=\05:wp=\n:ws=*:sd=d:tr=\r:\
    :ca=ANSWER TONE\r:cr=RINGING...\r:co=ON LINE\r:\
    :eh=\r:pw=k:si=i:\
    :n1#9:n2#6:n3#3:a1=NO ANSWER:b1=FAILED CALL:b2=NO_ANSWER:\
    :pl=sed1wssiwpwpd1sed1wssdwpwpphwpwptrwpwpwpcrn1wpcrn\
2wpcrn3wpcra1cab2wpcob1d1:
# Volksmodem 1200
vx|volks12|Volksmodem 1200:\
    :m1#9:m2#5:m3#2:a1=Destination busy:a2=Not responding:\
    :b1=Init Failed:b2=Hup Failed:b3=Call Failed:\
    :eh=\r:ph=ATDT:wr=\r:t1=+++:t2=ATH0\r:d1#25:d2#3:\
    :c0=\nATH0:c1=ATH0:c2=\nOK:c3=\nBUSY:c4=\nNO CARRIER:\
    :c5=\nCONNECT 1200:\
    :pl=t1d2t2wrc1m1wrwrc1m2wrc1m3c0b1wrwrc2b2phd1wrwrwrwrw\
    :
# Hayes Smartmodem using numeric result codes (Sw 2 down)
ha|hayes|Hayes Smartmodem:\
    :ps=AT:es=\r:ph=ATDT:wr=\r:\
    :s1=H0:s2=E0:s3=V0:s4=&m2:s5=&D2:s6=&C1:s7=M0:\
    :a1=BUSY:a2=NO DIALTONE:a3=NO CARRIER:a4=ERROR:\
    :b1=INIT FAILED:c0=0:c1=1:b2=2:c3=3:c4=4:c5=5:c6=6:\
    :c7=7:ca=10:cz=+++ATZ:tp=+++:tz=ATZ\r:d1#1:d2#2:da#10:\
    :m3#3:m1#1:m5#5:m7#7:\
    :pl=tpd2tzwrczm7c0m5wrczm3c0m1b1d1s1wrs2wrd1s3wrwrwrd1s4\
    wrc0b1s5wrc0b1s6wrc0b1s7wrc0b1phdawrc3a3c4a4c6a2c7a1c0a4c2a4:
# Hayes 2400 with numeric result codes
xx|hayestest|2400 with terse response|:\
```

```
:ps=AT:pe=\r:eh=\r:ph=ATDT:wr=\r:\
:c0=0:c1=1:c2=2:c3=3:c4=4:c5=5:c6=6:c7=7:c8=8:c10=10:\
:a4=ERROR:a6=NO DIALTONE:a7=BUSY:a8=NO ANSWER:\
:a0='0' UNEXPECTED:a2='2' UNEXPECTED:a3=NO CARRIER:\
:dl#20:pl=phdlwrc3a3c4a4c6a6c7a7c8a8c0a0c2a2:
```

acucap

The *acucap* facility is superficially similar to *modemcap* in that it uses a *termcap*-like capability syntax. However, in our opinion, it is much more cleanly implemented and much easier to use.

As in *modemcap*, capability definitions have up to three parts:

*   A two-character capability name.

*   An assignment operator (# for numeric capabilities, = for string capabilities).

*   The actual value to be assigned to the capability.

However, unlike *modemcap*, *acucap* includes a number of "Boolean" capabilities—that is, capabilities that are "on" or "off" and cause an action by their presence or absence.

The capabilities fall into three major groups:

*   Initialization

*   Dialing

*   Termination

And, of course, there are a number of miscellaneous capabilities that do not fall into any of these groups.

Initialization

The following capabilities are used to initialize the connection with the modem:

:ss=*str*:   Synchronization string. A string to be sent to the modem to see if it is operating. For the Hayes, AT.

:sr=*str*:   Synchronization response. What to expect from the modem in response to the synchronization string. For the Hayes, OK.

:sd#*nn*:   Synchronization delay. *nn* gives the time in seconds between synchronization string characters. This capability is not usually necessary.

:re: If present, this capability causes the modem to toggle DTR before beginning synchronization. In some cases, this can be used to reset the modem if its present condition is unknown.

Dialing

The following capabilities are used for dialing:

:cr: Carrier. Setting this capability causes UUCP or **tip** to wait until the modem senses a carrier before dialing.

:di=*str*:   Dial initialization. The string that is used to start a dialing sequence. For the Hayes, ATDT for touchtone dialing or ATDP for pulse dialing.

:dt=*str*:   Dial termination. The string that terminates a dialing sequence. Can contain standard UUCP escapes (e.g., \r for return).

:dr =*str*:   Dial response. What to expect from the modem if a dialing sequence that was just issued was successful. For the Hayes, DIALING.

:da#*nn*:   Dial acknowledge. The time (in seconds) to wait before looking for the dial response. Necessary only if the connection is timing out.

:dd#*nn*:   Dial delay. The time in seconds between dial characters. Not usually necessary.

:fd#*nn*:   Full delay. The time in seconds to wait for a carrier to be detected. If the call is not completed in this time, an error is returned.

:os=*str*:   On-line string. The string to expect from the modem once carrier has been detected. For the Hayes, CONNECT.

:rs=*str*:   Replacement string. This string is a single character that will be substituted for an equal sign (=) or dash (–) in the number to be dialed. Used to translate UUCP's standard delay characters to the delay characters expected by the modem. For the Hayes, a comma (,).

Termination

The following capabilities are used to close the connection:

:ab=*str*:   Abort. The string to be sent to the modem if **tip** is aborted. (This allows the modem to be reset, for example.)

:ds=*str*:   Disconnect string. The string to be sent to the modem when **tip** or **uucico** is done.

:hu: If present, this capability causes the modem to hang up the telephone if carrier is lost.

Miscellaneous Capabilities

The following miscellaneous capabilities may sometimes be necessary:

:db: Debug mode. Setting this capability causes the UUCP (or **tip**) dial routine to give more information as it dials.

:cd#*nn*:   Completion delay. The time to wait in seconds between completion string characters.

:cs=*str*:   Completion string. The string to expect from the modem after it receives the synchronization and dial strings. Use only if the modem has something to say at this point.

:ls: If this capability is present, use an internal sleep routine rather than **sleep** (3) for delays. All delays must then be given in microseconds rather than seconds.

:si: This modem is attached to a port that cannot return any characters until carrier is detected. Used only in special cases.

An acucap Entry for Hayes

The following simple *acucap* entry for a Hayes modem shows the use of the capabilities listed above:

```
#Hayes 1200 smart modem (touchtone dialing)
# switches = uuddduud (u=up, d=down)
hayes|h1200|smartmodem|smartmodem 1200(Touchtone):\
        :cr:hu:re:ss=AT\r:sd#1:sr=OK:di=ATDT:rs=,:\
        :dt=\r:dr=DIALING:fd#30:os=CONNECT:\
        :ds=+++ATZ\r:ab=+++ATZ\r:
```

That is:

:cr:	Wait for carrier before dialing.
:hu:	Hang up if carrier is lost.
:ss=AT:	Send AT to make sure the modem is connected.
:sd#1:	Give the modem 1 second to think about it.
:sr=OK:	Expect OK in response.
:di=ATDT:	Send the command ATDT before the telephone number.
:rs=,:	Replace an = in the telephone number UUCP or **tip** supplies with the , the Hayes uses for a pause.
:dt=\r:	Follow the number with a carriage return.
:dr=DIALING:	Expect DIALING in response.
:fd#30:	Give the modem 30 seconds to make the connection.
:os=CONNECT:	Expect the modem to say CONNECT when it makes a connection with a modem on the other end and goes on line.
:ds=+++ATZ\r:	When disconnected, return the modem to command mode (+++) and reset it (ATZ).
:ab=+++ATZ\r:	If **tip** is aborted, reset the modem.

If for any reason you find you do need to set the switches on the modem so that result codes are disabled, all you need to do is to add commands to re-enable them to your synchronization string:

```
:ss=ATE1Q0\r:
```

The modem reset command (ATZ) in the **ds** capability will restore the modem to its default state as defined by the switches.

Dialers

In BNU, the *Dialers* file contains the instructions for dialing the various modems supported by UUCP. (Some additional dialers, such as the original 801 dialer, are still part of the internal UUCP code and do not have descriptions in this file.)

The fifth field in a *Devices* file entry is used as an index to the *Dialers* file. In addition, each odd-numbered field beginning with the seventh field is used to match the first field of the *Dialers* file. If a match exists, negotiations can proceed. (This allows more than one "dialer" to be used in sequence, as when you must go through a LAN switch to reach a modem.)

Each entry in the *Dialers* file has the following format:

Dialers

```
dialer subs expect-send [expect-send] ...
```

Field	Function in *Dialers*
dialer	Type of dialer; must match the fifth or any additional odd-numbered fields in the *Devices* file. If this field contains the word "Direct" (for a direct wire), no additional fields in the entry are required.
subs	Translate string. The first of each pair of characters in the string is mapped to the second character in the pair in the telephone number dialed. It is usually used to translate the characters = and -, which are the characters UUCP uses to represent a "wait for dial tone" and a "pause" into whatever equivalent characters the modem uses.
expect-send	As defined in the *chat-script* field of file *Systems*. In addition to the character sequences listed in the table, the strings "\T" and "\D" are used to substitute the telephone number string passed to the dialing function. "\T" means to expand to the number in the *Dialcodes* file. "\D" means do *not* expand the string.

As shipped, the *Dialers* file on the 3B2 contains entries for the following smart modems and network switches:

Modems	Network Switches
Hayes	Micom
Penril	Develcon
Ventel	
Vadic	
Rixon	

Various escape characters can be used in the *Dialers* file. The list is similar but not identical to the list of escapes used in the *Systems* file.

Table B-1. Escape Characters in Dialers

Escape	Function
\c	No newline or carriage return.
\d	Delay for about two seconds.
\D	Telephone number or token without *Dialcodes* translation.
\ddd	Send octal number *ddd*.
\e	Disable echo checking.
\E	Enable echo checking for slow devices.
\K	Insert a BREAK.
\n	Send a newline.
\p	Pause for fraction of a second.
\r	Send carriage return.
\T	Send telephone number or token with *Dialcodes* translation.

It is very easy to add entries to *Dialers* once you have the hang of the very similar task of writing chat scripts in the *Systems* file.

The entry for a Hayes (assuming verbose result codes are sent back by the modem) looks like this:

```
hayes  =,-,  "" \dAT\r\c OK\r \EATDT\T\r\c CONNECT
```

That is, translate either an = or a - in the UUCP dial string to the , the Hayes uses for a pause (=,-,). When talking to the modem:

- Expect nothing (" ").

- Wait a second, then send AT followed by a carriage return but not a newline (\dAT\r\c).

- Expect OK followed by a return (OK\r).

- Enable echo checking so as not to send the telephone number too fast for the modem (\E), then send the dialing command ATDT followed by the telephone number, using dialcodes translation (ATDT\T), again finishing with a carriage return but not a newline (\r\c).

- If all goes well, expect CONNECT.

A problem frequently noted in setting up modems with BNU software running a "uugetty" is that the users will have the modem in "echo" mode. This causes the modem to send "RING" to the computer when an incoming call is received. This kicks the uugetty into reading the line. It reads the message in caps so it switches "login" into all caps mode and sends "PLEASE LOGIN:" instead of "Please login:". Since the calling system is expecting "ogin:", no handshake is completed.

The workaround is to have the modem in "no echo" mode or "partial echo" for TrailBlazers. Hayes modems must then have the "echo on" (AT E1) command in the Dialers chat script in order to get the expected OK's from the modem.

The Telebit TrailBlazer Plus

The Telebit TrailBlazer Plus is a Hayes-compatible modem capable of transmitting at speeds up to 19,200 bps. Features such as error correction, data compression, and UUCP protocol spoofing have made the Telebit popular among Usenet sites both large and small.

Like many modems, it has registers that can be set by the user to store configuration settings above and beyond those that are set via DIP switches. The TrailBlazer has no DIP switches, but it does have 255 registers! Fortunately, many of these are not used, and many more are "read-only," used for gathering statistics about connections.

Telebit's documentation provides thorough explanations of *what* each register does. In this section, we explain *why* we made the choices we did. We provide the *Dialer* entries we use and complete explanations of the most commonly changed registers.

We configure the modem by hooking it up to a terminal. We only have to do this once, as the external versions of the Trailblazer can save our configuration in battery-backed RAM.

```
AT &F S51=254 S52=2 S54=3 S55=3 S58=2 S64=1
AT S68=2 S111=1 S111=30 S130=2 S131=2 Q4 E0
AT &W
```

AT is the ATtention code for the modem, which must precede any commands to the modem. The Hayes S command is used to set a register. It has the form S*register=value*.

The use of the AT prefix can be disabled by setting S63=0. We prefer the familiarity of the Hayes-like command set.

&F recalls the modem's factory settings.

Register 51 determines the interface speed. The command S51=254 allows the data rate between the modem and the computer to be determined automatically. The modem examines the commands sent to it to derive the current interface speed, defaulting to 19200 bps. Register 66 determines whether the interface speed is "locked" or not. Locking the interface to 19200 bps (S51=5, S66=1) will improve throughput if, and only if, your computer supports hardware flow control properly. Ours is not trustworthy, so we set register 51=254 and allow register 66 to default to 0.

S52=2 causes the modem to reset (recalling the saved register settings) and hang up if the connection is dropped.

S54=3 causes the modem to relay break signals sent by the local system in sequence with the data stream. This allows break signals in UUCP chat scripts to work properly.

S55=3 causes the modem to relay the escape character (defined in register 2, it defaults to +) to the remote system in sequence with the data stream. We put this in the default profile because our modem is only used by UUCP. If your modem will also be used for interactive dial out, this is less than ideal, since the user will not be able to escape into the modem's command mode. One solution is to require the user to interact directly with the modem, setting register 55=0 before dialing out. Alternatively, you could define S55=0 by default, and set S55=3 as part of your UUCP chat script.

S58=2 tells the modem that the local system will be using RTS/CTS flow control (also known as hardware flow control) to control the data coming from the modem. This register defaults to XON/XOFF flow control, which is not usable with UUCP. See register 68 as well. Telebit recommends setting S58=0 (which disables all flow control), but S58=2 is what we use.

S64=1 causes the modem to ignore characters sent by the local system while the modem is dialing or answering.

S68=2 causes the modem to use RTS/CTS flow control to control the data coming from the local system. This register defaults to XON/XOFF flow control, which is not usable with UUCP. See S58 as well.

S110=1 enables data compression between Telebit modems.

S111=30 tells the modem to "spoof" the UUCP file transfer protocol support. Because the Telebit does very effective hardware error checking, the UUCP protocol's own error checking is unnecessary. If spoofing is in effect, the modem provides local acknowledgement of all UUCP's error checking and sends only data (with its own hardware error checking) out over the line. This speeds up UUCP transfers. We set S111=30 because the modem is used only for dialing out. A dial-in modem would want to allow S111 to default to 255 to accept whatever protocol the originating modem wants to use. However, if both modems have S111 set to 255, no protocol will be agreed upon and no spoofing will be done.

S130=2 controls the modem's interpretation of the DSR signal. According to Telebit's documentation, BNU requires S130=2 (the default), while other UUCP versions require S130=5. We have not been able to verify this.

S131=2 controls the modem's interpretation of the DCD signal. According to Telebit's documentation, BNU requires S131=2 (the default), while other UUCP versions require S131=1. We have not been able to verify this.

The Q4 command controls the reporting of result codes to the local modem. This is to prevent the "deadly embrace" problem we have already discussed. Some users report that Q6 works better on their systems.

The E0 command turns off the echoing of characters back to the local system while in command mode. This, too, is to prevent the "deadly embrace" problem.

The &W command saves the current configuration to non-volatile RAM, and executes the commands in the modem.

We have two entries in our *Dialers* file for our Telebits. The first, tbfast, is used when making connections to other Telebit modems. It sets S50=255 to force a high-speed connection. This is important if you are connecting to another Telebit which sends its PEP* tones at the end of its answering sequence, rather than at the beginning. (UUNET's modems do this, for example.) If you do not force a high-speed connection, the two modems will connect at 2400 bps. We also set S7=60 to allow the two modems time to connect. The second entry, tb, is used when connecting to non-Telebit modems at 1200 or 2400 bps.

```
tbfast     =,-,  "" \M\dATS50=255S7=60\r\c OK\r \EATDT\
    \T\r\c CONNECT-\d\c-CONNECT \m\c
tb   =,-,  "" \M\dATS50=0\r\c OK\r \EATDT\T\r\c\
    CONNECT-\d\c-CONNECT \m\c
```

If you have auto-answer problems when slow modems dial your Telebit modem, it may be because they time out on the modem's sequence of high-speed modulation tones as it searches for a matching data rate. To reserve the answering sequence, so that the tones for slower data rates are presented first, set S92=1. However, if you do this, incoming Telebit modems should have S50=255 to make sure that they don't agree to a lower rate, and wait for the high-speed PEP tones.

---

*Packetized Ensemble Protocol, a proprietary protocol.

C

More on RS-232

9-Pin Connectors
Distance Limits for RS-232 Cables

This appendix lists a few additional facts about RS-232 that you might find useful. These include pinouts for the 9-pin connector on the IBM PC/AT and the baud rate/distance tables for direct serial links.

9-Pin Connectors

Nine-pin connectors are becoming increasingly common on many microcomputers. The pins on these connectors have the same function as those on the more standard 25-pin connector, but of course, they fall in different positions. Table C-1 below shows the pinouts for the 9-pin connector on the IBM PC/AT. This is a DTE connector.

Table C-1. Pin Assignments on PC/AT 9-Pin Connector

Pin Number	Function
1	Data Carrier Detect (DCD)
2	Receive Data (RD)
3	Transmit Data (TD)
4	Data Terminal Ready (DTR)
5	Signal Ground (GND)
6	Data Set Ready (DSR)
7	Request to Send (RTS)
8	Clear to Send (CTS)
9	Ring Indicator (RI)

Distance Limits for RS-232 Cables

Although the RS-232 standard imposes an official limit of 50 feet on RS-232 cables, in practice, they can be much longer. The maximum workable length is dependent on baud rate. According to McNamara (*Technical Aspects of Data Communications*, Digital Press, 1982), the following distances have been determined, as shown in Table C-2.

Table C-2. Maximum Distances for RS-232 Connections

Baud Rate	Max Distance for Shielded Cable	Max Distance for Unshielded Cable
110	5000 feet	3000 feet
300	5000 feet	3000 feet
1200	3000 feet	3000 feet
2400	1000 feet	500 feet
4800	1000 feet	250 feet
9600	250 feet	250 feet

D

Useful Programs and Shell Scripts

Setting the Node Name
A uudemon.cleanup Script for the Korn Shell
What's in comp.sources

This appendix includes programs and scripts that may be useful to UUCP administrators. Rather than typing these scripts in, you can retrieve them from uunet via UUCP or FTP.

For UUCP, find a machine with direct access to UUNET, and type the following command:

```
uucp uunet\!~/nutshell/uucp/scripts.shar.Z yourhost\!~/yourname
```

The backslashes can be omitted if you use the Bourne shell (*sh*) instead of *csh*. The file should appear some time later (up to a day or more) in the directory */usr/spool/uucppublic/yourname*.

You don't need to subscribe to UUNET to be able to use their archives via UUCP. By calling 1-900-468-7727 (1-900-GOT-SRCS) and using the login "uucp" with no password, anyone may **uucp** any of UUNET's on-line source collection. (Start by copying *uunet!~/ls-lR.Z*, which is a compressed index of every file in the archives. *uunet!~nutshell/ls-lR.Z* contains a listing of the files contained in the nutshell subdirectory (example programs for our books.)) As of this writing, the cost is 40 cents per minute. The charges will appear on your next telephone bill.

To use FTP, you will need to (find a machine with direct access to the Internet. A sample session is shown, with commands in boldface.

```
% ftp uunet.uu.net
Connected to uunet.uu.net.
220 uunet FTP server (Version 5.99 Wed May 23 14:40:19 EDT 1990) ready.
Name (uunet.uu.net:ambar): anonymous
331 Guest login ok, send ident as password.
Password: ambar@ora.com (use your user name and host here)
230 Guest login ok, access restrictions apply.
ftp> cd nutshell/uucp
250 CWD command successful.
ftp> binary (you must specify binary transfer for compressed files)
200 Type set to I.
ftp> get scripts.shar.Z
200 PORT command successful.
150 Opening ASCII mode data connection for scripts.shar.Z.
226 Transfer complete.
ftp> quit
221 Goodbye.
%
```

To extract files once you have retrieved the archive, type:

```
% uncompress FILE.shar.Z
% /bin/sh FILE.shar
```

The files contained in the archive will be placed in your current directory.

Setting the Node Name

As discussed in Chapter 3, *Setting Up a Link*, before you can set up a UUCP network, you must give each system in it a unique name. Unfortunately, in some earlier UNIX systems, mechanisms that allow the administrator to change the name without recompiling the UNIX kernel are not always provided.

The following *sysname* program, written by Pat Wood of Pipeline Associates, works much the same way as **setuname**, **uname -S**, and **hostname**—it patches the name into the in-core image of the running kernel. As such, it should be executed from one of the system startup scripts, such as */etc/rc*.

The usage is:

```
# sysname yournode
```

We have only tested this program on our own System V system. However, it should work on any UNIX system. If your system is other than System V, define BSD or V7, as appropriate, instead of ATTSV. (In addition, on our system, *types.h* is located in */usr/include/sys* rather than */usr/include*; however, we thought it best to leave the program as Pat originally wrote it.)

```
#include <types.h>
#include <sys/utsname.h>
#include <fcntl.h>

#define KMEM "/dev/kmem"              /* kernel memory */

main (argc, argv)
int argc;
char *argv[];
{
    struct utsname uts;
    int memory;
    unsigned long nameloc;
    unsigned long unixname();

    if (argc !=2) {
        printf ("%s:  needs system name", argv[0]);
        exit(1);
    }
    if (strlen (argv[1]) > 8) {
        printf ("%s:  system name must be <= 8 chars", \r
            argv[0]);
    }
    nameloc = unixname ();
    if (nameloc =^= 0) {
        printf ("%s:  cannot get address for utsname", \r
            argv[0]);
        exit(1);
    }
    if ((memory = open(KMEM, O_RDWR)) =^= -1){
        printf ("%s:  cannot open %s", argv[0], KMEM);
        exit(1);
    }

    lseek (memory, nameloc, 0L);
    read (memory, &uts, sizeof (uts));
    strcpy (uts.sysname, argv[1]);
    strcpy (uts.nodename, argv[1]);
    lseek (memory, nameloc, 0L);
    write (memory, &uts, sizeof (uts));
}
/*
** unixname -- look up name in UNIX namelist
** argument is a string to look up in UNIX
** returns address
*/

#define ATTSV          /* define if running System V or V.2 */
/* #define BSD          /* define if running BSD */
/* #define V7          /* define if running V7 SYS3 or XENIX */
```

```
/*
**   name of the "utsname" structure changed
** as of System V from _utsname to utsname
*/
#ifdef ATTSV
# define UTSNAME "utsname"
#else
# define UTSNAME "_utsname"
#endif


/*
**   define UNIX to be name of unix object file,
**   e.g., /unix, /vmunix, /xenix.
*/
#define UNIX "/unix"

#if defined(ATTSV) || defined(BSD)
# include <nlist.h>
#else
# include <a.out.h>
#endif

unsigned long unixname ()
{
    struct nlist list[2];
    static char *name = UTSNAME;
/*
**   the following #ifdef is necessary due to a change of
**   the definition of the n_name element from an array
**   to a pointer
*/
#ifdef ATTSV
    /* set up name list array */
    char array[10];
    list[0].n_name = name;
    list[1].n_name = "";
#else
    /* set up name list array */
    strcpy (list[0] .n_name, name);
    list[1] .n_name[0] = 0;
#endif

    /* get name list entry for "name" */
    if (nlist (UNIX, list) =^= -1)
        return (0L);
    return ((long) list[0].n_value);
}
```

A uudemon.cleanup Script for the Korn Shell

As noted in Chapter Six, *UUCP Administration*, there is a bug in the administration scripts for early BNU versions. Due to differences in the Bourne and Korn shells, the script can change to another directory, and remove files there!

Here's a fixed version of the script, provided by Greg Woods of Elegant Communications and Uniforum Canada. He says that the script has been tested on a 3b1 (SVR 3.1.5.4), a 3b2 (SVR 3.1v2), and a 386/ix (Version 1.0.6). It should work well with all non-SVR4 HDB-UUCP's, though it currently uses */usr/lbin/mktable*, which is only found on systems with AT&T's SVR2/3 sysadm package. (*mktable* is just a simple sed script to remove comments and blank lines from a file, and could be replaced by the following commands:

```
sed ' /^[    ]*#/d
      /^[    ]*$/d
    '
```

(That's a <SPACE><TAB> between the []'s.)

The SVR4.0-1.1 uudemon.cleanup script is quite careful to check if a name is a directory, and in addition avoids the old bug by using "rm -fr" without the "cd ..;rmdir".

```
#!/bin/sh
:
#ident     "@(#)uucp:uudemon.cleanup     2.2.1.3 [eci386-local]"
#
#     This demon cleans up uucp directories using uucleanup.
#     It is started by /usr/spool/cron/crontabs/uucp;
#     It can be run daily, weekly, whatever depending on the system's
#        uucp load.
#     The log files can get large so you may have to up your ulimit.
#
#     e.g.:
# 45 23 * * * /usr/lib/uucp/uudemon.cleanu
#

#     defaults were: -D7 -C7 -X2 -o2 -W1
#
UUCLEANARGS="-D28 -C28 -X2 -o2 -W4"
UUCLEANDEF="-D28 -C28 -X2 -o2 -W4"
MAILTO="uucp"
MAILDIR=/usr/mail
TMP=/tmp/uu$$

export PATH
PATH=/bin:/usr/bin:/usr/lib/uucp:/usr/lbin
```

```
#
#       These are taken from the Makefile.  If changed in Makefile
#       they must be changed here also.
#
PUBDIR=/usr/spool/uucppublic
SPOOL=/usr/spool/uucp
LOCKS=/usr/spool/locks
XQTDIR=/usr/spool/uucp/.Xqtdir
CORRUPT=/usr/spool/uucp/.Corrupt
LOGDIR=/usr/spool/uucp/.Log
SEQDIR=/usr/spool/uucp/.Sequence
STATDIR=/usr/spool/uucp/.Status
WORKDIR=/usr/spool/uucp/.Workspace
ADMIN=/usr/spool/uucp/.Admin

#       OLD is the directory for archiving old admin/log files
OLD=$SPOOL/.Old
O_LOGS=$OLD/Old-Log

#       CLEANFILE is a list of "system<tab>args ..." for uucleanup
#       see uucleanup(1m) for a description of the available arguments
CLEANFILE=/usr/lib/uucp/Cleanup

mv $ADMIN/xferstats $OLD/xferstats
mv $ADMIN/audit $OLD/audit
mv $ADMIN/errors $OLD/errors
mv $ADMIN/Foreign $OLD/Foreign

> $ADMIN/xferstats
> $ADMIN/audit
> $ADMIN/errors
> $ADMIN/Foreign

#
#       The list in the for controls how many old LOG files are retained.
#       O_LOGS-2 goes to O_LOGS-3, O_LOGS-1 goes to O_LOGS-2.
#       Todays goes to O_LOGS-1
#
for i in  2 1 ; do
      j='expr $i + 1'
      mv ${O_LOGS}-$i ${O_LOGS}-$j
done

#
#       Combine all log files into O_LOGS-1.
#       Add a name separator between each system.
#
> ${O_LOGS}-1
for i in uucico uucp uux uuxqt ; do
      if [ ! -d $LOGDIR/$i ] ; then
            (
                  echo "Subject: uudemon.cleanup errors0
                  echo "uudemon.cleanup: $LOGDIR/$i directory does not exist,
```

```
                        remove if file"
                    echo "uudemon.cleanup: making a directory $LOGDIR/$i"
            ) | mail $MAILTO
            rm -f $LOGDIR/$i
            mkdir $LOGDIR/$i
            chmod 777 $LOGDIR/$i
            continue
        fi
        cd $LOGDIR/$i
        if [ "'pwd'" != "$LOGDIR/$i" ] ; then
            (
                    echo "Subject: uudemon.cleanup errors0"
                    echo "uudemon.cleanup: unable to chdir to $LOGDIR/$i"
            ) | mail $MAILTO
            continue
        fi
        for j in * ; do
            if [ "$j" = "*" ] ; then
                    break
            fi
            echo "********** $j **********" >> ${O_LOGS}-1
            cat $j >> ${O_LOGS}-1
            rm -f $j
        done
done

#     execute uucleanup for each system possibly with args from $CLEANFILE
#
for i in $SPOOL/[A-z]* ; do
        SYSTEM='basename $i'
        UUCLEANSPECIAL='mktable $CLEANFILE | grep "^$SYSTEM " | cut -d' ' -f2'
        if [ -n "$UUCLEANSPECIAL" ] ; then
                eval uucleanup $UUCLEANSPECIAL -s$SYSTEM
        else
                eval uucleanup $UUCLEANDEF -s$SYSTEM
        fi
done

#     Execute the system directory cleanup program
#     See uucleanup.1m for details.
#OLD: eval uucleanup $UUCLEANARGS

#     Use the grep instead of the mv to ignore warnings to uucp
#
grep -v 'warning message sent to uucp' $ADMIN/uucleanup > $OLD/uucleanup
#
#OLD: mv $ADMIN/uucleanup $OLD/uucleanup

if [ -s $OLD/uucleanup ] ; then
        (echo "Subject: uucp cleanup0; cat $OLD/uucleanup) | mail $MAILTO
fi
>$ADMIN/uucleanup
```

```
    # cleanup funny directories that may have been created in the spool areas
for d in $SPOOL/[A-z]* ; do
        # WARNING: for buggy 3.0 /bin/sh's, this loop will fail when ordinary
        # files exist in the $SPOOL directory.  For fixed shells, this loop
        # will potentially wipe out any world or uucp (or whoever runs this
        # script) writable directory on the system, depending upon the number
        # of consecutive files found.
        #
        #     woods@eci386 - Thu Mar 21 12:48:36 EST 1991
        #     - bug discovered by Chris Lewis on IBM RS/6000
        #     - fixed (was just [ -z "'ls $d'" ])
        #
        if [ ! -d "$d" -o -z "'ls $d'" ]; then
                continue
        fi

        # NOTE:  this will fail a buggy 3.0 shell when $d is a file
        # i.e. the shell will exit, and the rest of the script will
        # be ignored.  If the shell does not fail, and the above fix
        # is not applied, then all hell could break loose because of
        # the "cd .." below.
        #
        cd $d

        # we check that we are in the correct directory
        if [ "'pwd'" != "$d" ] ; then
                (
                        echo "Subject: uudemon.cleanup errors0"
                        echo "uudemon.cleanup: unable to chdir to $d"
                ) | mail $MAILTO
                continue
        fi
        for s in * ; do
                if [ "$s" = "*" ] ; then
                        break
                fi
                if [ -d $s ] ; then
                        rm -fr $s
                fi
        done

        # if it is now empty, remove it.
        cd ..
        rmdir $d
done 2>&1 >/dev/null

#
#     Find old cores
#
find $SPOOL -name core -print > $TMP
if [ -s $TMP ] ; then
        (echo "Subject: uucp cores0; cat $TMP) | mail $MAILTO
fi
```

```
#
#      Remove old files and directories
#
find $PUBDIR -type f -mtime +30 -exec rm -f {} ;
find $PUBDIR/* -type d -exec rmdir {} ;
find $SEQDIR -mtime +30 -exec rm -f {} ;
find $WORKDIR -mtime +1 -exec rm -f {} ;
find $STATDIR -mtime +4 -exec rm -f {} ;
find $CORRUPT -mtime +10 -exec rm -f {} ;

rm -f $LOCKS/LTMP*
rmdir $SPOOL/[A-z]* 2>/dev/null


#
#      Mail a daily summary of status
#
grep passwd ${O_LOGS}-1 > $TMP
grep "REQUEST.*/" ${O_LOGS}-1 >> $TMP
if [ -s $TMP ] ; then
      (echo "Subject: uucp requests0; cat $TMP) | mail $MAILTO
fi


awk '/(DENIED)/   {print prev}
            {prev = $0}' ${O_LOGS}-1 > $TMP

if [ -s $TMP ] ; then
      (echo "Subject: uucp DENIED0; cat $TMP) | mail $MAILTO
fi

#      Most people don't care about this one....
# uustat -q > $TMP
# if [ -s $TMP ] ; then
#      (echo "Subject: uu-status0; cat $TMP) | mail $MAILTO
# fi

ls $CORRUPT > $TMP
if [ -s $TMP ] ; then
      (echo "Subject: uucp $CORRUPT0; cat $TMP) | mail $MAILTO
fi

tail -20 $OLD/errors 2>/dev/null > $TMP
tail -20 $OLD/Foreign 2>/dev/null >> $TMP
if [ -s $TMP ] ; then
      (echo "Subject: uucp Admin0; cat $TMP) | mail $MAILTO
fi

#      Most people don't care about this one either....
# (echo "Subject: uucleanup ran; $SPOOL du0; du $SPOOL) | mail $MAILTO
```

What's in comp.sources

There are a number of other potentially interesting sources available in the *comp.sources.unix* and *comp.sources.misc* archives. We haven't tested them, but thought we should at least list them, so you can explore on your own.

The descriptions given below in Tables D-1 and D-2 are brief and often uninformative, but are all that are provided in the summary listings of the archive. Retrieve the file in question if you are interested in more information.

To obtain any of these sources, use anonymous ftp to UUNET as described in the first section of this appendix, and retrieve the files directly. The full pathname will begin with either *usenet/comp.sources.unix* or *usenet/comp.sources.misc*. The volume number shown in the table will be the second element of the pathname, and the filename itself the final element (unless the final component is itself a directory name). For example, you would find *uuencode* in the file *usenet/comp.sources.unix/volume7/uuencode* .

Table D-1. UUCP-related Programs in comp.sources.unix

Volume	Program	Description
volume1	uucpanz.s5	uucpanz for System V.
	uucpanz.v7	Another uucp status program: uucpanz.
	uuquei	A uuwizard's utility for uucp queue snooping.
volume2	uuhosts	uuhosts (updated).
volume3	times.awk	uucp info from LOGFILE (awk script).
	uuhosts2	Newer uuhosts (too many changes for diff listings).
	uuhosts3	uuhosts
	uuhosts4	uuhosts 1.69
	uumail	An opath/pathalias based uucp mailer.
	uumail2	uumail release 2.
	uumail2.fix	Fix to uumail release 2.
volume4	uumail3/part[1-2].	uumail 3.0
volume5	getmaps	Automated UUCP maps.
volume6	s3uuque	uuque for System III/V in C.

Table D-1. UUCP-related Programs in comp.sources.unix (continued)

Volume	Program	Description
volume7	paths.mk uucp+nuz.tulz uuencode	Makefile to build UUCP paths. Erik Fair's UUCP & Usenet toolbox. Uuencode and uudecode.
volume8	uucp.x25pad uumail4/part[01-04] uutty/part[01-02]	UUCP X.25 'f' protocol and PAD dialer. Uumail release 4.2. Bidirectional getty/login for System V.
volume9	uumail.pch	UUmail 4.X patch.
volume15	ultrix-modem uumailclean	UUCP/CU access on one modem. Clean-up backlogged UUCP mail.

Table D-2. UUCP-related programs in comp.sources.misc

Volume, Period	Program	Description
volume3 (1 January 88 - 20 April 88)	uuxqt-hack	A quick uuxqt fix for compressed news.
volume3 (24 April 88 - 19 July 88)	pcmail/part[01-08] pcmail/patch1	uucp mail for pc's. uucp mail for pc's: minor patch.
volume5 (22 October 88 - 29 December 88)	xenix-poll	Script to poll other uucp sites.
volume6 (18 January 89 - 22 May 89)	findpath.sh uupoll	UUCP Pathfinder v1.1 Uupoll
volume9 (4 November 89 - 6 January 90)	umdb/part[01-02] uustatus	UUCP Map Database. curses-oriented uustat (sort of).

Table D-2. UUCP-related programs in comp.sources.misc (continued)

Volume, Period	Program	Description
volume15 (October 90- 18 December 90)	getty_ps/part[01-05]	Enhanced SYSV Getty/Uugetty, Ver 2.0.
volume23 (20 Sep 91 - 23 Oct 91)	tua/part0[1-5]	tua - The Uucp Analyzer.

E

UUCP for MS-DOS and Macintosh Systems

UULINK for MS-DOS
Other MS-DOS Solutions
UAccess for Macintosh
UUCP for VMS

There are UUCP implementations for MS-DOS systems and the Apple Macintosh that allow you to perform most UUCP and Netnews operations. We have some functional familiarity with two of these solutions, UULINK for MS-DOS and UAccess for Macintosh. We also list some others that we know about in this section.

These non-UNIX UUCP solutions allow you to set up a UUCP mail and news node with more common and inexpensive computers, without the hardware and software overhead of a full UNIX system. For communication junkies who always need to be in touch, you can set up your laptop as a traveling UUCP node and be accessible through e-mail anywhere you can find a phone jack!

In general, these non-UNIX solutions mimic UNIX UUCP in configuration and setup. For example, the computer needs to have a system name and that name needs to be registered with other machines with which you want to communicate. You may need to develop a chat script that will allow you to log in successfully through UUCP. The correct directories (or folders, as for the Mac) need to exist

This appendix was written by Peter Mui of O'Reilly & Associates.

for the proper spooling and storage of incoming and outgoing mail and news and log files. In general, the setup and use of these implementations is less demanding than on a UNIX system, but each one has it's own distinct differences to be aware of.

If you're familiar with UNIX UUCP and its implementation, your experience will help you in setting up and using a PC-based UUCP system. If your first exposure to UUCP is through these systems, don't despair; the vendors of these solutions recognize that many of their users might be UUCP novices, and their documentation is geared appropriately.

UULINK for MS-DOS

UULINK is a commercial implementation of UUCP for MS-DOS published by Vortex Technology. Although it operates under MS-DOS, UULINK very closely mimics the setup, directory hierarchy, and operation of UUCP under UNIX. UULINK communicates with remote systems you put in \usr\uucp\sys, downloads mail and news into appropriate directories under \usr\spool, uploads your outgoing mail and news, and maintains optional log files. It contains mail and news readers, and **uuencode** and **uudecode** implementations for sending binary files. UULINK also contains a CRON system that lets your MS-DOS computer dial up remote machines at pre-determined times and poll for mail or news. UULINK recognizes multiple user names, allowing many people to receive and send mail from the same PC, and handles both UUCP addresses and Internet domain ("@") addresses.

Because of the lack of true, robust multi-tasking under MS-DOS, UULINK performs all of its operations in the foreground, so you can't do anything else on the computer while it's communicating with another site or while the CRON feature is active. However, it's kind of neat and somewhat reassuring to watch the queued mail and news get uploaded and downloaded.

By following the installation script provided on the distribution floppy, UULINK automatically creates the necessary hierarchy of directories under \usr that hold its executables, control files, and spooled mail and news. The most significant of these is \usr\uucp, which contains most of the executables and control files. The directory listing of this directory is:

```
Volume in drive A has no label
Directory of  A:\USR\UUCP

    .           <DIR>     4-22-91  10:30p
    ..          <DIR>     4-22-91  10:30p
ALIASES  LOC <DIR>        4-22-91  10:30p
```

```
SWITCHAR COM       152   12-29-87    9:05p
CHKMAIL  EXE     11904   12-29-87    9:05p
CLRUULOG EXE      6144   12-29-87    9:05p
ENABLE   EXE      7424   12-29-87    9:05p
LOGIN    EXE      8704   12-29-87    9:05p
MAIL     EXE     44416   12-29-87    9:55p
MSGSPLIT EXE     12800   12-29-87    9:05p
RDMAIL   EXE     35968   12-29-87    9:55p
UU       EXE     30080   12-29-87    9:55p
UUCICO   EXE     58368   12-29-87    9:55p
UUCP     EXE     24320   12-29-87    9:54p
EADCODE  EXE     15744   12-29-87    9:05p
UUMISC   EXE      7808   12-29-87    9:05p
UUNAME   EXE      8064   12-29-87    9:05p
UUXQT    EXE     42112   12-29-87    9:55p
CLOCKFIX SYS       384   12-29-87    9:05p
RDMAIL   HLP      2511   12-29-87    9:05p
ACCESS            2166    4-25-91   12:29a
ALIASES  GLB       996    6-16-91    1:28p
CRONTAB            619    4-25-91    1:11a
LOGMSG              35   12-29-87    9:05p
MODEM    INI         2   12-29-87    9:05p
NNGROUPS           113   12-29-87    9:05p
NNSEQ                8   12-29-87    9:05p
PASSWORD          1398    4-24-91   11:55p
PATHS             1535    4-22-91   11:03p
INSTALL  BAT       913   12-29-87    9:05p
REMOTE   BAT      1924   12-29-87    9:05p
SEQ                  9    9-19-91    1:11a
SITEINFO            95    4-25-91    2:11a
SYS               1693    6-18-91    8:29p
USERNAME             7    8-08-91   11:05p
ENABLE               1    4-24-91   11:50p
SIG           <DIR>       4-25-91   12:55a
        37 File(s)    5734400 bytes free
```

In addition to setting some shell variables in your CONFIG.SYS and AUTOEXEC.BAT files, you need to edit at least the following files properly before you can attempt to communicate with a remote system: ACCESS, PASSWORD, SITEINFO, and SYS. These files are analogous in both name and format to their UNIX counterparts that establish your system name, the names of known systems and modes of access, etc. The PASSWORD file defines valid login ids for UUCP use and allows them to have passwords, if desired. ACCESS limits a remote system's ability to read or write files locally.

The SYS file has UUCP-style entries for all of the systems you want to communicate with, as in:

```
ora 2 Any com1 2400 *P> ATDT555-1212\r *P10 NECT *P>2 \
        \r in: nuucp\r ssword: uupass\r
foobear 2 Any com1 2400 *P> ATDT555-1212\r *P10 NECT *P>2 \
        \r *P in: nuucp\r ssword: uupass\r
```

If you want your MS-DOS computer to communicate automatically at pre-determined times, you must also properly edit the CRONTAB file.

Reading and Sending Mail with UULINK

UULINK's LOGIN features allows many people to use the same MS-DOS computer to receive personal mail and maintain separate mail files. When you "log in" using the LOGIN command, UULINK sets you as the active user, and all outgoing mail is addressed from this user id. Note that if you're the only person using this computer, you never have to log in again: the one user name is always active.

Reading mail

To read mail, simply type "RDMAIL". Depending on how many messages you've received, it can take awhile before you see the <- prompt asking you to proceed. The commands for this mail reader can be obtained anytime by pressing "?". The more useful commands are shown below:

Command	Description
a	Answer a message (UUCP address parsing).
A	Answer a message (Internet address parsing [domain addresses]).
b	Backup—show the previous message.
d	Delete the current message.
d#	Delete message #.
e	Exit and save changes—note that q for quit does not save any changes!
h	Show the current header only.
ha	Show all message headers.
hu	Show undeleted message headers.
hd	Show deleted message headers.
l	List a message to a specified file (without RDMAIL message separators).
M	Mail a new message (note that it's capital M).
n	Show the next message.
o	Overwrite the active mail file.
p	List a message to a specified file (with RDMAIL message separators).
r	Read in a file (usually your mail.sav file—see below for details).

Command	Description
t#	Type message #.
z	Zap—delete the current message and show the next message.

To keep selected messages in your active mailbox as most UNIX mailers do, you have to use the "o" and "q" commands. You have to explicitly use the "o" (for overwrite) command to overwrite the active mailbox and actually perform your deletions. Then use quit. Note that if you use the "q" (for quit) command without preceding it with an "o" command, no changes will have been made to the mailbox and any message deletions (messages marked with "d") will be cancelled, so those messages will not be deleted.

If you use the "e" (for exit) command, it deletes deleted messages and appends undeleted messages into *a:/usr/spool/mail.sav/user_ID* (see "Saved mail" below).

Replying to mail

Type "a" or "A" to answer a message. You're prompted with the "Message reply sub-command" prompt. If you want to include the text of the message that was sent to you, type "F". Otherwise, press enter. Then follow the directions in "Sending mail" below.

Sending mail

From the MS-DOS prompt, type "mail". You will be prompted with To:, CC:, and Subject: fields, just like in UNIX. To end mail input, type CTRL-D or CTRL-Z. This will put you at the command prompt: it won't send the mail like in UNIX. You have to type "s" at this prompt to send it.

The commands for the mail sender can be obtained at this prompt by pressing **?**. The more useful commands are shown in the following table:

Command	Description
a	Abort the mail.
e	Edit the mail.
s	Send the mail.

Dialing out to upload mail

This step is really not necessary. Your outgoing mail will be queued for uploading the next time your site is in contact with the appropriate mail site or gateway site—regardless of whether the UULINK site calls the other site, or the other site calls the UULINK site.

Saved mail

Saved mail (via "s") is appended onto the save file for the active user. New mail will continue to be appended onto the user's main mailbox file. The user can then use RDMAIL to process mail from their mailbox file into their saved file as they wish. When you type "e" to exit RDMAIL, any undeleted messages are appended into a file named:

```
a:/usr/spool/mail.sav/user_ID
```

To look at this file again with RDMAIL, you have to use the "r" command in RDMAIL to read this file in. You MUST specify the full pathname, or it won't be able to find it.

This is different from UNIX mail, which marks read messages but continues to store them in your active mail file, appending new messages to the same file. The way to mimic UNIX mail readers under UULINK is to delete the messages you no longer want and then use the "overwrite" feature of RDMAIL to overwrite the existing mail file, eliminating those messages from the active mail file. Then use the RDMAIL "quit" command to leave RDMAIL instead of the "exit" command.

A Laptop Node Solution

Many people with UNIX mail and news at the office would like to continue to have access to these features while traveling. This section describes a real-world implementation of a "traveling UUCP node" using an MS-DOS laptop and UULINK software. This is not presented as the definitive or prescriptive solution, but to present some of the issues that arise from setting up such a system. It was implemented on a portable PC without a hard drive, and we think it can work on any MS-DOS compatible computer with minimal features; a single 720K floppy drive and 512K of RAM are all that are necessary, along with a modem or some other way to connect with the host system.

In brief, you'll have to properly configure the UULINK software on the laptop, and change certain restricted access files on your host system, probably by asking your system administrator. You may also have to create or modify your *.forward* file in your home directory on your host machine.

1. Decide what you need in your configuration. For the minimal system described, you probably won't have enough local storage to receive Netnews on the road. Depending on the size of your laptop's memory and the amount of mail and news you normally receive, the extent to which you duplicate your office-based communications capability may vary. We deal with a mail-only configuration in this discussion.

2. Set up a floppy (or your laptop's hard disk) containing the UULINK software and it's associated directory hierarchy. Look at the provided INSTALL.BAT program for hints on what's required. Make sure that you have appropriate parameters and variables set in your *config.sys* and *autoexec.bat* files, as described in the UULINK documentation.

   Depending on your space requirements, you may decide you don't need certain features of UULINK, and will be able to delete specific files from \usr\uucp, freeing up some space.

   Check with the UULINK documentation on the function performed by each file before deciding that you don't need it. However, some of our recommendations are shown in the following table:

Name	Size	Comments
SWITCHAR COM	152	Not necessary.
CHKMAIL EXE	11904	Not necessary.
CLRUULOG EXE	6144	Not necessary.
ENABLE EXE	7424	Not necessary—you can set ENABLE manually.
LOGIN EXE	8704	Not necessary if you're the only user.
MAIL EXE	44416	Keep.
MSGSPLIT EXE	12800	Not necessary.
RDMAIL EXE	35968	Keep.
UU EXE	30080	Keep.
UUCICO EXE	58368	Keep.
UUCP EXE	24320	Keep.
EADCODE EXE	15744	Not necessary if you don't receive or send binary files.
UUMISC EXE	7808	Not necessary.
UUNAME EXE	8064	Not necessary.
UUXQT EXE	42112	Keep.
CLOCKFIX SYS	384	Not necessary.
RDMAIL HLP	2511	Keep.
ACCESS	2166	Important for receiving UUCP files.
ALIASES GLB	996	Keep—you'll probably want local aliases.

Name	Size	Comments
CRONTAB	619	Don't need this if you're not going to automate.
LOGMSG	35	Not necessary if you're only dialing out.
MODEM INI	2	Keep.
NNGROUPS	113	Not necessary.
NNSEQ	8	Not necessary.
PASSWORD	1398	Keep.
PATHS	1535	Important for Internet-style domain addresses.
INSTALL BAT	913	Not necessary.
REMOTE BAT	1924	Not necessary.
SEQ	9	Keep.
SITEINFO	95	Keep.
SYS	1693	Keep.
USERNAME	7	Keep—set by LOGIN.EXE.
ENABLE	1	Keep—set by ENABLE.EXE.

For example, if you're the only person using the laptop, you can delete LOGIN.EXE once you execute it once. If you're going to dial up manually, you can delete CRONTAB. The software and control files can reasonably be reduced to about 200 to 300K. You'll have to be responsible for making sure that all the paths point to the right drive: the A: drive if you've got a floppy based solution, or the C: or D: drive for a hard drive solution.

A nice feature of UULINK is that log files, which can grow to gargantuan proportions on traditional UNIX systems, are optional under UULINK: if they exist, they're appended to, but if they don't exist, they're not created. For this minimalist system we kept the log files active while debugging the system, but deleted them once we were satisfied with its operation.

3. Add a PC text editor to the floppy. You probably don't want a full-featured text editor with a lot of features and a long start-up time. If you're used to vi, use one of the public-domain vi implementations for the PC which are available, or MKS-vi. Configure UULINK to use it as the editor for editing mail and mail replies. Once again, be sure that the paths are set up properly for MAIL and RDMAIL to find it.

4. Pick a system name for your traveling node, and ask your system administrator to add it to the list of systems that your current mail node (your "host" node) recognizes. Your traveling node will become a remote site to this system. Because your phone number will be constantly changing, you should set up the entry so that the host system never calls you, but waits for you to call it. If you're acting as the system administrator, see the section of this book on setting up remote sites.

Pick your system name carefully: at the very least, you don't want it to conflict with any other systems you communicate with. If you want to be really
safe, check the UUCP and Internet maps for systems with the same name: a
conflict may occur between your node and a node with the same name somewhere else.

5. To forward your mail to the traveling node, there are several options. You can
ask your system administrator to create a new entry in the */usr/lib/aliases* file
to re-route mail to the new node. However, this means that you have to bother
the system administrator each time you want to change the mail path.

If your UNIX mail handler supports it, the better solution is to add a *.forward*
file to your home directory. Edit this file to forward mail to the traveling node
while on the road, and edit this file again to unforward your mail once you
return to the office. Optionally, you can use the *.forward* file to "fork" the
mail to the traveling node while continuing to hold it in your default mailbox
at the same time. For example, the following *.forward* file forks mail to two
nodes at once: the local, host node and the remote, traveling mode:

```
# A "#" at the front of a line disables the line or
# denotes a comment
# The following line sends mail to the user's default
# mailbox on the host
\user_id
# The following line (currently disabled) sends mail to
# another office machine
# office2\!user_id
# The following line (currently enabled) sends mail to
# the "traveling laptop node"
remote\!user_id
```

6. As an added enhancement, UULINK's SITEINFO file can be "improperly" configured to make the return address in the header field of outgoing mail point to
the host node rather than to the traveling node. This has the advantage that
mail recipients who reply to your mail using the "reply" feature of their mail
program have it sent to your host node by default: your return address stays
consistent regardless of where you are, with all mail being received by your
host machine.

For example, the SITEINFO file on the laptop might be (without the comments):

```
wanderer# this remote site's name
host.com# here's where we cheat: this SHOULD be
wanderer.host.com
newshost# the node that acts as your news feed
Bogus Inc., Cambridge, MA#site id:
expansion# ignore this
expansion# ignore this
```

Note that this little trick does not work if people sending you mail route it explicitly to the traveling node. For example, mail addressed to ora!bob goes to the host node named ora, which can determine if any further routing to *wanderer* is necessary, but mail explicitly addressed to *ora!wanderer!bob* will be passed through ora automatically.

We've glossed over many of the details of completing the configuration: setting up the chat scripts, etc. Also, if you create this configuration on the minimalist system, you'll have to be careful about how much mail you keep around, and be responsible for deleting mail before you run out of memory. See UULINK's documentation for more information on the specific details of the setup, and the other appropriate sections of this book for establishing a reliable link.

Where to Get UULINK

UULINK is available from:

> Vortex Technology
> P.O. Box 1323
> Topanga, CA 90290-1323
> Tel: 310-455-9300
> Fax: 310-455-2364

Other MS-DOS Solutions

We know of four other UUCP systems designed to work under MS-DOS: FSUUCP, UUPC/extended, RamNet/UUCP, and UFGATE.

FSUUCP

Fubar Systems UUCP (FSUUCP) Version 2 is a shareware UUCP package available from many MS-DOS bulletin boards. According to the authors, the software system is as close to UNIX standard as it could be made without sacrificing functionality. It can be considered a subset of the UNIX utilities of the same name, but with certain enhancements and/or compromises.

Among the executables included with FSUUCP are the following:

UUCICO.EXE   implements a standard *g* protocol transfer mechanism.

BATCHER.EXE — "batches" news into the proper files for transmission and places them in the appropriate directories to await transmission.

EXPIRE.EXE — removes news articles that are "n" days old.

UUXQT.EXE — places incoming data files from UUCP transfer in the proper directory structure (i.e., mail is delivered to the proper mailbox and news is placed in the proper directory).

MAIL.EXE — is an RFC-822 compliant mailer subset. This program is as close to UNIX(tm) mail as possible.

POSTNEWS.EXE — allows you to post news to the network.

READNEWS.EXE — is a subset of the standard **readnews** system.

UULOG.EXE — displays UUCP log entries for systems or users from the LOGFILE.

UUSNAP.EXE — displays a "snapshot" list of all UUCP jobs queued and ready for transfer.

UUQ.EXE — displays detailed information about the list of all UUCP jobs queued and ready for transfer.

FSUUCP is downloadable from many MS-DOS bulletin boards. Additional information is available from:

Fubar Systems
1742 Lima Drive
San Luis Obispo, CA 93405-6817
Tel: 805-542-0336
e-mail: *chris@hypnos.calpoly.edu*

UUPC

UUPC is a public domain program readily available via ftp from many archive sites. The following information is culled (and often quoted directly!) from the information files distributed with uupc.

UUPC/extended is a small but free package for MS-DOS and OS/2 that allows mail to be exchanged between a PC and any system using the UUCP *g* protocol (i.e., UNIX systems). It includes a UUCP command for binary transfers, it currently does *not* include USENET news support.

The distribution includes the following EXE files with the following functionality:

MAIL.EXE — is the mail user agent (MUA); it is used for both sending and receiving mail.

UUCICO.EXE — acts as the mail transport agent by exchanging files with other systems via the serial port (modem). It can both call out (active polling) and wait for another system to call (passive polling).

UUXQT.COM — processes requests received via UUCICO, invoking RMAIL.COM or other programs to process data. It should be run after each UUCICO.EXE invocation.

RMAIL.COM — is called by both MAIL.EXE and UUIO.EXE to deliver mail; as such, it must be called RMAIL.COM.

UPOLL.COM — serves as a driver for UUCICO and UUXQT, invoking UUCICO to answer the phone and/or dial out on regular basis and then automatically invoking UUXQT to process any files received; this permits unattended operation of UUPC/extended, allowing it, for example, to call another system in the middle of the night.

UUCP.COM — is an experimental version of a command to copy binary files between two systems without going through mail.

UUSTAT.COM — is a utility to report on and update the status of jobs queued for other systems.

UUPC/extended 1.11f is available via:

- Anonymous FTP from *sun.soe.clarkson.edu*, directory *pub/uupc*.

- Anonymous FTP from *wsmr-simtel20.army.mil*, directory *PD1:<MSDOS.UUCP>*.

- An automated mail server running on *sun.soe.clarkson.edu* at Clarkson University.

- Clarkson University BBS

FTP programs vary from system to system; contact your local system support staff for instructions on anonymous FTP. Note that because of simtel20's popular archives, *sun.soe.clarkson.edu* is generally easier to connect to via anonymous FTP.

Send mail to *archive-server@sun.soe.clarkson.edu* and ask for help. Once you read the read help message, you can request files using commands such as "send uupc uupc11fr.zip".

The Clarkson University Bulletin Board is a Xenix system, and can be reached 24 hours a day at 315-268-6667, 8N1, 1200/2400 Baud. To get the "login:" prompt, you may have to send a BREAK. New users should download *00readme.bbs* from the root directory.

The files available are shown in the following table:

Name	Description
uupc11fw.zip	Formatted documentation files for UUPC/extended.
uupc11fr.zip	Required run time files for MS-DOS.
uupc11fo.zip	Additional (optional) run time files for MS-DOS.
uupc11f2.zip	Required executable files for OS/2.
uupc11f3.zip	Additional (optional) executable files for OS/2.
uupc11fs.zip	Source files for UUPC/extended.
uupc11fd.zip	Raw documentation files for UUPC/extended.
howtoget.doc	This file. (Only available on *sun.soe.clarkson.edu.*)
announce.doc	A summary of the new release. (Only available on *sun.soe.clarkson.edu.*)

The file *uupc11fs.zip* includes the source, *makefiles* for Borland C++, and MS C 6.0. Most MS-DOS users will want *uupc11fr.zip*, *uupc11fo.zip*, and *uupc11fw.zip*. Most OS/2 users will want *uupc11f2.zip*, *uupc11f3.zip*, and *uupc11fw.zip*. Both *uupc11fs.zip* and *uupc11fw.zip* include the same sample files.

The *uupc11fs.zip* file should be PKUNZIPed with the unpack directory (-d) option.

The filenames change with each release, to include the release number in the filename, but the last character of the suffix is the same for each file in every release.

RamNet/UUCP

RamNet/UUCP is a commercial program offering full UUCP and Netnews functionality. To make configuration easy, the makers of RamNet will automatically send e-mail to your host system's system administrator telling them what they have to do to connect with your node. You can choose between a menu-driven or command-line driven mail interface based on BSD mail. The Newnews interface is based on **rn** and offers a subset of **rn** functionality. RamNet/UUCP is designed as a terminate-and-stay-resident (TSR) program, which allows it to operate as a background task most of the time.

RamNet/UUCP is available from:

> Software Concepts Design
> P.O. Box 908
> Margaretville, NY 12455
> Tel: 607-326-4422
> Fax: 607-326-4424

UFGATE

UFGATE is a shareware system that implements a gateway between the FidoNet and UUCP electronic mail systems. Mail from FidoNet can pass into the UUCP electronic mail network, and vice versa. UFGATE can also take UUCP mail from one uucp system and forward it to another. When this package is used with an appropriate FidoNet mailer, the system it runs on becomes a full member of both the FidoNet and UUCP electronic mail communities. UFGATE also allows its FidoNet compatible host to participate in Usenet.

UFGATE has no message entering system itself; it relies on a FidoNet mailer/BBS for this. It assumes that you have a FidoNet compatible mail system up and running.

UFGATE is available from:

> Late Night Software Co.
> 671 28th Street
> San Francisco, CA 94131
> Tel: 415-695-7727

UAccess for Macintosh

UAccess is a Macintosh-based UUCP system. It takes advantage of the Mac's friendly user interface to allow you to configure your system and access all of the program's functionality through pull-down menus. Setting up your UUCP node involves finding the right menu items to select and entering the appropriate information rather than editing configuration files directly.

UAccess allows you to select separate Mail and News servers, and has a built-in terminal feature. It has an automatic "expect"/"send" feature for your chat script which will probably work in most cases, but also allows you to create your own chat script by hand if you find that necessary.

UAccess can be set up to dial up your Mail and News servers automatically as background processes.

All of your site-specific information and preferences are stored in a single configuration file, and you can keep multiple configuration files under different names. Because of this, it's possible to work around some limitations of the program. For example, UAccess supports only one user (there is no login feature) and one mail server. However, having multiple configuration files with different user ids specified allows many people to use the same Mac to receive personal mail. By specifying different mail servers in different configuration files, you can have the software access many systems for both. Simply load or launch the application with different configuration files as you see fit.

UAccess for Macintosh is available from:

> ICE Engineering, Inc.
> 8840 Main Street
> Whitmore Lake, MI 48189
> Tel: 313-449-8288
> Fax: 313-449-9208

Other Macintosh UUCP Systems

There are two other implementations of UUCP for the Macintosh that we know of: a Mac port of Gnuucp, from the Free Software Foundation, and a Mac port of UUPC. Both are freely available.

Mac/Gnuucp is (that is, it should be—Stanford purges it occasionally) available from *sumex-aim.stanford.edu*; failing that, try *rascal.ics.utexas.edu*. Try the mail reader Fernmail (also at *sumex-aim*) as an alternative to the HyperCard stack that comes with Mac/Gnuucp.

The Macintosh port of UUPC should be available at the same places as Mac/Gnuucp, although it is reportedly harder to find, and harder to get working.

UUCP for VMS

UUCP is also available for DEC VAX systems running VMS. For information, contact:

> DECUS
> Public Domain Software Library
> 219 Boston Post Road (BP 02)
> Marlboro, MA 01752-1850
> Tel: 508-841-3564

F

Frequently Asked Questions

How Do Domain Names Work?
How Do I Find Someone's E-mail
  Address?
How Do I Get on the Internet?
How Do I Use Anonymous FTP?
Miscellaneous Netnews Questions
Miscellaneous UUCP Questions

Parts of this appendix are based on material originally published by UUNET under the title *UUNET Answer Booklet*. UUNET ships *Managing UUCP and Usenet* to each of their new customers, but there were a number of questions that they found were still asked frequently. Material taken from the UUNET booklet was originally Copyright © 1991 by UUNET Technologies, Inc., and is reproduced with permission. Note that there have been numerous editorial changes and additions. In some cases, the "question" was taken from the UUNET booklet, but the answer was written from scratch because the UUNET answer was customized for their subscribers.

Some parts of this appendix duplicate material elsewhere in this book, and simply give it emphasis. Other parts cover areas that overlap with UUCP but are not, strictly speaking, part of the subject matter for this book. The bulk of the appendix is actually about mail addressing and Internet access, but I couldn't resist having Appendix F be *Frequently Asked Questions* and Appendix G *The UUCP G Protocol*.

And really, these questions are frequently asked.

How Do Domain Names Work?

E-mail is a hot topic today, even in corporate America. People in the mainstream are realizing what scientists and hackers have known for years: nothing beats e-mail for communicating with a lot of people simultaneously, especially when those people are spread all over the world.

Unfortunately, the spreading popularity of e-mail has made some of the problems of the "way it's usually done" glaringly apparent. In particular, there is no way to get "directory information" for individual customers like you can for phone numbers. In fact, there isn't even a good way to get the equivalent of country-codes or city exchanges!* Here's the problem, with a bit of historical perspective:

When UNIX e-mail was started, there were a small number of systems, each with only a small number of users. In fact, there was so little thought of expansion when UNIX mail was created that users were (and still often are!) simply addressed by their first names.

If you were on the same system, you could send mail to another user named Tim simply by saying:

```
% mail tim
```

and then typing in your message. If Tim was a user on another system, you simply had to use the system name as a prefix. UUCP, which served as a mail transport agent, uses ! as a separator, so to reach Tim on a system named *isla*, you could type:

```
% mail isla!tim
```

That was fine for a while, but before long, people were typing things like:

```
% mail apple!ames!garp!bloom-beacon!ora!isla!tim
```

This is more or less equivalent to telling Federal Express, "Fly this letter from Boston to your Memphis hub, then fly it to San Francisco, then truck it to Santa Rosa, and from there to Sebastopol, where you'll find Tim out on Barnett Valley Road."

---

*Actually, there is, in the form of a directory published by O'Reilly & Associates, called *!%@:: The Directory of Electronic Mail Addressing & Networks*. But that book is only the beginning of the story, since it's your system—not just you—that needs to know how to reach remote sites.

As a result, software was developed for registering computer systems and sites, using *domain names*. An address equivalent to the above, using the domain system, rather than an explicit routing path, is simply this:

```
% mail tim@isla.ora.com
```

or perhaps just:

```
% mail tim@ora.com
```

In the domain system, all possible systems are grouped into subgroups called domains. Each domain is divided into subdomains. Ideally, what this means is that from the outside, a system routing e-mail only needs to know how to reach the top-level domain that a user belongs to. Then, it is up to the domain to know how to reach the subdomain, and for that subdomain to reach each of its own subdomains, and so on. For example, the above address says that *tim* can be found on machine *isla*, in the domain *ora.com*, which is assigned to *com*mercial organization called O'Reilly & Associates. The shorter form means simply that ora.com knows not only how to reach each of its own subdomains, but also each of its users. This is probably true for a small organization like O'Reilly & Associates, but is probably not true for a large one like IBM or HP.

This is pretty much analogous to the postal system. If Happy Camp has only 200 residents, you can probably post a letter to Kerri Bonasch with no more address than Happy Camp, CA, and have a reasonable chance of getting it there. But don't try doing that with someone in San Francisco or New York!

At any rate, in order for this domain system to work, there has to be a system for registering domains, and there has to be some kind of a database that explains how to reach at least each top-level domain. Some people have suggested that domains parallel the geographic system used by the post office, which is intuitively obvious, at least to people with a rudimentary sense of geography.

Using this approach, Tim might be addressed as *tim@isla.sebastopol.ca.us*. This kind of system is used in Europe, and it does simplify things. Unfortunately, the domain system was already well entrenched in the U.S. before the idea got this far. To understand how this happened, you have to understand a bit about the history of the domain system, which had its roots in the research network known as the Internet.

The Internet once used a "flat" (nonhierarchical) name space. But the Internet quickly outgrew this system, and it became clear that a replacement was needed. This was the Domain Name System, or DNS. Six top-level domains were created: *.com* for commercial sites, *.edu* for educational institutions, *.gov* for U.S. governmental institutions (remember, the Internet was a project of the U.S. Government), *.mil* for military agencies, *.net* for administration of other networks, and categories (such as professional institutions). Most of the domain names used today fall under the *.com* and *.edu* domains.

Be that as it may, Internet domain addressing now seems established as the dominant way to address e-mail.*

Keep in mind, though, that the domain system hides vast differences in the underlying transport of mail. The domain system means that the user doesn't need to know how to get mail from one site to another ... but someone (or something) does.

Underneath it all, there are a variety of physical routing mechanisms—actual networks that connect individual systems—and there needs to be a vast, and constantly-updated database that tells how to get mail from one site to another.

Since domain addressing is actually used on different networks, the underlying mechanisms are different.

The next two subsections describe the mechanisms both for the Internet proper, which for the most part uses TCP/IP, and the UUCP network, which of course uses uucp.

How Domain Addressing Works on the Internet

The Internet grew out of a U.S. Government-sponsored experimental network known as the ARPANET. The mission of the ARPANET was to experiment with connecting distant computers together via leased lines. The protocols and software that were developed on the ARPANET are still being used on the Internet. Today's Internet is a group of *inter*connected *net*works (hence the name Internet) which span the globe.

The predominant communication protocols used by the Internet are TCP and IP. IP stands for Internet Protocol, and is a mechanism that provides unreliable packet delivery. TCP, which stands for Transmission Control Protocol, is built on top of IP, and provides reliable connection-oriented service.

One fundamental aspect of IP is that each machine is given a unique numeric address. For example, *ruby.ora.com* has the number 140.186.65.25. This numeric address is used both for local area networks using TCP/IP, and the broader Internet. Internet numbers, like domain names, are assigned by an organization called

---

*At least until some proposed international standards, known as X.400 and X.500, are actually implemented and widely available.

the Network Information Center (NIC), which is run by Government Systems, Inc. (GSI) of Chantilly, VA.*

When one Internet site wants to connect to another, the sending system has to translate from the hostname (such as *ruby.ora.com*) to the Internet address (140.186.65.25). This translation is done by a program called *named* (for name daemon). *named* on the sending site asks the Internet's so-called *root name servers* for the name of the server that keeps track of ora.com's names.† It then asks that server for the address of *ruby.ora.com*, receives the answer, and uses it to make the connection.

When e-mail is sent from an Internet site to a site that's not on the Internet, things work slightly different. Say, for example, you are sending mail to *isla.ora.com*, which is not directly on the Internet. *named* locates the name server for *ora.com* as we described above, but instead of asking for the address of *isla.ora.com*, it asks where mail for isla should be sent. In this case, the answer is *ora.ora.com*. *named* continucs by looking up the address of *ora.ora.com*, and delivers the mail there. An MX record (MX stands for Mail eXchanger; a *record* is a piece of data in the DNS database) is what allows mail bound for one site to be redirected to another.

How Domain Addressing Works with UUCP

UUCP sites don't have the same infrastructure that makes domain addressing work on the Internet. What's more, the Usenet‡ doesn't have any central coordinating authority like the NIC, nor a network of name servers. Everything on the Usenet is donc by redundant anarchy. So why should addressing be any exception? Everyone joining the Usenet is asked to fill out a site registration form, which is forwarded to the UUCP Mapping Project at Rutgers University (*uucpmap@rutgers.edu*). This ensures that your UUCP name is unique, and places your routing information in the database, but it doesn't get you a domain name. (More information on that subject later.)

---

*For many years, the NIC was run by SRI International, Menlo Park, CA. The host nic.ddn.mil will continue to be the place where requests are sent via e-mail.

†Note that this server isn't necessarily part of the ora.com domain; it can be another site that's agreed to keep track of ora.com's routing information.

‡Technically, the Usenet is defined as the set of machines which receive Netnews, by whatever fashion. In colloquial use, it is also used to refer to the set of machines which speak UUCP (there is a lot of overlap between the two sets, but they're not identical). We're using the term "Usenet" because, although it's not as technically precise as, say, "UUCPnet", it's a lot easier to say.

The maps produced by the UUCP Mapping Project contain information about what other sites the registering site communicates with, and the cost of each connection.

The entire database of maps is posted monthly, on a rotating basis, to the Usenet. Any site that wants to keep track of how to reach all other sites needs to continually download the updated maps, and process them into a database that defines the "shortest path from my site to everywhere else."

This is done using a set of public domain programs that is also posted to the net. *uuhosts* helps you unpack the maps, and display them when you want to peruse them. *pathalias* parses the unpacked maps into a database that shows the shortest path from your site to every other site in the maps. Then you need a "smart mailer"—a mail agent that will actually parse the domain style address and route the mail according to the database produced by *pathalias*. The most popular of these agents is a public domain program called *smail*. If you need to deliver mail over both TCP/IP and UUCP, you will have to integrate *smail* with the program you use to send mail via TCP/IP (typically *sendmail* or *mmdf*).

Fortunately, there are alternatives that don't involve anywhere near as much work. In the past couple of years, a number of commercial services have sprung up that will keep track of all the network information, and will route mail for you. For example, if you route your mail through UUNET, you can leave the address routing to them. Because they run pathalias daily, you should be able to send mail to *uunet!anysite!anyuser* and have it delivered. (You may still need to set up sendmail or smail to understand domain-style addresses, but you can rely on these other hosts to actually find the most effective path to route your mail.)

Setting up sendmail or smail is beyond the scope of this book. Books on these programs, as well as on the Internet Domain Naming System (DNS), are planned for release from O'Reilly & Associates in 1992.

How Do I Register a Domain Name?

Domain names are registered by the Network Information Center (NIC) at Government Systems, Inc. in Virginia. You must fill out an electronic form for domain registration. This is somewhat tedious, and requires you to know something about the Domain Naming System. You must also find another site already on the Internet that is willing to act as your mail forwarder.

UUNET will provide to subscribers, free, an electronic copy of the domain registration form that is largely filled out and ready to register. You need only fill out the required, site-specific blocks and return the form to UUNET via e-mail. UUNET can act as the mail forwarder for your domain. Your domain name will be registered by the NIC in about four weeks. UUNET also provides this service to non-subscribers for a one-time fee of $50.00. For further information on domain registration, send mail to *uunet!info*.

The domain registration form is also available via anonymous UUCP or ftp in the file *uunet!~/uunet-info/domain-info*.

Note that getting a registered Internet domain name is not the same thing as actually being on the Internet. It simply gives you a name that Internet sites can use to find you.

Also note that registering with the UUCP mapping project, as described at the end of Chapter 8, *Installing Netnews*, is not the same as Internet domain name registration. If you run UUCP, you should register with the UUCP mapping project, even if you are also on the Internet.

What are Those Funny Addressing Symbols?

Because not every system understands domain addressing, there are several "hacks" that are used when routing mail across networks that use dissimilar addresses. Here are a few of the special characters that are used in mail addresses:

.   There are two uses of ".". The major, and most appropriate, use is as a level separator for domain names under the Internet Domain Name System. The dot is being used as a valid DNS domain separator only if the top-level (rightmost) domain is COM, EDU, GOV, MIL, NET, or a valid two-letter ISO country code. For example:

```
uunet.uu.net
wheaties.ai.mit.edu
fernwood.mpk.ca.us
```

The other common use is in what you could regard as a "pseudo-domain." The domain name actually specifies the network where the domain-like address is valid for messages gated between distinctly different networks. Some networks that might appear in this type of address are ARPA, BITNET, CSNET, DEC, SPAN, and UUCP. The remainder of the domain-like address may look like a DNS address, but usually uses a single level under the ".". For example:

```
sahara.uucp
psuvm.bitnet
```

!   Should only be used when sending via UUCP. This should be the only special character in the address (called a path). The path indicates each site through which mail will be routed, starting at the left and going towards the right. Mixing ! with @ is not considered good. That is, use:

```
uunet!ucbvax.berkeley.edu!smith
```

not:

```
uunet!smith@ucbvax.berkeley.edu
```

@   Denotes a domain-style address. All DNS addresses use this to specify the actual domain name. Many addressing schemes on networks other than the Internet use @ as well, although not specifically as a domain name separator. Many UUCP systems use this too, with "uucp" as the domain name, but this often causes problems for sites without a smart mailer since they are unable to determine the physical return path. Example uses are:

```
smith@ucbvax.berkeley.edu
usenet@grinch.uucp
```

Mixing @ and ! can result in ambiguously addressed mail and should be avoided. Many UUCP-only sites interpret such an address as a path, thus basing routing on the left-most part, while UUCP systems with a smart mailer and Internet sites properly interpret it as a domain address, routing to the right-most part first. Except for any '.'s in a domain address, the @ should always be the right-most and first-interpreted special character.

%   Should only be used with DNS addresses when addressing a site that can't be reached directly from the Internet. This is a hack often used to allow sending to a site that either lacks a direct Internet connection, such as one linked via UUCP, or is behind a broken name server, such as some older Arpanet sites. For example:

```
joe%oduvm.bitnet@psu.edu
```

Converting Address Formats Manually

You may find that you can only use one addressing style if you're at a UUCP site lacking a smart mailer. Everything will have to be path-oriented to be of use. This does not restrict you from sending or receiving mail with Internet sites. It just means you have to convert domain address into UUCP paths (or set up a smart mailer).

You can use an Internet domain in your UUCP path, just as long as it's a proper hostname and is delimited by !'s. Basically, you convert the domain address into a path by reversing it and prepending the path to a preferred Internet/UUCP forwarder, such as *uunet*, just prior to where the Internet hostname is referenced.

A generic template might be:

```
internet-forwarder-path!internet-hostname!username
```

Here's an example conversion using *uunet* as the forwarder from a site one hop away from *uunet*:

Domain address to send to: *john@ucbvax.berkeley.edu*

Path to use: *unet!ucbvax.berkeley.edu!john*

Here's a somewhat more involved example:

Domain address to send to: *mary%dragon@sun.com*

From site: *raider.uucp (uunet!tiamat!mjbtn!raider)*

Path to forwarder: *mjbtn!tiamat!uunet*

Path to use: *mjbtn!tiamat!uunet!sun.com!mary%dragon*

By applying this conversion process in reverse, you can construct a valid domain address for yourself. You only need to know the proper Internet address of your Internet forwarder and the path to your site from there.

For more information on mail addressing and networks, see the Nutshell Handbook *!%@:: A Directory of Electronic Mail Addressing & Networks*, by Donnalyn Frey and Rick Adams.

How Do I Find Someone's E-mail Address?

A very thorough answer to this question has been written by Jonathan Kamens of MIT, and is posted to the net on a regular basis. A copy of the most recent posting (message id <finding_addresses_690710436@athena.mit.edu>) is reproduced below, with some minor edits.

A question which appears frequently on the USENET is, "I know someone's name, and I think they might have an electronic mail address somewhere. How can I find it?"

There are many different techniques for doing this. Several of them are discussed below. Your best bet is to try the pertinent methods in this posting in the order in which they are listed (well, sort of; at the very least, please try all the pertinent methods that do not involve posting queries to *soc.net-people* before resorting to that).

I've listed "Direct contact" near the end of this list because, for some reason, people seem to be reluctant to call people on the telephone or write them a paper-mail letter asking what their e-mail address is, as long as there is even a remote chance that it might be found without asking. This attitude is somewhat counter-productive, since in most cases, it is much easier to get someone's e-mail address by asking them than it is by following the other methods outlined below. Furthermore, even if you do manage to find an e-mail address using one of the on-line methods described below, it is not guaranteed that the person at the other end of the line checks that address regularly or even that it is the correct address.

Therefore, if you do have a telephone number that isn't too expensive to call, or if you have a paper-mail address and aren't in too much of a hurry, you can probably save yourself a lot of trouble by skipping all of the on-line methods listed below and going directly to "Direct contact."

College E-mail Addresses

The posting entitled "College Email Addresses" in the *soc.college* newsgroup describes the account and e-mail address policies for graduate and undergraduate students at many Universities and Colleges. If you are looking for a University/College student, check that posting for the University or College in question and follow its instructions for finding out more.

If the posting has expired at your site or has not been posted recently, you can get a copy of it using the instructions below (in the "References" section).

Inter-Network Mail Guide

If you know which network/service your target has an account on (e.g., CompuServe, Fidonet), then the "Inter-Network Mail Guide" posting in *comp.mail.misc* may be able to provide you with some help, although it probably will not be particularly helpful unless you have some sort of address to start with (a small number of networks use full names as addresses, and the posting mentions when this is the case, but it doesn't apply in very many cases).

No updated version of this posting has been posted recently, but you can get a copy of it using the instructions below.

Usenet-addresses Server

If you think that your target may be on the USENET and may have posted a message to the USENET at some point in the past, you might be able to find his/her address in the USENET address database on the machine *pit-manager.mit.edu.*

To query the database, send an e-mail message to *mail-server@pit-manager.mit.edu* with "send usenet-addresses/name" in the body or subject of the message, where "name" is either the first or last name of the person for whose address you are searching. Non-alphanumeric characters in names (such as apostrophes in Irish names) should be replaced with a period. For example, "send usenet-addresses/o.brien". The search will be done in a case-insensitive manner.

Note that multiple requests can appear (on separate lines) in mail to the mail server, but each request will be answered in a separate message.

In many cases, you will get a list of quite a few matching addresses, and you will have to go through it looking for ones that may be the one you're looking for.

NIC.DDN.MIL whois Database

The "whois" database on NIC.DDN.MIL contains the addresses of many military personnel, as well as the addresses of "prominent net.personalities." If your target is active on the Internet, he may be in the NIC database.

If your system has the "whois" program, you can use that to query the NIC database. If not, but you have Internet access, you can telnet to *nic.ddn.mil* and run the command "whois" once you are logged in (help is available). If you do not have Internet access, you can send mail to *service@nic.ddn.mil* to query the "whois" database; send a message with "help" in the body to find out more information.

Note, furthermore, that some sites run local "whois" databases to provide information about people inside their organizations. The only way to find out if your site runs such a database is to ask someone locally about it (see "Get more help locally" below), and the only way to find out about such databases at other sites (assuming, of course, that those databases are not mentioned in any of the other sources listed in this document) is to contact responsible individuals at those sites and ask (see "Finding a hostname and asking someone there for help" below).

IBM's Directory of Users

The IBM Corporate Internet Gateway provides a directory of users (which I believe contains only IBM employees, although I'm not certain) that is available to anyone who can send e-mail to it. If your target works for IBM (or you suspect he/she does), then this might be useful to you.

To use it, send mail to *nic@vnet.ibm.com* with the command "whois lastname firstname" or "whois lastname, firstname" in the subject or body of the message. If you use the former syntax, then both the last name and first name specified can be a prefix of the name rather than the entire name. If you use the latter syntax, the comma indicates that the last name is complete (but the first name is still only a prefix). For example, "whois Smith R" would return all people with a last name starting with "Smith" and a first name starting with "R", while "whois Smith, R" would return only those people with exactly the last name "Smith" and a first name starting with "R".

Other Directory Services

There are several other directory services you may be able to use to search for your target.

First of all, many Bitnet sites have name servers that can be queried in one way or another. To get a list of them with documentation, send a mail message to *listserv@bitnic.bitnet* (a.k.a. *listserv@bitnic.educom.edu*) with the command "send bitnet servers" in the body of the message.

RPI runs a white pages server for people interested in the field of communications. To find out how to use it, send mail to *comserve@rpiecs.bitnet* (or *comserve@vm.ecs.rpi.edu*) with "help" in the body of the message.

BITNIC (the BITNET Network Information Center) runs a name server of more general interest. To find out how to use it, send mail to *netserv@bitnic.bitnet* (again, *bitnic.educom.edu* can also be used) with "help" in the body of the message.

Finding a Hostname and Asking Someone There for Help

If you know the organization, company, or whatever at which your target's account is likely to be located, then you might be able to get your hands on the hostname of a machine at that location. Once you've done that, you can usually write to someone responsible for e-mail support at the site and ask for help finding the address you are seeking.

There are three main sources from which you can get hostnames. The first is the NIC "whois" database, which contains site and organization information as well as information about individuals. For more information about using it, see above. Organization entries in the NIC database will usually list an administrative, technical and/or zone contact person, with his/her address, to whom you can write. You can also write to "postmaster" at almost any Internet host to get in touch with someone responsible for e-mail.

The second is a network directory published by the University of Texas. Although it hasn't been updated in a few years, it still provides a useful list of many site names. It is available for anonymous ftp from several different locations, including */net.directory/1988.netbook* on *emx.utexas.edu*. It is BIG, so you might not have room to store it locally, unless you ask someone in charge to set up some space for it. You should NOT transfer it to */tmp* every time you need it, or something like that; that's a horrible waste of network bandwidth. Contact people are usually listed in the site entries in the net directory, but you might want to try "postmaster" first.

The third is the UUCP maps in the *comp.mail.maps* newsgroup. See the posting "UUCP map for README" in that directory for more information. You can grep in the news spool or use your news reader's search facilities to search for a particular string (e.g., an organization name) in the *comp.mail.map*s postings. Each UUCP map entry lists the contact person for the entry.

Once you've got a hostname and the person to contact, you need to figure out how to get the mail there, if it's on a network you don't know how to reach. See the "Inter-Network Mail Guide" posting referenced above if you need help with that.

If you do go this route, make sure you provide as much information as you can about the person whose address you are seeking; remember that the more detailed (and polite!) you are, the more likely it is that the person you are contacting will be able to help you. Remember, too, that the person you are contacting is probably very busy, and responding to requests like yours is probably not one of his/her highest priorities, so be patient.

Knowbot Information Service

The "Knowbot Information Service" (KIS) is a "white pages" service that allows you to query one service and have it search several other address databases of various sorts for addresses matching your query.

Two hosts running KIS servers are *nri.reston.va.us* and *sol.bucknell.edu*. Either can be reached on the Internet via telnet at port 185 (e.g., *telnet nri.reston.va.us 185*), or via electronic mail to *netaddress@host* (e.g., *netaddress@nri.reston.va.us*). For more information about Knowbot, use the "man" command after connecting via telnet or in the body of your e-mail message.

Direct Contact

If you have a paper mail address or telephone number for your target, call them or write to them and ask for an e-mail address.

In that case, you might encounter the somewhat common situation where your target knows he has an e-mail address, but he doesn't know what it is. If this happens to you, then give him your e-mail address and ask him to send you mail (and if he can't figure out how, tell him to get someone at his site to help). The odds are that when you get his message, it'll contain a valid return address in it.

Get More Help Locally

Often, the postmaster at your site (or whomever is responsible at your site for answering mail-related questions) has a large amount of knowledge that will help him to help you find the answer to your question. If you have been unable to find the answer for yourself, check with people locally and see if one of them can help you out.

The Last Resort—soc.net-people

If all the methods above have failed, you can consider posting a message to *soc.net-people* asking for help locating your target. Before doing so, however, you should read the "Tips on using soc.net-people" posting in that newsgroup. If it has expired, you can get a copy using the instructions below (note that the name in the instructions below may change when a new version with a new date is posted, so you may need to ask for an index of the *soc.net-people* archive to find out the name of the most recent version).

Note that this is listed as THE last resort, to be tried even later than using a telephone number or paper mail address. Any posting to the USENET uses the resources of the sites on the USENET and of the networks that carry it; certainly, the total cost of transporting a USENET message is more than the cost of a stamp or a short phone call. Since the benefit gained is to you and not to the USENET as a whole, you should avoid posting if you possibly can.

References

If you want to learn more about computer networks and how they interact with each other, these books might be interesting and useful to you:

- *!%@:: A Directory of Electronic Mail Addressing and Networks*
    by Donnalyn Frey and Rick Adams
    ISBN 0-937175-15-3
    (published by O'Reilly and Associates, Inc., e-mail nuts@ora.com)

- *The Matrix: Computer Networks and Conferencing Systems Worldwide*
    by John S. Quarterman
    ISBN 1-55558-033-5 (Digital Press)

The following USENET postings may also be useful to you:

- Subject: College Email Addresses
    Newsgroups: *soc.college,soc.net-people*

- Subject: Inter-Network Mail Guide
    Newsgroups: *comp.mail.misc*

- Subject: Tips on using soc.net-people [l/m 26/05/91]
    Newsgroups: *soc.net-people*

These postings are available via anonymous ftp from *pit-manager.mit.edu* (18.72.1.58) in the files:

```
/pub/usenet/soc.college/College_Email_Addresses
/pub/usenet/comp.mail.misc/Inter-Network_Mail_Guide
/pub/usenet/soc.net-people/Tips_on_using_soc.net-people_[l_m_26_05_91]
```

They are also available from *mail-server@pit-manager.mit.edu* by sending a mail message whose body contains any or all of the following lines:

```
send usenet/soc.college/College_Email_Addresses
send usenet/comp.mail.misc/Inter-Network_Mail_Guide
send usenet/soc.net-people/Tips_on_using_soc.net-people_[l_m_26_05_91]
```

Send a message containing "help" to get general information about the mail server.

Credits

The following people provided useful comments, information, and/or suggestions:

Randall Atkinson	<atkinson@itd.nrl.navy.mil>
Mark Brader	<msb@sq.com>
Mark-Jason Dominus	<mjd@central.cis.upenn.edu>
Arthur K. Ho	<artho@kgnvmw.vnet.ibm.com>
Patrick Hoepfner	<hoepfner@heasfs.gsfc.nasa.gov>
Jonathan Kochmer	<nwnetman@u.washington.edu>
Paul D. Nanson	<pdn@msnvm1.vnet.ibm.com>
Ellen Keyne Seebacher	<elle@midway.uchicago.edu>
Robert Ullmann	<ariel@relay.prime.com>
Peter M. Weiss	<pmw1@psuvm.psu.edu>
Bill Wohler	<wohler@sap-ag.de>
Peter J. Woodrow	<woodrow@ijsapl.enet.dec.com>

How Do I Get on the Internet?

In the old days, this was one of those "if you have to ask, you can't do it" kind of questions. First of all, only large organizations could afford the kind of high-speed links required for a wide-area TCP/IP-based network. Secondly, because much of the cost of running the Internet is subsidized by government grants, Internet use is restricted to organizations doing government sponsored or approved research and development.

However, some of the restrictions have been relaxed recently, and there are now several "resellers" of what effectively amounts to Internet access. Three major resellers that we are aware of include:

> AlterNet
> UUNET Technologies, Inc.
> 3110 Fairview Park Drive, Suite 570
> Falls Church, VA 22042 USA
> Tel: 703-876-5050
>   800-488-6383
> e-mail: _alternet-info@uunet.uu.net_

> PSINet
> Performance Systems International, Inc.
> 11800 Sunrise Valley Drive, Suite 1100
> Reston, VA 22091
> Tel: 703-620-6651
> e-mail: _info@psi.com_

> CerfNet
> California Education and Research Federation Network
> San Diego Supercomputer Center
> General Atomics
> P.O. Box 85608
> San Diego, CA 92138 USA
> Tel: 619-534-5087
> e-mail: _cerf-help@sds.sdsc.edu_

These resellers provide their own high-speed networks (in reality, lines leased from one of the long-distance telephone companies), so commercial traffic is allowed. This is ideal for institutions with offices in several locations wishing to put together a high-speed, IP-based wide-area-network. (For example, using AlterNet, O'Reilly & Associates could run NFS between its systems in Cambridge, MA and Sebastopol, CA.) In addition, if you are willing to agree to certain restrictions on commercial use, you can be gatewayed to the "real Internet."

Physically, there are usually four levels of access:

*   T1—a 1.5 megabit/second leased line.

*   A 56 kbit/second leased line.

*   A 9.6 kbit/second leased line.

*   Dialup access with a 9.6 kbit/second modem and a system running SLIP (serial-line IP) software.

Except for the last category, which requires only a V.32 modem, these levels of access require installation of special equipment (Cisco routers and high-speed modems) at each site, plus a leased-line circuit from each site to the long-distance carrier's nearest "Point of Presence" (POP). After initial setup costs ranging from $2,000 (for SLIP) to $5,000 (for T1), monthly costs range from $250 (for 9600 dialup service) to $2000 (for T1 service), plus the local phone company's circuit cost (which depends on speed and the distance to the POP).

56k and T1 service may not be available in all locations, since it depends on what the phone company can provide.

How Do I Use Anonymous FTP?

Those new to Usenet sometimes read with hungry eyes notices of software available by "anonymous ftp." What is it, and how do you get it?

ftp is a file-transfer utility used with TCP/IP networks. Many systems provide a guest login, to which an ftp user can log in with username "anonymous". Once logged in, one can retrieve software and whatever other files are made available in the ftp area.

UUNET has one of the largest anonymous ftp archives available anywhere. Its files are also available via anonymous uucp to a 900 number, for which you are charged by the minute. Of course, UUNET subscribers can uucp the files using their established connection to *uunet.uu.net*.

For details on using anonymous ftp or anonymous uucp to uunet, see Appendix D, *Useful Programs and Shell Scripts*, which includes instructions on how to retrieve the scripts shown in this book.

If you are a subscriber, UUNET will also ftp files from other sites for you (if you can't use ftp yourself), and uucp you the resulting files. Send mail to *uunet!ftp-request*, and include the host where the file resides, and the pathname of the file(s) to be retrieved.

For example:

```
Please send me
        pub/dir/file1.txt
        pub/src/file2.tar.Z
from
        ucbvax.berkeley.edu (128.32.133.1)

Thanks,
        site!user
```

UUNET will try to get the file for you, as soon as possible. If the file does not exist, if they can not find it, or if they can not connect to the host, they will tell you. If they can get the file for you, they will normally UUCP/uuto it to you via UUCP to the directory ~*uucp/receive/USER/uunet* on your computer. Note that USER is your username. If you have the **uupick** command, you can use this command to retrieve the file. Otherwise, you will have to get it manually.

You should receive mail when the file arrives. Please check in the public directory on your system in a day or three if you don't get mail. Remember that UUNET will not go on treasure hunts for you. You must give exact references and filenames.

Please note that there are a large number of files already on *uunet* available for you to UUCP. Check to be sure the file you want is not already on *uunet*.

UUNET also provides portions of its 2.0 gigabit source archive on tape. These archives are distributed in four different formats: on three 6250-bpi 1/2 inch tapes; on eight 1/4 inch cartridge tapes (QIC-24, 60 megabyte tapes, Sun compatible); on one Exabyte 8mm tape; or on four 1/4 inch (QIC-150, 150 megabyte) tapes. All files are compressed (except the compress program itself) to save space.

All sources are the latest available versions at the time the tape is written. Included on the tape are the MIT X Window System, Version 11 Release 5 plus fixes and lots of contributed software (200 megabytes); the complete *comp.sources.unix* archive (85 megabytes); the T$_{E}$X text processing system (40 megabytes); all available GNU software (90 megabytes); the complete *comp.sources.games* archive (45 megabytes); the freely redistributable software from the 4.3BSD-Reno release of Berkeley UNIX (26 megabytes); various networking related programs (250 megabytes); all the Internet RFCs (20 megabytes); the *comp.std.unix* standards archives (10 megabytes); and lots more.

To obtain the tape distribution or for further information send mail to *uunet!archive-tapes*.

Miscellaneous Netnews Questions

Here are some of the frequently-asked questions UUNET faces from news subscribers.

Why am I getting newsgroups that I don't want and did not ask for?

If you are getting articles for newsgroups that do not match the newsgroup patterns in your news *sys* file, then those articles were most likely cross-posted to one of the newsgroups that you did ask for.

If you are receiving newsgroups that do not match the newsgroup *patterns* that you asked your feed to send to your site, then you may not have asked for the newsfeed that you thought you did.

Remember, a *sys* entry is composed of patterns for hierarchical structures and not just newsgroup names. Your feed may be sending you subgroups of a newsgroup you requested if you didn't explicitly request not to have the subgroups sent.

Why am I getting newsgroups that I don't want after I have stopped the full newsfeed or shortened my newsgroup list?

You may still have batched news waiting for your computer which dates back prior to your newsfeed change. If you do not want these newsgroups, you must contact your newsfeed (at UUNET, *uunet!news-request*) and ask for all news batched for your site to be deleted. You will then start with a fresh newsfeed with only the groups you requested.

How do I stop newsgroups from going to junk?

Remember:

*   Your newsfeed's *sys* entry for you controls what is sent to you.

*   Your site's *sys* entry for you controls what you accept.

*   Your site's *active* file controls what newsgroups will be kept.

If a newsgroup is not listed in the *active* file *and* a pattern matching that newsgroup is not in your *sys* file, then articles for that group will be thrown in the junk directory. "junk" is NOT included in a feed.

Your newsfeed(s) should be sending you just those newsgroups that you want (or at least what you asked for). To find out which newsgroups your feed is sending you, send them a *sendsys* control message. (See next question.)

What newsgroups am I currently receiving?

If you want to see what newsgroups your feed is currently sending you, you can send a sendsys news control message. This will send to you, by return e-mail, a copy of all of your feed's *sys* file. Current versions of news also support a *sendsys SITENAME* version of the sendsys control message. This will return just

SITENAME's portion of *uunet's sys* file. B News 2.11 has supported this since Version 18. For example (using B News only):

```
date | inews -c sendsys ora -n to.uunet
```

(where *ora* and *uunet* would be replaced by your hostname and your feed's hostname, respectively.)

Please remember that the newsgroups you are getting are a function of the entries that your feed has in its *sys* file, NOT the entry you have in your own *sys* file.

If you are being fed by UUNET, you can also retrieve copies of their *sys*, *active*, and *newsgroups* files via uucp or anonymous ftp. The files can also be found in *uunet!˜/news/* (e.g., *uunet!˜/news/sys*).

How can I get newsgroups added to my newsfeed?

All of the newsgroups that your feed currently has are listed in its *active* file. For UUNET, this is in *uunet!˜/news/active*.

A description of most of the newsgroups (but not all) is in the *newsgroups* file. For UUNET, this is in *uunet!˜/news/newsgroups*.

Once you have decided on all of the newsgroups that you want, mail a list of them to your feed (for UUNET, to *uunet!news-request*) and they will change your newsfeed accordingly. If you already have a newsfeed, and you want to change it slightly, just specify the newsgroups to add or delete instead of sending the whole list again.

Please remember that the administrator at your newsfeed can not read your mind (and most likely will not try). Your feed will try to interpret the list of newsgroups that you send us as if news was reading the list. In particular, this means that if you ask for a newsgroup that has subgroups (e.g., if you ask for *comp.unix*), you will also get all of the subgroups (e.g., *comp.unix.questions*, *comp.unix.aix*, and so forth).

A few examples:

1. You want to get just the newsgroups *comp.unix* and *comp.unix.questions*, but you do not want any of the other subgroups under *comp.unix*. If you ask for:

    ```
    comp.unix comp.unix.questions
    ```

    you will get EVERY sub-newsgroup under *comp.unix*. Instead, ask for:

    ```
    comp.unix !comp.unix.all comp.unix.questions
    ```

2. You want all of the newsgroups of a particular category, as in every *sci* group.

    Do NOT list them all out! Just ask for *sci* and you will get every *sci* group.

3. You want to receive *misc.jobs.contract, misc.jobs.offered, misc.jobs.misc,* and *misc.jobs.resumes*.

   To make your feed's life easier, and your entry in their *sys* file shorter, instead of asking for:

   ```
   misc.jobs.contract misc.jobs.offered misc.jobs.misc misc.jobs.resumes
   ```

   just ask for:

   ```
   misc.jobs
   ```

   and you will get all four newsgroups.

   You can use this method to make your list of newsgroups shorter. This is a great help to your feed! The *sys* file at major feed sites like UUNET is huge and is getting longer every day.

Please be aware of the distinction between newsgroups and distributions. An article must match both a newsgroup in your *sys* file entry *and* a distribution in your *sys* file entry before that article will be sent to you. Unfortunately, the field in the *sys* file that lists newsgroups is usually the same place where distributions are listed (this depends on the version of news that is running). Also, unfortunately, some newsgroups are also distributions. For instance, there are "alt" newsgroups, and alt is also sometimes used as a distribution.

If you ask for a distribution, you will also get all of the newsgroups. For instance, if you ask for the distribution "dc" you will also get all of the dc.* newsgroups, unless you ask for:

```
dc !dc.all
```

If no distribution is given in an article, then the default distribution is *world*.

Please do NOT send your feed the "local" distribution. The distribution local means local TO YOUR SITE and should NOT be sent to any other site. Note that *all* includes local. Don't use *all* in your sys file; you should use *all,!local* instead.

Miscellaneous UUCP Questions

Here are some of the common UUCP questions that UUNET receives from new customers:

What does an error exit(65) from uucp mean?

When uux returns exit(65) in a rmail job, it usually means that you sent mail via uucp without the first line being a "From" line.

This normally means that you are running something other than a standard mailer, and that you didn't set it up right. It may also mean that you changed something and did not make the change completely. It could also mean that your system has a broken mailer. If you recently had a system upgrade, note that some vendors supply broken mailers.

When I connect, I get an OK on startup, then a few seconds later the line disconnects. My error log shows the message "assert error uucico arg is less than five." What could this be?

The first file you are trying to send to *uunet* is probably corrupted. Delete it from the queue and try again.

Why do I get the message "Shere=uunet" when I try to log in to my new UUNET account?

You tried to log in yourself, rather than having UUCP log in. UUNET does not support individuals logging in directly to *uunet*. You must have your computer log into *uunet* via UUCP to pick up your news and mail and drop off news or mail. The message Shere=uunet is the connection message for UUCP.

G

The UUCP G Protocol

G Protocol Packet Formats
G Protocol (Data Link Layer) Initialization
G Protocol Data Transfer and
    Acknowledgement
Data Link Layer: Cases, Notes, and War
    Stories
Role Exchange
Sending Messages and Files
    (Presentation Layer)
G Protocol Shutdown
Over and Out
A Complete Session
References and Acknowledgements

The following description of the UUCP *g* Protocol was written by Jamie Hanrahan of Kernel Mode Consulting, San Diego, after he implemented a version of UUCP for VMS. This description of the *g* Protocol was presented as a paper at the Fall 1990 DECUS Symposium in Las Vegas.

A portion of the paper relating to work file contents, which is covered elsewhere in this book (Appendix A) was omitted.

Initial Handshake (Shere Exchange)

- Occurs after call placement and login.

- Initiated by answering system.

- All messages begin with 20 (CTRL-P, also known as DLE) and end with 00 (NUL).

- Sent and received in "raw mode" (no carriage returns, line feeds, etc.).

```
Caller                                          Answerer
------>                                          <--------

(places call, gets carrier,
gets login prompt, logs in)
                                    (uucico program starts)
                                      20Shere=hostname 00
  20Shostname 00
                                              20ROK 00
```

- Hostnames are the respective systems' uucp hostnames.

- Caller's Shostname message may include any or all of the following optional elements:

  Shostname -Qseq -xdbg -pgrade -vgrade=grade

  — "seq" = call sequence number (or 0).

  — "dbg" is a digit, answerer sets its debug level accordingly.

  — "grade" indicates what class of files are being transferred (e.g., mail, news, arbitrary files). Taken from systems file entry; not sent or supported by all systems. Some implementations support -p, some support -v, some both, some neither. (See discussion of "C." files later on.)

- Old answerers may send just Shere instead of Shere=hostname.

- The "ROK" message says that the answerer has accepted the call. Instead, the answerer may reject the call with any of the following messages:

  — RLCK. Answerer thinks it's already talking to that caller.

  — RCB. Answerer wants to call the caller back (to avoid imposter callers).

  — RBADSEQ. Call sequence number is wrong (caller is an imposter, or more likely, sequence numbers weren't updated properly at one end or the other).

  — RLOGIN. Caller's login name (username) isn't known to answerer's uucp (USERFILE or Permissions file).

— RYou are unknown to me. (Yes, it really does send all of that.) Caller's hostname isn't known to answerer (as determined by *L.sys* or *Systems* file).

If caller receives any of these, it simply hangs up. (The answerer hangs up after sending the reject message, possibly waiting a few seconds so that the modem disconnect won't prevent the message from reaching the caller.)

If answerer "accepts the call":

```
Caller                                        Answerer
------>                                        <---------

                                              Pprotlist
Uprot
```

where:

— "protlist" is a list of the protocols (each identified by a single letter, e.g., *g*) supported by the answerer.

— "prot" is a single protocol from protlist selected by the answerer.

• Caller can send UN (and then hang up) if it supports no protocols in common with answerer.

At this point the two machines have agreed on a protocol. We'll assume that it's the *g* protocol, so that the last two messages may have been something like the following:

```
Caller                                        Answerer
------>                                        <---------

                                              Pfgt
Ug
```

At this point both systems call the *gturnon()* function, which causes the *g* data-link protocol to start up.

G Protocol Packet Formats

All subsequent communication (until after the *g* protocol shutdown) is in "packet mode".

- Each packet has a six-byte header.

- Control packets have only a header.

- Data packets have a header and a data segment.

Packet Header Format

```
+--------+--------+--------+--------+--------+--------+
|  DLE   |   K    |  cklo  |  ckhi  |  ctl   |  XOR   |
+--------+--------+--------+--------+--------+--------+
```

The first byte is always DLE (octal 020, hex 10).

The second byte is the "K byte." For a control packet it is always nine (i.e., a tab character). For data packets it indicates the transmitted (physical) length of the following data segment, as shown:

K-byte Value	Data Segment Length (bytes)
1	32
2	64
3	128
4	256
5	512
6	1024
7	2048
8	4096
9	control packet

The third and fourth bytes are the low and high bytes, respectively, of a checksum computed on the data segment (if any) plus the control byte. (The checksum computation is described later.)

The fifth byte is a bitmapped command byte, described in the next section.

The last byte is a simple XOR of the middle four bytes. The first and last bytes perform a framing and validation function for headers.

The Control Byte

The "control" byte is bit-mapped as follows:

```
   7   6   5   4   3   2   1   0
  +-------+------------+------------+
  | T   T | X   X   X | Y   Y   Y |
  +-------+------------+------------+
```

The T field denotes the type of packet:

```
T Value     Packet Type
-------     --------------------------------------------
0           control packet
1           alternate channel data packet (unused in uucp)
2           long data block
3           short data block (to be described later)
```

The interpretations of the X and Y fields vary with the packet type (control versus data).

For control packets the X field is the type of control packet and the Y field is a parameter, as shown:

X Value	Name	Y Field Interpretation
1	CLOSE	No significance.
2	NAK	Last correctly received packet number.
3	SRJ	Packet number to retransmit.
4	ACK	Last correctly received packet number.
5	INITC	Maximum window size to use.
6	INITB	Maximum data segment size to use.
7	INITA	Maximum window size to use.

The "data segment size" on the INITB packet is encoded like the KBYTE but with numbers one lower; e.g., an INITB packet with a Y field of 1 indicates a data segment size of 64 bytes.

Most descriptions of uucp refer to types 2 and 4 as "RJ" (reject) and "RR" (receiver ready), respectively.

SRJ ("selective reject") is not used in known implementations.

Data Packets

For data packets, the X field is the sequence number of the packet, and the Y field is the "ACK number"—the sequence number of the last packet correctly received by the system sending the data packet. (See the section on data transfer and acknowledgement.)

A data packet header is always followed by a data segment of size indicated by the Kbyte.

Long data packets

If the packet type is "long data", all "n" bytes of the data segment (where "n" is denoted by the Kbyte) contain data.

Short data packets

If the packet type is "short data", the data segment is still sent in its entirety, but the first one or two bytes indicate the difference between its physical (transmitted) length and the number of bytes to be passed to the presentation level (its "logical length"):

```
 7   6   5   4   3   2   1   0
+---+----------------------------+
| 0 | length difference (1-127)  |
+---+----------------------------+
```

or, if the difference is too large to fit in seven bits,

```
 7   6   5   4   3   2   1   0   7   6   5   4   3   2   1   0
+---+----------------------------+--------------------------------+
| 1 | length difference(lo bits) | length difference (high bits)  |
+---+----------------------------+--------------------------------+
      first byte of data segment      second byte of data segment
```

For example, a data packet with a physical segment size of 64 (Kbyte=2), but an effective (logical) length of zero, would be sent by sending a "short data" packet where the data segment consisted of a byte with the numeric value 64, for example:

```
 7   6   5   4   3   2   1   0
+---+----------------------------+
| 0 | 1   0   0   0   0   0   0  |
+---+----------------------------+
```

followed by 63 additional bytes (whose contents would be ignored by the receiver).

G Protocol (Data Link Layer) Initialization

The *g* protocol is initialized via an exchange of the INITA, INITB, and INITC packets. A simple approach:

*   Each system starts sending INITA's to the other.

*   Upon receiving an INITA, send an INITB.

*   Upon receiving an INITB, send an INITC.

*   When both have sent and received an INITC, initialization is complete.

When the INITx packets are received each system sets its uucp parameters (data segment size and maximum transmit window size) to the smaller of what it can handle and what it gets from the packet.

G Protocol Data Transfer and Acknowledgement

After initialization, data packets are exchanged. Thus, all subsequent traffic consists of Shortdata, Longdata, ACK, and NAK packets (until the end of the session, when CLOSE packets are exchanged).

*   Each data packet must be acknowledged by the receiver.

*   Data packets can only be acknowledged in sequence.

*   If a data packet arrives corrupted (as determined via checksum), the receiver sends a NAK (requesting retransmission) or simply does not send an ACK, allowing the sender to time out awaiting an ACK (which has the same effect).

*   The first packet sent by each transmitter has sequence number one. Packet sequence numbers are modulo 8 (i.e., 1, 2, ..., 7, 0, 1, ...).

*   UUCP (in most implementations) uses a transmit window size of more than 1 (typically 3, maximum 7 due to the three-bit packet sequence numbers).

    — After sending one data packet the sender need not wait for an ACK before sending the next data packet, until window size unACK'd packets have been sent.

    — Colloquially this is known as a "windowed" protocol. (As opposed to stop-and-wait, e.g., most Kermit implementations.)

— After the transmit window is full (i.e., window size unACK'd packets have been sent), transmitter must wait for an ACK of (at least) the first packet in the transmit window before sending another packet.

— *g* protocol's receive window size is 1—at any given time there is only one packet which is valid to be received.

- An ACK provides the number of the last correctly-received packet, and implies that all earlier packet numbers have also been correctly received. Thus a single ACK may acknowledge multiple packets.

- The "ACK number"—the number of the most recent correctly- received message—also appears in the Y field of the headers of data packets. If a system is about to acknowledge a packet, but happens to have a data packet to send, it need not send an explicit ACK; putting the number of the packet to be ACK'd in the Y field of the data packet is sufficient. This doesn't happen often, because uucp's "upper layers" don't use the link in both directions at once.

- A NAK provides the same number as an ACK but requests retransmission of all outstanding packets with higher (modulo 8) numbers.

- Both ACKs and NAKs provide acknowledgement for not only the indicated packet but also all previous packets in the transmit window ("stacked ACKs").

This is known as a "go back n" protocol. It is relatively easy to implement but performance suffers when errors occur.

More complex protocols allow a receive window size of greater than one with "selective reject", and this was in fact the intent of the SRJ control packet. An SRJ says "retransmit this one packet, I didn't get it right". This avoids having to resend an entire transmit window to correct an error in just one packet.

A Simple Data Exchange

```
Sender                              Receiver
------>                             <--------

Data 1
                        (receives Data 1 ok)
                                       Ack 1
Data 2
                        (receives Data 2 ok)
```

```
                                              Ack 2
(receives Ack 1)
Data 3
                          (receives Data 3 ok)
                                              Ack 3
(receives Ack 2)
Data 4
                      (receives Data 4 in error)
                                              NAK 3
(receives Ack 3)
Data 5
               (receives Data 5 ok but out of seq.)
(receives NAK 3)
(resends everything in window)
Data 4
Data 5
                          (receives Data 4 ok)
                                              Ack 4
Data 6
                          (receives Data 5 ok)
                                              Ack 5
(receives Ack 4)
Data 7
                 etc...
```

Data Link Layer: Cases, Notes, and War Stories

Corrupted Packet Headers

When looking for a packet, the receiver should scan for a DLE, then read the next five bytes following and check the XOR.

- If the XOR check fails, the "packet header" cannot be trusted. Scanning for the next DLE begins at the next byte following the current DLE (not six bytes after it).

- If the XOR check succeeds, but something's wrong with the header (illegal Kbyte value, for example), the receiver should treat this the same as an XOR failure. (XOR checks aren't all that robust.)

Corrupted Data Segments

If the header on a data packet is good (XOR is okay), but the checksum indicates that the data segment is corrupt:

- Send a NAK to indicate receipt of a corrupted data packet (but see below).

- Rescan the input looking for the next control packet, starting with the first byte of the data segment.

This seems counterintuitive; if we can trust the header it seems that we ought to be able to trust it to tell us how long the data segment is, and just skip it.

Suppose the file being received is a copy of just one direction of a uucp data transfer. If we pay no attention to what's inside the data segments we see this (assuming 32-byte data segments, K = 1):

```
HHHHHH DDDDDDDDDDDDDDDDDDDDDDDDDDDDDDDD HHHHHH DDDD...
```

but since the data contains a uucp packet stream, the data fields contain:

```
HHHHHH ddddhhhhhhddddddddddddddddddddddddd HHHHHH ddddddddddhhhhhh

1       2                                   3      4    5
```

Now, suppose that the header at 1 gets corrupted in transmission, so the XOR check fails. We junk it and start looking for another DLE, and we find the "embedded header" at 2. It passes xor, so we interpret it as a data header, and read the next 32 characters. If it happens to be the right packet number it will fail on checksum, but more likely it's the wrong packet number; whatever, we send a NAK to tell the sender what we want, and resume scanning. Since we rescan all of (what we thought was) the data segment, we'll find the DLE at 3 . . . and we're back in sync.

If instead we had said "bad data segment, skip 32 characters" we'd be looking for the next header starting at 4. We'd then find the next embedded header at 5 . . . . We'd eventually get back in sync, but it might take a LONG time!

4.2.3—Missing Packets (out-of-sequence Packets) The UUCP *g* protocol employs a receive window size of one; that is, there is only one packet that may be received at any time (the next one that follows the previous correctly-received packet).

If an out-of-sequence packet is received the correct response is to send a NAK (with the Y field, as always, being the number of the last good packet).

4.2.4—Too many NAKs. It is not good to send a NAK for every error condition. Let's revisit the simple data exchange diagrammed previously:

```
Sender                                          Receiver
------>                                          <--------

Data 3
                                 receives Data 3 ok)
                                            Ack 3
(receives Ack 2)
Data 4
      (data 4 is corrupted on the link)
                            (receives Data 4 w/error)
                                       NAK 3 (#1)
(receives Ack 3)
Data 5
                           (receives Data 5 out of seq.)
                                      NAK 3 (#2)
Data 6
                           (receives Data 6 out of seq.)
                                      NAK 3 (#3)
(receives NAK 3 #1)
Data 4
Data 5
Data 6
                            (receives Data 4 ok)
                                       Ack 4
(receives NAK 3 #2)
Data 4
Data 5
Data 6
(receives Ack 4)
                           (receives Data 4 out of seq.)
                                      NAK 4
                  etc...
```

UNIX uucps address this by being very "shy" about sending NAKs, mostly just letting the sender time out.

This works but hurts throughput.

DECUS uucp keeps track of the number of received error packets and sends the NAK only if the number modulo the window size = 1. Thus we send the first NAK right away, but no more until at least a window-size worth of packets have been received.

4.2.5—Duplicate Packets. If a packet is received with a number that's already been received and ACKd it's either:

• A duplicate of one we got earlier; our ACKs got lost, so the sender timed out and is resending its window.

- A future packet, and the intervening seven packets were bad (but this can't happen, since maximum window size is seven, not eight).

Since packets must always be acked in sequence, the only correct thing is to send a NAK indicating the last good (in sequence) received packet.

Miscellaneous

Control packet priority

The control packet types denote the priority of the packets. That is, if several control packets are to be sent, the lower-numbered ones are sent first. (CLOSE before anything else, for example.) Control packets in turn have priority over data packets.

Varying physical packet lengths

Although the protocol allows for data packets with different K values (physical lengths) to be sent in a session, in practice, both ends always use the value negotiated at the start of the session.

Interpacket noise

The DLE that begins a packet should follow right on the heels of the previous packet. Berkeley 4.3 uucp has a bug that causes it to send two null bytes between packets. A robust implementation will not report errors when it encounters two null bytes while looking for a DLE.

Common parameters

Almost all implementations seem to use a window size of 3 and a data packet physical length of 64 bytes (Kbyte = 2). Some implementations will agree to use a larger window size or packet length, but do not do so correctly.

Checksum details

The checksum that is placed in the packet header for data packets has the value:

```
MAGIC - (chksum(buf,len) ^ (0xFF & cbyte))
```

For control packets, the checksum value is simply:

```
MAGIC - (0xFF & cbyte)
```

where:

> "buf" is the data segment
> "len" is its (physical) length
> "chksum()" is shown below
> "cbyte" is the value of the control byte
> "MAGIC" is 0125252 (octal) (i.e., alternating bits set)

If a data packet is resent, the checksum must be recalculated, as the checksum includes the control byte and the Y field (last good received packet number) of the control byte might change between transmissions of the same data packet.

```
/*
 * the checksum routine, copied from G. L. Chesson's article,
 * modified by John Gilmore to reflect actual behavior
 * (see References)
 */

int
chksum(s,n)
register unsigned char *s;
register n;
{
        register short sum;
        register unsigned short t;
        register short x;

        sum = -1;
        x = 0;
        do {
                if (sum < 0) {
                        sum <<= 1;
                        sum++;
                }
                else
                        sum <<= 1;
                t = sum;
                sum += *s++ & 0377;
                x += sum ^ n;
                if ((unsigned short)sum <= t)
                        sum ^= x;
        } while (--n > 0);

        return(sum);
}
```

File Transfer Messages (Application Layer)

The data packets and acknowledgements form a reliable data link which the two uucico programs use to exchange messages and files.

At the start of a uucp session the caller is in master mode and the answerer is in slave. The caller searches its uucp spool directory for work (queued requests to send or receive files). Each such "work request" results in an "S" (request to send), "R" (request to receive), or "X" (remote request for uucp) message being sent to the slave:

> S srcfile_on_master targetfile_on_slave ...

> R srcfile_on_slave targetfile_on_master ...

> X srcfile uucphost!targetfile ... (not covered here)

The slave will respond with one of:

> *(for send requests)*
> SY   Ok
> SN2   Not permitted
> SN4   Can't create temporary file
>
> (for receive requests)
>
> RY<mode>   Ok (gives protection mode of file)
> RN2   Not permitted

If the master receives any of the reject messages it simply looks for its next queued work request.

If the master receives an "Ok", the master (for file send requests) or the slave (for file receive requests) sends the file to the other side. The receiver of the file then sends one of the following messages:

> CN5   Couldn't move temp file into place
> CY   File received Ok

to the sender.

Role Exchange

When the master has no more queued work requests it asks the slave if it wants to hang up. The slave then looks for work and, if any is found, the two systems exchange master and slave roles.

Example: Slave has no work, hangup is agreed upon:

```
Master                                              Slave
------>                                             <-----

H
                                                      HY
HY
          (at this point both systems invoke
          the g protocol shutdown routine)
```

Example: Slave has work, roles are exchanged:

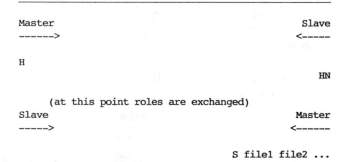

```
Master                                              Slave
------>                                             <-----

H
                                                      HN

          (at this point roles are exchanged)
Slave                                              Master
----->                                             <------

                                          S file1 file2 ...
```

When the new master runs out of work it will again ask the former master if it wants to hang up (as more work may have been queued on that side during its tenure as slave). The process repeats until neither system finds any work for the other.

Sending Messages

- Messages (S, SY, SNn, R, RY, RNn, CY, CNn, H, HY, HN) are sent in long-data packets.

- Some uucps send the last (or only) part of a message in a shortdata packet.

- As many packets as necessary for the message are used.

- The message is terminated by a null byte.

- Only one message is sent at a time.

- Some uucps seem to expect the rest of the packet to be padded with nulls.

Sending Files

- Since UNIX, and therefore uucp, has no concept of "file attributes," the file is simply copied, byte for byte, into packets and transmitted. (The file protection mode is sent either as a parameter on the S message or with the RY message.)

- Transmission of a shortdata packet with logical length of zero indicates end of file (that is, the previous packet contains the last bytes in the file).

These details are specific to the *g* protocol—thus *g* includes both the data link and presentation layers.

G Protocol Shutdown

When both systems have agreed (via H, HY, HY message exchange) to hang up, they each call the *gturnoff()* function, causing CLOSE control messages to be exchanged:

```
(either)                                    (either)
-------->                                    <--------
                                             CLOSE
CLOSE
```

Over and Out

After the data-link layer has exchanged "CLOSE" messages, one more set of "over and out" messages is exchanged:

```
Caller                                  Answerer
------>                                  <--------

OOOOOO  (six "O"'s)
                          (seven "O"'s)  OOOOOOO
```

Note that since the g protocol has already been turned off, these message are not preceded by six-byte headers. They are, however, preceded by DLE and terminated by NUL, as were the Shere, Shostname, Pprots, etc., messages at the beginning of the session.

A Complete Session

Here the caller sends one file and receives one, after which the answerer sends one file. (ACKs, NAKs, and retransmits for the g protocol are not shown.)

```
Caller                                  Answerer
------>                                  <--------

(places call, logs in, etc.)
                             (uucico program starts)

    (subsequent transmissions are framed by DLE .... NUL)

                              Shere=hostname
Shostname
```

```
                                              ROK
                                              Pfgt
Ug

     (subsequent packets have "g" protocol headers)

Control(INITA)                        Control(INITA)
Control(INITB)                        Control(INITB)
Control(INITC)                        Control(INITC)
Longdata(S fromfile1 tofile1 ...)
                                      Longdata(SY)
Longdata(file contents)
Longdata(file contents)
          ...
Shortdata(last few bytes of file)
Shortdata(logical length 0)
                                      Longdata(CY)
Longdata(R fromfile1 tofile1 ...)
                                      Longdata(RY)
                              Longdata(file contents)
                              Longdata(file contents)
                                     ...
                      Shortdata(last few bytes of file)
                          Shortdata(logical length 0)
Longdata(CY)
Longdata(II)
                                      Longdata(HN)
                      Longdata(S fromfile1 tofile1 ...)
Longdata(SY)
                              Longdata(file contents)
                              Longdata(file contents)
                                     ...
                      Shortdata(last few bytes of file)
                          Shortdata(logical length 0)
Longdata(CY)
                                      Longdata(H)
Longdata(HY)
                                      Longdata(HY)


Control(CLOSE)                        Control(CLOSE)

     (subsequent transmissions are framed only by DLE .... NUL)

OOOOOO
                                      OOOOOOO
```
___

References and Acknowledgements

UUCP Protocols

(The following two papers were instrumental both in preparing this article and in implement uucp *g* for VMS. I believe that all of the material in these two papers is incorporated in this article. I could be wrong.)

Chuck Wegrzyn posted a Usenet article (date unknown) that described the Shere exchange, over-and-out exchange, and the application layer.

"Packet Driver Protocol" by G. L. Chesson of Bell Laboratories (October 5, 1988), distributed via Usenet and Internet, is the standard reference on the *g* protocol data-link layer.

The UUCP System

Managing uucp and Usenet by Tim O'Reilly and Grace Todino, (O'Reilly and Associates, Newton, MA 02164), has a good description of the Shere exchange and of work file and execution file contents.

UUCP Implementation Description, by D. A. Nowitz, part of most complete UNIX documentation sets (check the Supplementary Documents volumes, if present) provides a general description of each program in the uucp suite.

"HoneyDanBer UUCP—Bringing UNIX Systems into the Information Age" by Bill Rieken and Jim Webb, ;login: (journal of the Usenix Association), Volume 11, Numbers 3 and 4 (May/June and July/August, 1986). Describes "external" features of one of the newest UNIX uucp implementations, including new filename conventions, logging, and error handling.

General

A widely-recognized work on the subject of data communications protocols is *Computer Networks* by Andrew S. Tanenbaum (Prentice-Hall). Algorithms are included for several different types of windowed data-link protocols.

Kermit, A File Transfer Protocol, by Frank da Cruz (Digital Press), provides a very lucid description of the sliding-window extension to Kermit. Although windowed Kermit differs in several important ways from uucp *g*, this material was of great assistance in designing the windowed *g* implementation for DECUS uucp and in understanding the subtle nuances of windowed protocols.

Critiques and Proofreading

The following people graciously reviewed and send comments on early versions of this paper:

- Christopher J. Ambler, *chris@fubarsys.slo.ca.us*, *cambler@polyslo.cal-poly.edu*

- Jordan Brown, *jbrown@jato.jpl.nasa.gov*

- Eric Johansson

- Nick Pemberton, Lsuc, *uunet!mnetor!aimed!nick*

- Mark Pizzolato, *decwrl!infopiz!mark*

Index

!, addressing symbol, 293
%, addressing symbol, 294
25-pin connectors, 13
9-pin connectors, 257
@, addressing symbol, 294
., addressing symbol, 293

A

-a option, uusub, 128
ABORT keyword, 92
ACCESS file, 273, 277
ACK packet, 314, 316
active file, 182, 306-307
ACU (Automatic Call Unit), 8, 22
acucap file, 4, 65, 237, 248-251
acucntrl, 30
addgroup command, 152, 197

addresses, converting formats, 294
  domain (see domain addresses)
  network, 290
  return; and traveling nodes, 279
  symbols used in, 293-294
administration of UUCP, 122-144
administrative login, 97
  (see login ids)
aliases, 118
aliases file, 187
ALIASES.GLB, 277
alt newsgroups, 147
AlterNet, 303
anonymous ftp, 304-305
arbitron program, 202
ARG COUNT assert error, 234
ARPANET, 290
articles, batching, 196

sci newsgroups, 146
security, 95-121
  and L.cmds, 106
  and passive systems, 135
  BNU, 109-119
  conversation count checks,
    107-108
  filesystem access, 100-105;
    controlling, 116
  login ids, 97
  modes and ownership of UUCP
    files, 119
  remote command execution, 117
  requiring call back, 101, 104
  verifying remote system name,
    118
  Version 2 UUCP, 96, 99-109
sendbatch program, 151, 181,
  196
sendbatches program, 153, 196
SENDFILES option, Permissions
  file, 110, 114
sendmail program, 152
sendsys control messages, 306
SEQ file, 277
sequence count checks, 96
sequence (SEQF) files, 223, 235
serial communications, 32
serial ports, configuration, 21, 23,
  29
  device names in Xenix, 31
  login prompt on, 22, 29
  naming conventions, 21
service definitions, in Sysfiles, 56
setuname program, 43
shar file, 167
shell scripts, for automatic maintenance, 130-135
Shere exchange, 310
Shere=uunet message, 309
short data packets, 315
Shortdata packets, 316
Shostname, 311
signals, RS-232, 14
SITEINFO file, 277
SITENAME control message, 306

slave mode, uucico, 71
slave role, exchanging with master
  role, 324
smail program, 148, 202, 292
soc newsgroups, 146
software, Netnews, 202;
  obtaining patches for, 203
special characters, used in
  addresses, 293
special permissions, 103
speed, modem, 46, 63
  specifying range of, 46, 63
speed labels, 29
spool directory, 10, 222
  BNU, 124
  BSD 4.3, 125
  checking, 126
  congestion in, 126
  contents of, 123-125
  in Version 2, 123
SPOOLDIR, 161
spooling, 3.
SQFILE, 96, 99, 107-108
SRJ packet, 314
Starlan network, 93
start bit, 33
STAT FAILED assert error, 234
statistics files, 235
status messages, 138-139
status (STST) files, 5, 72, 124,
  223, 230
  format of, 80
  location of, 138
stop bit, 33, 37
STST files, (see status files)
su program, 99, 162
subgroups, adding, 307
superuser, xxi
SWITCHAR.COM, 277
symbols, used in addresses,
  293-294
sys entry, 306
sys file, 150, 155, 177, 180
  retrieving, 307
  sample, 177-178
SYS file (DOS), 277

UUPC, Mac port of, 285
UUPC/extended, 281-283
uusched program, 3, 123, 133
uusend program, 108
uustat command, 127
uusub program, 127-128
Uutry program, 68, 82
uux program, 1, 101
UUXFLAGS, 162
uuxqt program, 7
UUXQT.COM, 282
UUXQT.EXE, 277, 281
UXMIT, 165

X

Xenix, and automatic system
maintenance, 134
serial device names, 31
systemid file, 44
uuinstall program, 41
XON/XOFF, 37
.XQTDIR, 124

V

VALIDATE option, Permissions
file, 110, 114
Version 2 UUCP, and spool directory congestion, 126
forwarding, 96
security, 96, 99-109
VMS, UUCP for, 286
vn program, 202
Vortex Technology, 280

W

windowed protocol, 316
word size, 33
work (C.) files, 3, 123, 224-225
working files, 222-236
working login, 10, 97
world distribution, 308
WRITE option, Permissions file,
110, 116
**WRONG MACHINE NAME status
message**, 139
**WRONG TIME TO CALL status
message**, 139

About the Authors

Tim O'Reilly is founder and president of O'Reilly & Associates, publisher of the X Window System series and the popular Nutshell Handbooks on UNIX. Tim has had a hand in writing or editing many of the books published by O'Reilly & Associates.

Tim's long-term vision for the company is to create a vehicle where creative people can support themselves by exploring interesting ideas. Technical book publishing is just the first step. Tim graduated cum laude from Harvard in 1975 with a B.A. in Classics.

Grace Todino is currently residing somewhere in the Middle East. She was one of the original authors of the Nutshell Handbooks *Managing UUCP and Usenet* and *Using UUCP and Usenet* while working as a technical writer at O'Reilly & Associates.

Colophon

Our look is the result of reader comments, our own experimentation, and distribution channels.

Distinctive covers complement our distinctive approach to UNIX documentation, breathing personality and life into potentially dry subjects. UNIX and its attendant programs can be unruly beasts. Nutshell Handbooks help you tame them.

The animal featured on the cover of *Managing UUCP and Usenet* is a grizzly bear. The grizzly inhabits the colder regions of the Northern Hemisphere. In North America it is found in Canada and northwestern US. Though not as big as some of the brown bears, a full grown grizzly can weigh up to 700 pounds, and is the most aggressive of the bear family. Although they are omnivores, grizzlies prefer to eat meat whenever possible. Also, though heavy, thickset animals with a lumbering gait, grizzlies are capable of moving at 25 m.p.h. over short distances.

Grizzlies are solitary except during mating or when females are rearing cubs. However, they seem to "communicate" using "bear-trees." Bears will tear a piece of bark off certain trees whenever they pass. It is not known what this signifies, but the bear-tree does serve as some kind of signal.

Edie Freedman designed this cover and the entire UNIX bestiary that appears on other Nutshell Handbooks. The beasts themselves are adapted from 19th-century engravings from the Dover Pictorial Archive.

The text of this book is set in Times Roman; headings are Helvetica; examples are Courier. Text was prepared using SoftQuad's *sqtroff* text formatter. Figures are produced with a Macintosh. Printing is done on a Tegra Varityper 5000.

O'REILLY & ASSOCIATES, INC.

UNIX Text Processing

Learning
GNU Emacs

Debra Cameron and Bill Rosenblatt

O'Reilly & Associates, Inc.

UNIX Programming

Programming
perl

By Larry Wall and Randal Schwartz

O'Reilly & Associates, Inc.

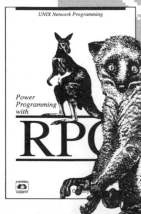

UNIX Network Programming

Power
Programming
with
RPC

Help for UNIX System Administrators

TCP/IP
Network Administration

By Craig Hunt

O'Reilly & Associates, Inc.

UNIX BOOKS

OTHER TITLES
FROM O'REILLY & ASSOCIATES, INC.

Understanding DCE

By Ward Rosenberry, David Kenney, and Gerry Fisher

Understanding DCE is a technical and conceptual overview of OSF's Distributed Computing Environment for programmers and technical managers, marketing and sales people. Unlike many O'Reilly & Associates books, *Understanding DCE* has no hands-on programming elements. Instead, the book focuses on how DCE can be used to accomplish typical programming tasks and provides explanations to help the reader understand all the parts of DCE.

150 pages (estimated), ISBN 1-56592-005-8

Guide to Writing DCE Applications

By John Shirley

The *Guide to Writing DCE Applications* is a hands-on programming guide to OSF's Distributed Computing Environment (DCE) for first-time DCE application programmers. This book is designed to help new DCE users make the transition from conventional, nondistributed applications programming to distributed DCE programming. Covers RPC, name service, security services, threads, and other major aspects of DCE, and also includes practical programming examples.

282 pages, ISBN 1-56592-004-X

TCP/IP Network Administration

By Craig Hunt

TCP/IP Network Administration is a complete guide to setting up and running a TCP/IP network for practicing system administrators of networks of systems or lone home systems that access the Internet. It starts with the fundamentals: what the protocols do and how they work, how to request a network address and a name (the forms needed are included in an appendix), and how to set up your network.

After basic setup, the book discusses how to configure important network applications including sendmail, the r* commands, and some simple setups for NIS and NFS. There are also chapters on troubleshooting and security. In addition, this book covers several important packages that are available from the net (like gated).

Covers BSD and System V TCP/IP implementations.

350 pages (estimated), ISBN 0-937175-82-X

System Performance Tuning

By Mike Loukides

System Performance Tuning answers one of the most fundamental questions you can ask about your computer: "How can I get it to do more work without buying more hardware?" Anyone who has ever used a computer has wished that the system was faster, particularly at times when it was under heavy load.

If your system gets sluggish when you start a big job, if it feels as if you spend hours waiting for remote file access to complete, if your system stops dead when several users are active at the same time, you need to read this book. Some performance problems do require you to buy a bigger or faster computer, but many can be solved simply by making better use of the resources you already have.

336 pages, ISBN 0-937175-60-9

Essential System Administration

By Æleen Frisch

Like any other multi-user system, UNIX requires some care and feeding. *Essential System Administration* tells you how. This book strips away the myth and confusion surrounding this important topic and provides a compact, manageable introduction to the tasks faced by anyone responsible for a UNIX system.

If you use a stand-alone UNIX system, whether it's a PC or a workstation, you know how much you need this book: on these systems the fine line between a user and an administrator has vanished. Either you're both or you're in trouble. If you routinely provide administrative support for a larger shared system or a network of workstations, you will find this book indispensable. Even if you aren't directly responsible for system administration, you will find that understanding basic administrative functions greatly increases your ability to use UNIX effectively.

466 pages
ISBN 0-937175-80-3

COMPUTER
SECURITY
BASICS

Deborah Russell and G. T. Gangemi Sr.
O'Reilly & Associates, Inc.

Practical UNIX Security

By Simson Garfinkel & Gene Spafford

If you are a UNIX system administrator or user who needs to deal with security, you need this book.

Practical UNIX Security describes the issues, approaches, and methods for implementing security measures—spelling out what the varying approaches cost and require in the way of equipment. After presenting UNIX security basics and network security, this guide goes on to suggest how to keep intruders out, how to tell if they've gotten in, how to clean up after them, and even how to prosecute them. Filled with practical scripts, tricks and warnings, *Practical UNIX Security* tells you what you need to know to make your UNIX system as secure as it can be.

"Worried about who's in your Unix system? Losing sleep because someone might be messing with your computer? Having headaches from obscure computer manuals? Then *Practical Unix Security* is for you. This handy book tells you where the holes are and how to cork'em up."

"Moreover, you'll learn about how Unix security really works. Spafford and Garfinkel show you how to tighten up your Unix system without pain. No secrets here—just solid computing advice.

"Buy this book and save on aspirin."—Cliff Stoll
512 pages, ISBN 0-937175-72-2

Computer Security Basics

By Deborah Russell & G.T. Gangemi Sr.

There's a lot more consciousness of security today, but not a lot of understanding of what it means and how far it should go. This handbook describes complicated concepts like trusted systems, encryption and mandatory access control in simple terms.

For example, most U.S. government equipment acquisitions now require "Orange Book" (Trusted Computer System Evaluation Criteria) certification. A lot of people have a vague feeling that they ought to know about the Orange Book, but few make the effort to track it down and read it. *Computer Security Basics* contains a more readable introduction to the Orange Book—why it exists, what it contains, and what the different security levels are all about—than any other book or government publication.

464 pages, ISBN 0-937175-71-4

Managing UUCP and Usenet

10th Edition
By Tim O'Reilly & Grace Todino

For all its widespread use, UUCP is one of the most difficult UNIX utilities to master. Poor documentation, cryptic messages, and differences between various implementations make setting up UUCP links a nightmare for many a system administrator.

This handbook is meant for system administrators who want to install and manage the UUCP and Usenet software. It covers HoneyDanBer UUCP as well as standard Version 2 UUCP, with special notes on Xenix. As one reader noted over the Net, "Don't even TRY to install UUCP without it!"

The Tenth Edition of this classic work has been revised and expanded to include descriptions of:

- How to use NNTP (Network News Transfer Protocol) to transfer Usenet news over TCP/IP and other high-speed networks
- How to get DOS versions of UUCP
- How to set up DOS-based laptop computers as travelling UUCP nodes
- How the UUCP 'g' protocol works

368 pages, ISBN 0-937175-93-5

termcap & terminfo

3rd Edition
By John Strang, Linda Mui, & Tim O'Reilly

The *termcap* and *terminfo* databases are UNIX's solution to the difficulty of supporting many terminals without writing special drivers for each terminal. *termcap* (BSD) and *terminfo* (System V) describe the features of hundreds of terminals, together with a library of routines that allow programs to use those capabilities. This book documents hundreds of capabilities and syntax for each, writing and debugging terminal descriptions, and terminal initialization.

"*termcap & terminfo* has been invaluable at explaining what all those strange characters mean in /etc/termcap. The real value of this one would come if I decided to build my own terminal type. I haven't done that, but the book has surely won back its purchase price by helping me add some flashy screen handling to simple shell scripts."
—UNIX Today

270 pages, ISBN 0-937175-22-6

Using UUCP and Usenet

By Grace Todino & Dale Dougherty

Using UUCP shows how to communicate with both UNIX and non-UNIX systems using UUCP and *cu* or *tip*. It also shows how to read news and post your own articles and mail to other Usenet members. This handbook assumes that UUCP and Usenet links to other computer systems have already been established by your system administrator.

While clear enough for a novice, this book is packed with information that even experienced users will find indispensable. Take the mystery out of questions such as why files sent via UUCP don't always end up where you want them, how to find out the status of your file transfer requests, and how to execute programs remotely with *uux*.

210 pages, ISBN 0-937175-10-2

!%@:: A Directory of Electronic Mail Addressing & Networks

2nd Edition
By Donnalyn Frey & Rick Adams

This book is designed to answer the problem of addressing mail to people you've never met, on networks you've never heard of. It includes a general introduction to the concept of e-mail addressing, followed by a detailed reference section, which provides information for over 130 different networks around the world.

For each network, the book shows: general description, address structure and format, architecture, connections to other networks or sites, facilities available to users, contact name and address, cross references to other networks, future plans and the date of update. Appendixes include indexes to second-level domains, network names, country names, country codes, and a description of how Internet addresses are handled by UUCP sites.

If you routinely send e-mail and want concise, up-to-date information on many of the world's networks, this book is for you.

438 pages
ISBN 0-937175-15-3